# The

# Coronapanic

# Debacle

Ben Irvine

Oldspeak Publishing.

First published in 2022.

# A long time ago, in a Britain far, far away...

Don't forget, even if you get this illness, for the overwhelming majority of people, even in the elderly groups... it will be mild to moderate.

– Prime Minister Boris Johnson, March 5, 2020

It is clear that the risk is very heavily weighted towards older people. But I think people translate that into 'if I'm old and I then get it, I'm likely to pass away'. Actually, the great majority of people will survive this, even if they're in their eighties... It's worth reiterating: the great majority of people will be managed at home. The great majority. They'll be fine... Even in the most vulnerable oldest groups in a very stressed health service, which Hubei was at the point when most of the data come out of, the great majority of people who caught the virus, and not everybody will, survived it. The great majority... It's easy to get a perception that if you're older and you get this virus then you're a goner. Absolutely not. The great majority of people will recover from this virus. Even if they're in their eighties.

– Chris Whitty (the UK government's Chief Medical Officer), March 5, 2020

I also want at this stage to speak directly to older people, because this disease is particularly dangerous for you, for older people, even though the vast majority of older people will experience a mild to moderate illness.

– Boris Johnson, March 12, 2020

It's not possible to stop everybody getting it and it's also actually not desirable, because you want some immunity in the population. We need to have immunity to protect ourselves from this in the future.

– Patrick Vallance (the UK government's Chief Scientific Advisor), March 12, 2020

We want to suppress it, not get rid of it completely, which you can't do anyway... and also allow enough of us who are going to get mild illness to become immune to this, to help with the whole population response, which would protect everybody... We think this virus is likely to be one that comes back, year on year, becomes like a seasonal virus, and communities will become immune to it. And that's going to be an important part of controlling this longer term... 60 per cent is the figure you need to get herd immunity... We've been working on this since the beginning of January... What we don't want to do is to get into knee jerk reactions where you have to start doing measures at the wrong pace because something's happened.

– Patrick Vallance, March 13, 2020

The great majority of people who have this infection will actually have a mild or moderate infection and will be managed at home and indeed will not need any testing... The great majority of people who get this disease, irrespective of age, will recover from it.

– Chris Whitty, March 16, 2020

All references and links to sources are available from
**www.benirvine.co.uk**

# Preface

This book contains three long essays about the period of Covid-19 restrictions in Britain between March 2020 and February 2022. The first essay was written in the summer of 2021, the second was written in the winter of 2021 and the third was written in the summer of 2022. I opened the book by quoting those early words of reassurance from Boris Johnson and his chief science advisors not because I believe that Britain's Covid-19 restrictions would have been justified if the virus had been unmild – I do not – but because the contrast between the mildness of the virus and the severity of the restrictions calls out for an explanation. These three essays are attempts to provide the explanation.

A note about terminology: in what follows I have mainly used the words 'Britain / British'. In fact, 'the UK / UK' would have been more accurate, because strictly speaking Britain doesn't encompass Northern Ireland. However, if I had used the word 'UK' as both adjective and noun, there would have been so much repetition, the writer in me would have been offended. I hope no one in Northern Ireland will be offended if I say Britain / British without intending to exclude them from the discussion. In any case, I have probably *over*generalised in many instances by using the word

Britain; most of the discussion is about England, my own country; you could write four separate books about the experiences of each of the home nations.

Although much has happened since I wrote the first two essays, and they have a campaigning tone which the third does not, since it was written after the debacle had ended, I have not attempted to rewrite the first two essays or to splice all three essays together. Each essay stands alone, and together they represent my understanding as it evolved throughout the coronapanic debacle. As you progress from one essay to the next, you get a sense of a deepening scandal, as my research gave me possession of more and more information and detail. You could think of the first essay as a bird's-eye view and the second and third essays as zooming in on certain aspects of the debacle. There is some repetition of content between the essays, but, given that the media has completely ignored the facts and events that I discuss here, perhaps this repetition is no bad thing.

If I could change anything about these essays, I would make it so that they never needed to be written in the first place.

Ben Irvine
September 6, 2022

# Contents

# The Unions and the U-turns

This is an essay about the driving role that public sector unions have played during the coronapanic debacle in Britain. It's a long essay, but I hope you'll stay with me, because the topic is extremely important.

I'm going to reveal to you some shocking incidents that you may not know about. For instance, you may not know that the first lockdown was set in motion the day after the largest teaching union threatened unilateral schools closures. Or that numerous teaching unions refused to return to work during the first lockdown. Or that, in the summer of 2020, a transport workers union threatened to strike unless the government mandated masks on trains. Or that, in the same summer, a retail workers union pressured the government into mandating masks in shops. Or that the third lockdown happened the day after there was a colossal teaching mutiny with tens of thousands of teachers refusing to return to work in January 2021. Or that the reason why children have been cruelly masked in schools was that mutinous teaching unions demanded it. And these are just some of the known incidents of unions making demands or threats; I will also reveal a huge amount of circumstantial evidence on this matter.

But before I start talking about the unions in detail, I want to provide some background context.

The first thing I want to point out is something that everyone, on every side of this Covid debate agrees on. During the coronapanic debacle, the government has acted indecisively and indeed capriciously. Boris Johnson and his ministers have done countless U-turns, and this has left the public in a state of confusion and exasperation. The impression you get from all this U-turning is a government that's not really been in charge. They've been buffeted this way and that. Reacting rather than leading.

There are two main theories as to why this has been the case. On the left, the most popular theory is that Johnson is in hock to the world of business. Socialists seem to think that Johnson never does enough to protect us from Covid-19. They say he prefer profits over people, that his powerful friends in the business sector lobby him to prioritise the economy over health. The socialists believe that they themselves have been the only thing that has stood between the status quo and Armageddon. If they hadn't kept urging Johnson to put stringent virus-control measures in place, the socialists allege, Johnson would have let the virus rip, and there would been death on a colossal scale. According to this theory, Johnson U-turns because the socialists keep making him do the sensible thing.

But there is another theory. This alternative theory is popular among lockdown sceptics. There are many who argue that the whole coronapanic debacle was deliberate – that it was planned from the start, by way of an international conspiracy. There are different suggestions as to who exactly the conspirators were. The Chinese Communist Party, the World Health

Organisation, the World Economic Forum, Bill Gates, Big Pharmaceutical Companies, or perhaps all of the above. But whoever was responsible, the general idea is the same; that the Covid-19 outbreak was not just a pandemic but a plandemic. In other words: it was all planned. The virus was deliberately engineered and deliberately released, with the world's governments always planning to follow China's example and lock down. Naturally, you may wonder why anyone would want to unleash such mayhem. The lockdown sceptics who believe there was a global plan – let's call them plandemic theorists – argue that the conspirators were trying to do a 'Great Reset'. This is a phrase that has been popularised by the work of a German academic called Klaus Schwab. Schwab has argued that nations should cooperate to shut the world's economy down and start again in a greener, more sustainable fashion. Supposedly, the Covid-19 outbreak was planned in order to do just this very thing – a Great Reset to make the entire world economy greener.

The Plandemic theory offers an explanation as to why Johnson has done so many U-turns. Plandemic theorists say that the conspirators behind the Great Reset have been giving Johnson instructions all the way through the plandemic. And when those instr-uctions have conflicted with his own decisions, he's simply reversed those decisions and done what he's told. Some plandemic theorists go as far as to allege that the U-turns themselves were part of the plan. They say that Johnson was deliberately trying to sow conf-usion, to demoralise the public, to make them feel out of control by asking them to do one thing and then the opposite, with seemingly no rhyme or reason to the instructions. The plandemic theorists call this a 'psy-op' – a psychological operation to subdue the public while the Great Reset was in progress.

Personally, I find the plandemic theory deeply implausible, indeed ridiculous. For one thing, I don't believe that a conspiracy on this grand scale, involving so many officials and politicians in so many countries, would have been possible without someone leaking the news, whether before or during the pandemic. I also don't think the coronapanic debacle has looked anything like a Great Reset. As economies have reopened, they've carried on more or less exactly as before, from an environmental perspective. And some governments didn't shut their economies down in the first place, or they shut them down and then admitted it was a mistake. Plandemic theorists often say 'it's been the same the world over', but this is simply not true. There have been similarities the world over, but every country has reacted differently to the coronapanic. The one thing every country has in common is that there was a global panic. A global panic about Covid-19 was bound to have some similar effects across nations, especially when governments were under so much pressure from their own citizens. With a few exceptions, governments didn't want to be the odd one out. They didn't want to be seen to be allowing millions of their citizens to die. Many governments copied China's lockdown because public demand for lockdown spread as the panic spread.

I'll return to the plandemic theory later. But let me note something else first, something very important. By focusing on the plandemic theory, lockdown sceptics have overlooked the first theory: that the reason Johnson has kept doing all these U-turns is that socialists have kept pressurising him into it. You can believe this theory without being a socialist. I am not a socialist. I do not endorse the rhetoric that the socialists use to describe Johnson's approach to Covid-19. He is not some sort of plutocratic monster who thinks money is more important than people's lives. But I do believe he has been listening to the socialists all the way through the coronapanic debacle. Indeed, I believe he has been capitulating to them. And I believe that nothing is more obvious, or more important. Understanding the role of socialists in the coronapanic debacle is key to unlocking this whole sorry mess.

What I am going to do in this essay is reconstruct the events of the last 18 months and show how socialist public sector unions have been pushing Johnson into repeated U-turns. Although I think it's obvious that this has been the general dynamic, there are some astonishing revelations when you delve into the details. And once you've taken in all the details, the whole landscape of the coronapanic debacle is transformed: you realise that almost every step on Britain's path into Covid lunacy has been driven by socialists. No socialism, no coronapanic debacle.

So let's go back to the start. In late January 2020, the Chinese government locked down Wuhan. This alerted the world to the fact that a new coronavirus was on the loose. What followed was a gradual ramping up of fear, with the media playing a big role. A trickle of scare stories grew into a tsunami as the media warned of mass death on a scale not seen since the Spanish Flu a century ago. Of course, the truth was rather different. The virus was basically just a new version of a cold. The average age of death from Covid-19 was soon calculated to be around 82. This is slightly older than the normal average age of death of around 81. Old, frail and sick people have always been vulnerable to respiratory viruses such as colds and flus. In this sense, Covid-19 was nothing out of the ordinary.

Even the scare stories indicated this, if you looked closely enough. Much was made of an outbreak on the Diamond Princess, a cruise ship which was carrying thousands of tourists, mainly pensioners. The ship was quarantined with everyone on board from late January until March 1. It was like a petri dish for the virus. However, out of a total of around three thousand seven hundred passengers and crew, only 14 people died. Indeed, most of the people onboard didn't become infected, and most of the people who did become infected didn't have any symptoms. Moreover, the youngest who died was 60. The rest were in their 70s and 80s. The outbreak on the Diamond Princess pointed towards a flu-like condition, nothing worse. There were no grounds for panic.

Unfortunately, at this point, not many people were keeping cool and looking at the known facts. One person who was, however, was our Prime Minister, Boris Johnson. On March 3, he told the press that he was continuing to shake hands with people. He said he'd been to a hospital where there were some coronavirus patients and he'd shaken hands with everybody. He was clearly playing down the threat. Dominic Cummings, his former adviser, has said that, at this stage, Johnson thought Covid-19 was a scare story, like Swine Flu. He thought it was a panic that would blow over. Cummings has even suggested that Johnson wanted to be infected with Covid-19 live on TV to show that the virus was 'nothing to be scared of'. Johnson's science advisers who flanked him in press conferences were merely recommending that people washed their hands; no talk of lockdowns yet.

This relaxed attitude was reflected in the government's official policy in the first weeks of the outbreak. The government pursued a 'herd immunity' strategy. The plan was to let the virus spread fast through the young and healthy population, so that later in the year, during the more dangerous months of the winter, the virus wouldn't be able to spread as readily, because most people had already acquired immunity through the initial spread. Meanwhile, vulnerable people – old and sick people – could stay out of harm's way for a while, if they wanted to. The sooner the virus had spread through the young and healthy population, the sooner the older people could emerge from hiding. A sensible plan; keep the economy open, and keep the vulnerable people safe. And indeed, this is how things normally work when it comes to respiratory viruses. Old people don't normally go to nightclubs. They stay indoors drinking Horlicks and watching TV.

Admittedly, Johnson never publicly came out and said that he was pursuing herd immunity. The closest he came was in a TV interview on March 5 when he said herd immunity was 'one of the theories' the government was looking at. Famously, he said: 'Perhaps you could take it on the chin, take it all in one go, and allow the disease, as it were, to move through the population, without taking as many draconian measures'. But we know for sure that herd immunity was not just one theory; it was official government policy. Dominic Cummings has confirmed this. Also, in early March the Italian PM told Channel 4 that herd immunity was Johnson's policy choice. And, as late as March 12, the government's chief science advisor Patrick Vallance was on TV and on the radio elaborating and defending the herd immunity strategy.

Alas, we know that this resolve didn't last. During the first few weeks of March, the idea gradually took hold that Covid-19 patients would 'overwhelm the NHS' if the government pursued a herd immunity strategy. There were doctors, scientists, campaigners, politicians, journalists and regular members of the public repeating this warning like a mantra. It soon became an entrenched principle; allowing Covid-19 to spread was unacceptable because the NHS could be overwhelmed. Johnson and his colleagues tried to play down this notion too – offering the usual platitudes about the NHS being the best health service in the world, and well prepared, etc. But note: this defence of the NHS was already a sign that the government was caving in, because they were not challenging the idea that protecting the NHS was the be all and end all. What the government should have said is this: an overwhelmed NHS, or indeed a potentially overwhelmed NHS, is no excuse for confiscating people's freedom. It's no excuse for stopping family members from seeing each other. It's no excuse for destroying businesses. It's no excuse for blighting the lives of young people and children, who were virtually invulnerable to Covid-19. Additionally, the government should have said this: apart from causing catastrophic damage, lockdown won't make any difference to anything, because whether or not there's a lockdown, sick people will stay in their houses. But hardly anybody made these rational points because the idea of overwhelming the NHS rapidly become a taboo – an unthinkable outcome.

As this NHS obsession gripped Britain, and the panic grew, Johnson's government caved in further. Their messaging became more equivocal. Not so much of the brazenly shaking hands in hospitals. Now Johnson began talking about 'taking the right measures at the right time'. The government had started to hedge its bets – preparing for a possible U-turn. When Italy locked down on March 9, a clamour grew for Britain to do likewise. But it's important to note that the government didn't capitulate immediately. Johnson continued to resist what he called 'draconian measures'. His science advisors continued to point out that even big public gatherings didn't have much of an effect on transmission. As late as March 12, Johnson was still saying: 'We are considering banning major public events like sporting fixtures. The scientific advice is this has little effect on the spread – but it does place a burden on other public services.' I invite you to pause and consider that statement carefully. It is very revealing. The government ultimately *did* ban major public events (and more). And the stated reason wasn't the scientific advice. It was because of the potential burden placed on public services, as Johnson put it.

So what happened behind the scenes to make Johnson prioritise the public sector over the science? I think it goes without saying that the NHS was pressurising Johnson into lockdown. With all those nurses dancing, and all the clamour for PPE, and the public being encouraged to protect the NHS, and clap the NHS, our health service became a veritable lockdown cult over the next few months. We can also assume that public sector workers generally supported draconian action, because Johnson was in discussions with them about the 'burden' that would be placed on public services; he must have been given the impression that public services weren't able to cope with the so-called burden. There was also pressure from academia. On March 14, 200 academic scientists – none of whom were leading experts in epidemiology – wrote an open letter to the government warning that herd immunity was risking lives. And on the same day, at least one teaching union called for the government to take draconian measures. The National Education Union wrote an open letter on March 14 asking why the government wasn't closing schools. The NEU is the largest teaching union in Britain, with around 450,000 members. In their letter, the NEU claimed that the government was considering taking legal action to keep schools open. There was obviously a battle taking place between Johnson and unionised teachers. We are entitled to speculate as to whether similar battles were taking place between the government and other public sector unions in early and mid-March. At that point, the unions were a little less publicly vocal about their views on the pandemic than in subsequent months.

It's also worth noting that the atmosphere among socialists generally in early March 2020 was febrile, certainly if social media is anything to go by. On Twitter, I was defending the government's efforts to keep the country open. I received an almighty backlash from socialists. They were calling me a 'selfish murderer', and worse. This backlash is relevant because socialists dominate Britain's public sector and its unions, as well as academia and the media. And the whole principle behind the lockdown was inherently socialist. Socialists told us we should all be forced by the government to pull together in the collective interest to protect the NHS. The idea that individuals should freely take responsibility – whether for their own health, or for supporting each other – has been taboo throughout the coronapanic debacle, because personal responsibility is always taboo on the left. And what a calamity that taboo always is! Without personal responsibility, society falls apart. During the Covid-19 pandemic, the right thing to do – and the government knew it – was for young and healthy people to take personal responsibility, to go out and face the music, to continue working, to keep the country open, and protect the vulnerable. On March 12, the government started advising vulnerable people not to venture out. Johnson made this announcement almost apologetically, as though it was a massive imposition on people's lives. Of course, much, much worse was to come.

On March 16, Professor Neil Ferguson published his ridiculous prediction that 500,000 people could die from Covid-19. In the evening, the Prime Minister made a statement asking people to work from home where possible, avoid unessential travel and unessential social contact, and not congregate in social venues. The media went ballistic, and the panic shifted up a gear. But there was still no lockdown. At this point, the government was dishing out stern advice, not rules. Indeed, on the same day, Johnson expressed a willingness to keep schools open. He said: 'We think on balance it is better that we can keep schools open for all sorts of reasons but this is something we need to keep under review.' Meanwhile, again on March 16, representatives from the Association of School and College Leaders and the National Association of Head Teachers met privately with the Education Secretary Gavin Williamson and warned him that it was 'likely' that schools would have to close due to staff isolating. The pressure from the teachers was growing.

On March 17, the NEU wrote another open letter to the government, now explicitly calling for all schools to be closed. And this time the NEU upped the ante. Like the ASCL and the NAHT, they noted that some of their members would have to stay away from school, as per the government's advice on protecting the vulnerable, and this might mean that the schools didn't have enough staff to function. This was surely an exaggerated fear; whatever the potential inconvenience schools faced, the proper attitude among the non-vulnerable teachers should have been to keep calm and carry on. They should have taken responsibility for keeping kids in school. But the NEU saw things differently. They warned that they would support any headteachers who unilaterally closed schools. This warning was tantamount to a threat of mutiny. There would have been chaos if schools had started closing unilaterally, chaos that the government wasn't willing to face.

Let me make this point very clear, because it's extremely important. The government was under siege in mid-March – there was massive public support for locking down, and similar support from the NHS and other public services, as well as from academia and the media. Johnson was politically vulnerable. He was being vilified, being told that he would be personally responsible for people's deaths. He was being called a butcher. The Labour Party backed the lockdown, as did the largest union in the country, Unite, with 1.3 million members. Much of Johnson's own party did. His chief advisor Dominic Cummings was pressuring him to lockdown. Indeed, Cummings has disclosed that he and other ministers had been plotting against Johnson from the very first days after the general election. Johnson may not have survived the chaos of trying to keep schools open amid a teaching mutiny and a possible cabinet mutiny. I think there is every chance that Johnson would have been pushed out if he hadn't capitulated in mid-March, in which case the lockdown would have happened anyway. And let's remember what was at stake: he was elected to deliver Brexit. Brexit might have been thwarted if Johnson had been unseated. He faced a horrible dilemma.

And let me also make this clear: Johnson faced this dilemma almost completely alone. The vast majority of mainstream conservative journalists offered zero support for keeping Britain open. Aside from a handful who entered the fray in mid-March when the pressure on Johnson was already unsustainable, mainstream conservative journalists simply abandoned the principle of freedom. As did many conservative voters. While Johnson pursued herd immunity, most conservatives offered at best a stony silence, and at worst, active support for lockdown. Let me ask you this: How can a general win a fight if he runs over the top of a trench and the soldiers choose to stay behind in the trench? The idea that one man, with almost zero support, could instruct an entire nation, including six million unionised public sector workers, to keep calm and carry on when most people adamantly didn't want to keep calm and carry on is a fantasy. Mainstream conservative journalists failed Boris Johnson and failed Britain in March 2020. Most of the conservative public did the same; very few people spoke out in support of freedom.

And so it was that Johnson pulled the trigger on

lockdown. On March 18, the day after the NEU's threat, Johnson announced that all schools would close. The schools would close on March 20 – a Friday. On the Friday evening, the PM announced that the economy was shutting down. The timing of this is significant. The stay home order came four days later, but in effect the lockdown began on the day that the schools shut. You cannot keep a country open if people can't go to work; and people can't go to work if their children are not being supervised. The NEU's intervention directly caused the first lockdown. It was the tipping point, whereby Johnson had no choice but to lockdown if he wanted to stay in power. You could think of him as bending like the proverbial blade of grass in a hurricane. Unlike an oak tree that stays firm but gets blown over in a hurricane, a blade of grass bends and lives to fight another day. Even the rhetoric of the first lockdown hints at the government's desire to ride out the storm. 'Three weeks to flatten the curve', we were told. Why just three weeks, if a terrible pandemic is raging? A paraphrase would be: three weeks to try to get everyone to calm down and see that they are overreacting; three weeks to get the teachers back to work; three weeks to get the public and the public sector onside for herd immunity.

After Johnson had announced the lockdown, there was one very revealing moment in a press conference. A journalist asked him if the lockdown would be enforced by the police. Johnson blustered back an incredulous question– 'the police!?' He was stunned that anyone in Britain would suggest such a thing. By locking down, he was obviously going against his own judgement. You could see in his tortured eyes that he knew that what he was doing was wrong. But events were spiralling out of his control. The first lockdown was accompanied by a massive fear campaign, eagerly supported and branded by the NHS, along with zealous buy-in from the whole apparatus of British government. When I think of this, I think of a remark by Steve Hilton, a former chief advisor to David Cameron. Hilton said: 'the bureaucracy masters the politicians'. In other words, when he and Cameron were in power, they would often read in the newspaper about new initiatives that had been adopted by the public sector without the government even being consulted. The public sector has a life and an energy of its own. Of course, I am not suggesting that Johnson had completely lost control of the government in mid-March. But the lockdown with all its associated rules and measures happened with such rapidity and momentum, much of the impetus must have been distributed across the whole of the public sector, including the NHS. I also suspect that some sort of pre-existing emergency plan for an Ebola-type outbreak had been triggered, which hampered Johnson's capacity to reacquire much control over the situation. The Coronavirus Act that passed through Parliament without a vote on March 23 probably reflected such a plan. Johnson was tied up in legislation and public sector zealousness. Moreover, if he had tried to reverse course, the socialists who shrieked him into the lockdown would have shrieked even louder, and probably succeeded in forcing him out of office. He remained politically vulnerable as long as he remained sceptical.

Another factor that leant momentum to the lock-down was, ironically, lockdown sceptics themselves. Most lockdown sceptics actually supported the lockdown when it happened; they only gradually became sceptical. But unfortunately, most of the newfound lockdown sceptics had been too busy panicking at the start to notice that Johnson had ever pursued herd immunity. Either that, or they were too ashamed to admit that they had supported the lockdown. So they too started shrieking at him, holding him solely responsible for the lockdown. They called him a Marxist, a fascist, a dictator. And, as we have seen, many of them suggested that he had been following a global plan all the way through – a Great Reset, with Klaus Schwab the architect. Supposedly, herd immunity had all been a ruse, a psy-op. Supposedly, Johnson had never intended to keep Britain open.

The problem with all these notions is obvious: by ignoring what actually happened at the start, lockdown sceptics helped keep the public in the dark, and this helped perpetuate the lockdown. For one thing, lockdown sceptics who favoured the plandemic theory were hardly likely to convince the public that the lockdown was crazy when their own theory was even crazier. And more importantly: Johnson wasn't about to announce that socialists had pressurised him into abandoning herd immunity, and if lockdown sceptics weren't willing to make that announcement on his behalf, the public would never get to find out that the lockdown was based on politics not science. Of course, the public aren't stupid. They knew that Johnson had pursued herd immunity and changed direction under pressure. The socialists knew it too. By refusing to explain that this capitulation was a bad thing, most lockdown sceptics allowed the socialists to own the narrative of what happened at the start. The public were given no alternative to the socialists' narrative of Johnson being a free market butcher who had grudgingly yielded to the science.

Lockdown sceptics were so furious with Johnson, they may actually have discouraged him from being honest. At best they were threatening to kick him out of office as soon as the truth emerged. At worst they were threatening to put him in jail. Going back to my previous analogy, most lockdown sceptics were like soldiers who'd stayed in the trench while their general had run over the top alone. When Johnson inevitably surrendered, his soldiers started calling him a traitor. And even the few who did acknowledge that Johnson had faced a monstrous barrage were calling him weak, conveniently ignoring the fact that he had been slightly stronger than most of them.

Let me put these psychological points another way. If you want to get someone to admit a mistake, the best thing to do is flatter them. You could tell them, for instance, that admitting a mistake takes bravery. Or that the mistake was understandable in the circumstances. And if that person initially did the right thing, before making the mistake, you should certainly focus on that. Given that Johnson had initially done the right thing by pursuing herd immunity, lockdown sceptics should have admitted this, and admitted their own failure to support him. They should have extended an olive branch to him, cleared the air. They should have said 'You were right, Johnson, and we were wrong; go back to your initial herd immunity strategy; and we'll support you this time'. Instead, most lockdown sceptics vilified Johnson to make themselves look braver. They were massive hypocrites. Perhaps he decided that he'd rather not fall on his sword to appease them, especially when the furore from socialists would probably have seen him replaced him with a lockdown hawk anyway. The hypocrisy of most lockdown sceptics helped trap Britain in the coronapanic debacle. They were doubly unbrave. Not only did they succumb to the mass panic at the start, they were then not brave enough to admit that they had panicked. In heaping all the blame on Johnson, they obscured the truth about his ongoing capitulation to the socialists.

As soon as Johnson had sanctioned the lockdown, he was trapped in lies. His political survival depended on him continuing to pretend that the coronapanic debacle was justified. This fact is extremely important because it made him vulnerable to further mutinies from the public sector. He couldn't confront those mutinies without telling the truth. And he couldn't politically survive telling truth.

What followed was 18 months of public sector threats and government U-turns. The story of these threats and U-turns is largely unknown, because no one in the media will report on it. So let's go through the whole chronology.

For a start, let's consider the fact that the first lockdown didn't only last three weeks. The National Education Union continued to resist the idea of teachers going to work. Remember, this was crucial: because if the schools weren't open properly, the country couldn't reopen. There is direct evidence that teachers were resisting returning to work during the first lockdown. On May 8 the Trades Unions Congress (TUC) published a joint statement on behalf of six unions with teaching members. The statement included a series of tests that the government must meet before schools could reopen. Yes, they did use the word 'must'. The tests included additional PPE and 'No increase in pupil numbers until the full rollout of a national test and trace scheme'. At that time, only the children of key workers were in school. By demanding the 'full rollout' of test and trace, the teachers were in effect refusing to return to work. Four days later, there was another statement, this time from nine teaching unions; three more had got in on the act. The statement demanded adequate social distancing in schools, which was contingent on small class sizes. Again, this was in effect a refusal to reopen schools as normal. The statement included this phrase, which just drips with cowardice: 'We do not know enough about whether children can transmit the disease to adults. We do not think that the government should be posing this level of risk to our society.' On May 15, the British Medical Association (BMA) also threw its weight behind the teaching unions, and called for schools to stay shut, although several days after that the BMA changed its mind. On May 30, the NEU issued another press release calling for the government not to reopen schools properly.

They got their way. Schools never did reopen fully during the first lockdown. Which is a main reason why the first lockdown continued for so long. Restrictions were gradually lifted during May and June, but Johnson didn't implement an easing of the working from home guidance until July 17. This is a very significant date, because it was the day after the schools had closed for the summer. Johnson waited until he wasn't going to get into a confrontation with teachers before properly reopening the economy. All the while, he was also dealing with other unions, for instance, Unite. On May 5, Unite's General Secretary Len McCluskey wrote to the union's membership to inform them that he was in discussions with the government about reopening the economy, and he would put safety first. And on May 4, Britain's three rail unions – the RMT, ASLEF and the TSSA – wrote to the PM urging him not to lift the lockdown and not to run more trains. No wonder Johnson took so long to get Britain open again. But when he finally did, he predicted that the country would see a 'significant return to normality' from as early as November. It might be possible, he said, to move away from the social distancing measures.

So it seemed that life was heading back to normal last summer. Unfortunately, public sector unions had other ideas. The coronapanic lunacy escalated.

On May 18, the rail workers union, the RMT, which has 80,000 members, called for mandatory face masks on trains. Led by General Secretary Mick Cash, the RMT threatened strike action if the government didn't comply with this demand. As Cash explained: 'If that's what needs to be, to keep people safe then we will stop trains'. He insisted that staff were entitled to refuse to work if they didn't feel safe. At the same time, another union, Unite, was likewise calling for masks on all public transport, specifically mentioning buses and trams.

And what happened? Lo and behold, the government caved in again. The threat of industrial action crippling critical transport infrastructure is enough to make any government think twice. On June 4, there was a government announcement that masks would be mandatory on all public transport from June 15 onwards. ASLEF welcomed the announcement. So did the TSSA, and of course the RMT. The transport unions had got their way. The government had been blackmailed into a policy that ministers didn't agree with.

And worse was to come. On Jul 24, masks were mandated in shops. This demented measure seemed to come out of the blue. Like most people, I was stunned. Why on earth had there been no mask mandate throughout the first few months, but now that the first wave was over, and life was going back to normal, suddenly we were being forced to adopt a measure that we'd been told all along wasn't necessary? Even in the weeks leading up to the mandate, government spokes-people had told us that masks in shops weren't necessary. And then a U-turn.

By now, I hope you can guess what was behind the U-turn. That's right: lobbying by a large union. In this case, it was the Union of Shop, Distributive and Allied Workers (USDAW), the retail workers union, with 400,000 members. USDAW had spent months lobb-ying the government for mandatory masks, social distancing, one-way systems, and cleaning stations in shops. On May 1, the Telegraph reported that the government faced possible industrial action over this issue. USDAW and the British Retail Consortium had joined forces to compile a submission to the gov-ernment about how the retail sector could reopen without any threat of industrial unrest. The gov-ernment ultimately caved in. Mandatory masks in shops were announced in mid-July, coming into force on July 24. It's worth pausing to reflect on how incredible this is. For the next year, shops were turned into madhouses, with masked shoppers shuffling around, one-way systems, arrows on the floor, instructions everywhere, little circles telling you where to stand to keep two metres apart, boxes piled up in supermarket lobbies to create barriers for separate entrances and exits, hand sanitiser dispensers at the front of shops, and often, a masked goon at the entrance instructing you on how to behave. None of this would have happened if it hadn't been for the retail unions.

Perhaps you disagree. Perhaps you might argue that all this would have happened without the lobbying of the unions. Some people say that after Johnson himself contracted coronavirus, a week after the first lockdown, he became a convinced zealot for draconian measures. I don't think so. The case of the second lockdown suggests that Johnson become more sceptical over time, not less. England's second lockdown happened in mysterious circumstances. I do not know for sure what caused it. What we do know is that Dominic Cummings has said that Johnson tried to convince his own colleagues that another lockdown was a bad idea. In WhatsApp messages he sent at this time, Johnson said he no longer believed 'all this NHS overwhelmed stuff'; he said that all the people dying were over 80, and that hardly anyone over 60 had ended up in hospital. Dominic Cummings has also claimed that Johnson was regretful after the first lockdown, saying 'I should have been the Mayor of Jaws and kept the beaches open'. Moreover, during a discussion with his colleagues about the prospect of a second lockdown, Johnson apparently shouted 'no more fucking lockdowns' and 'no, no, no, I won't do it'. A book by a former SAGE member Jeremy Farrar even quotes Johnson as stating after the first lockdown: 'I don't believe in any of this, it's all bullshit.' When the second lockdown came, it was leaked to the press in advance. There are suggestions that Johnson was still unconvinced and was 'bounced' into the lockdown by the press leak. According to Cummings, Johnson subsequently declared that he'd rather see 'bodies piled high in their thousands' than oversee a third lockdown.

There was something very fishy about the circumstances of the second lockdown. It started on November 5 and was announced on October 31. Two weeks before that, the NEU had been up to their tricks again, making demands. The NEU wanted what they called a 'circuit breaker', whereby the school half term, which came at the end of October, would last for two weeks instead of the usual one week. This was to 'allow the government to get in control of the test, test and trace system'. The NEU's demand for a circuit breaker was refused, and the school term resumed as usual on Monday November 1. However, within days of this resumption, a cruel new measure was introduced in schools. On the Thursday, the government announced that pupils in all secondary schools were now required to wear masks in school corridors. Masks in schools had been demanded by teaching unions earlier in the summer. It seems they finally got their way on November 5 – the same day that the second lockdown started.

I think this is all too coincidental for us not to speculate about the circumstances of the second lockdown. The government presumably was facing another teaching mutiny, with teachers making absurdly unreasonable demands. This time, perhaps, the government decided that keeping schools open was the absolute priority. You can imagine ministers proposing that instead of closing the schools for a short period, a national lockdown would be introduced for a short period. After all, the teaching unions were complaining about the 'infection rate'. A national lockdown might have placated them, if it reduced the infection rate. Likewise, the teaching unions would have been placated by the masks in corridors rule; they had been demanding mandatory masks in schools since the summer. In my opinion, on November 5 the teaching unions received a package of measures that convinced them to stay at work. It's even possible that the November 5 mask mandate was thrown in as an added extra, after the teachers had returned to work on Monday 1 but were still restless. Interestingly, after the second lockdown was announced, teaching unions proceeded to insist that schools should close too. But without the blackmail leverage of potentially forcing the economy to close – the economy was already closing! – this further demand was rebuffed by the government. Goodness knows what went on behind the scenes. But what I do know is that probing questions need to be asked about all this. The events of the second lockdown were sinister. Somehow, despite having a PM who said 'I don't believe in any of this, it's all bullshit', we ended up in lockdown again with the nation's schoolchildren being tormented by cowardly unionised teachers.

When the second lockdown ended on December 2, Britain reverted to a 'tier system' where the extent of local restrictions was determined, apparently, by the infection rate in each area. At this point, Johnson seemed to be hell bent on making sure Christmas wouldn't be ruined by too many restrictions. The original plan was for three households to be able to meet for five days over Christmas in tiers 1-3, which was most places. But suddenly, on Dec 19, the allotted time that households were allowed to spend together was changed to just a single day. And much of the country was plunged into tier 4, which meant no indoor mixing or travel at all. The U-turn was breathtaking. Only days before in Parliament, Johnson had been mocking Kier Starmer, who was calling for tougher restrictions over Christmas. Johnson said: 'All he wants to do is to lock the whole country down. He is a one-club golfer; that is the only solution he has.' Johnson's lockdown sceptic colours were on full display in this instance. Then suddenly: almost the entire country was in lockdown again over Christmas.

So what on earth happened? Well, you know the drill. It's a case of trying to work out which union pressurised the government into the U-turn. On this occasion, I think the culprits were the British Medical Association, which has over 150,000 members, largely doctors and consultants. In the days preceding Dec 19, the BMA went into campaign mode, producing a strongly worded press release saying that the government must review its plans for the Christmas period. Yes, that word 'must' again. The Chair of the BMA, Chaand Nagpaul, spoke to the radio and TV, stoking fears and demanding tougher measures over Christmas. He told the Times 'We need to hear from the government very soon'. Don't you think that's somewhat menacing language? Was a mutiny on the cards? I don't know, but I do know that in 2016 the BMA supported a junior doctors' strike, over working conditions. Given that working conditions for NHS staff were central to the whole coronapanic debacle, it is not beyond the realms of possibility that the BMA threatened to strike during the Christmas period of 2020 if the government didn't tighten the Covid restrictions. Whatever the BMA said to the government, Johnson caved in again, humiliatingly.

So Christmas came and went – a lockdown squib. And the coronapanic debacle rumbled on. Indeed, it escalated again. What followed was the most extraordinary episode of the whole debacle. It was doubly extraordinary because most lockdown sceptics simply ignored it and its significance.

At the end of December, Michael Gove said he was confident that England's schools would reopen in January. The plan was to reopen primary schools on January 4, and to allow pupils in years 11 and 13 to return in the first week, with the rest going back in the following weeks. On January 3, Johnson went on national TV and said: 'There is no doubt in my mind that schools are safe'. Also on January 3, Gavin Williamson, the Education Secretary, wrote in the *Daily Mail*: 'We must all move heaven and earth to get children back to the classroom'. Alas, on the same day, an utterly astonishing event took place which meant that the government had no hope whatsoever of reopening schools. The NEU held an online Zoom meeting viewed by a combined 400,000 teachers and members of the public. Yes, you heard that right. 400,000 people attending a trade union meeting. The NEU noted in a subsequent press release that it was the biggest trade union meeting in history. The advice agreed by the executive at this meeting was that teachers should not return to their classrooms. In the words of the NEU itself: 'The NEU advised its members on Sunday, 3 January that it would, in our view, be unsafe for you to attend the workplace in schools and colleges which were open to all students.' This was a teaching mutiny on an unprecedented scale.

Meanwhile, the National Association of Head Teachers called for all schools to move to home learning, and recommended that Heads should take no action against staff who felt too unsafe to return to work. Another teaching union, the NASUWT, likewise called for remote learning. Since late December, they had been calling for schools to remain closed until the spring.

Before I tell you about the inevitable government capitulation, let me note that the government had already bowed out of one similar battle. The government had planned to reopen primary schools in 10 London Boroughs, while other boroughs remained under tighter restrictions. But eight of those ten councils were Labour-led and – supported by the NEU – they lobbied the government to stop the schools from reopening. So the government backed down and announced that all schools in London would remain closed.

It was throughout the rest of the country that the government hoped it could get schools open again. But when the NEU advised its members not to return to work, and the NAHT advised Heads not to take any action against staff who didn't return to work, the government was in a hopeless position. You can't just make tens of thousands of people go to work if they refuse to. Especially when most of them are socialists and they hate you. The schools reopened as planned, but there must have been chaos on January 4. By the end of that same day, the government was in panic mode. They suddenly announced another national lockdown, citing all the usual nonsense about a new variant and stopping the spread. Obviously, it was an extremely cynical political move, to rapidly shift the narrative to avoid disclosing that the teaching unions had openly defied the government. No government can afford such a humiliation. They U-turned, to give the illusion of staying in control. This is the same government that 24 hours before was insisting that schools were safe. Now suddenly everyone was in lockdown purely because teachers had refused to return to work. It's staggering. Beyond belief. And what is most staggering of all is that the circumstances of this U-turn were barely remarked upon in the press. Even lockdown sceptics generally ignored what had happened. Most of them chalked it up as another 'psy-op'; the government supposedly was deliberately trying to confuse everyone again. Even half a year later, I can hardly get any lockdown sceptics to engage with this episode, even to admit that it happened. As I said earlier, it's because most lockdown sceptics desperately want to blame everything on the government, and to ignore the dynamics between the government and the unions. Otherwise, these lockdown sceptics would have to face up to the fact that they didn't support the government at the very start, in March 2020 when the first capitulation happened. It's easier to blame everything on Johnson or a Great Reset than to face up to one's own shortcomings.

So England had returned to lockdown for no reason other than teachers refusing to go to work. It turned out to be longest lockdown of the three. It was also the most insane, from the beginning to the end. The shenanigans from the unions escalated from the start. On January 17, the UCU, the academic union, threatened strike action to stop the government from reopening universities properly. The UCU had been resisting the reopening of universities at least since

August 2020, when they warned of an 'avalanche' of Covid-19 cases if universities returned to normal. With no face-to-face teaching, and students often being quarantined in their dorms, universities became madhouses. The UCU intended to keep it that way. Meanwhile, on January 11 the RMT had demanded an upscaling of protections on the London Underground, despite the fact that only so-called essential workers were using it.

And the teaching unions were continuing to run amok. Bear with me; I know this is an exhausting litany, but that's the reality of it. In December, the NEU had demanded that children wear masks in classrooms. In January, the NEU reiterated the demand, although they were now resisting any sort of reopening of schools. On February 19, nine teaching unions issued a press release saying that the government's plan to reopen schools on March 8 was 'reckless'. Recall that in October 2020, the teaching unions had called for a test and trace system to be in place before schools reopened. This demand remained on the table too. In the end, the government managed to persuade the teachers to return to work in March, but the teachers' two main demands were met. When the schools reopened, kids were being tested thrice-weekly and whole groups were being sent home based on one child having a positive test without any symptoms. Utter madness. And if this wasn't mad enough, schoolchildren were now being forced to wear masks in classrooms. Nothing has made me angrier since the start of the whole coronapanic debacle – the sight of children being forced to wear masks for hours upon end, because some cowardly psychotic socialist teachers are scared of a cold. It was child abuse, pure and simple. I'm flabbergasted that any parent tolerated it. Those poor tormented kids. Surely some of them will be scarred for life.

On February 22, the government announced a 'roadmap' out of the third lockdown. This longwinded plan was designed purely to give the government an opportunity to cave in again if the unions caused trouble. By the end of March, the strict lockdown was over – the 'stay home' order had been rescinded, although people were still being advised to work from home, and public venues only gradually reopened thereafter. In May, the government announced that children would no longer be required to wear face masks in schools. Led by the NEU, five teaching unions wrote an open letter to protest this, but the government managed to uphold the ruling. Many schools simply ignored it, and continued to force the children into masks anyway. On June 8, four teaching unions piped up again, again led by the NEU, demanding the reintroduction of the masks. The government held firm again. Maybe the fact that many Heads were unilaterally enforcing the mask rule was enough to stop the unions from mutinying again.

Or *did* the government hold firm? The roadmap was supposed to be completed on June 21. The plan was that in England there would be an end to all measures on that date, including no more mandatory social distancing, no more masks, and no more capacity limits for venues. But the government postponed the reopening by a month, citing 'scientific evidence'. The BMA had also demanded a delay, which perhaps influenced the government. At this point, most lockdown sceptics were in despair, thinking that the debacle would never end. I was more optimistic. I couldn't help noticing that the revised end of the roadmap coincided with the final week of the school term. Freedom Day, as it became known, was on Monday July 19, when all schools were either shut for the summer or winding down, just days away from shutting. I am speculating here, but maybe the government had thrown teachers another sop: warding off their latest demand for face masks by upholding infection control measures throughout the country. As usual, the teaching unions were obsessed with the infection rate; if the government could prove to the teachers that it was taking the necessary action to keep the infection rate down outside of schools, perhaps the government wouldn't have to do another U-turn on masking the children.

Whatever the truth of this matter, July 19 was the new date for Freedom Day. On July 5, when Johnson first explained exactly what Freedom Day would entail, he seemed more bullish than he had been since 18 months ago when he had boasted about shaking hands with people in the hospital. On July 12, he made another statement about Freedom Day. He noted – tellingly – that if he delayed the reopening until September, the school term would be upon us. He mentioned this point twice, calling the school holiday a 'natural firebreak'. I'm sure by now you can appreciate the deep exasperation in that comment. 'It's now or never' was a phrase that Johnson kept saying around this time. The plan was that all legal restrictions would be lifted on July 19, although the NHS test and trace system and border restrictions would remain in place. Johnson also emphasised that wearing a mask would become a matter of 'social responsibility'. This was a classic Johnson fudge, but it was also ingenious. He knew there was opposition from the unions to Freedom Day, and he knew they would attempt their own unilateral mask mandates. Rather than be obligated to oppose these unilateral efforts, his social responsibility fudge enabled him to both endorse and not endorse mask wearing and wash his hands of the whole debate. In the process, he would allow the public to see exactly who was driving the coronapanic debacle, namely, the public sector unions, not the government. Wherever there were still mask mandates, the public would know exactly who was behind them.

In the run up to Freedom Day, there was an almighty demented outcry from the unions. It's hard to do justice to the scale and intensity of this outcry, but here's a list of just a few unions that called for continued restrictions. The UCU, Prospect, the TUC, Unison, the Royal College of Nursing, the Chartered Society of Physiotherapy, the Royal Pharmaceutical Society, the NAHT, Equity, the National Police Chiefs Council, The British Dental Association, the Transport Salaried Staffs' Association, the National Education Union, the RMT, USDAW, ASLEF, GMB, the PCS Union, Community Union, Unite, various NHS organisations including NHS Confederation, NHS Employers and NHS Million, and the BMA, the union for doctors and consultants. There was a chorus of the usual accusations – that Johnson was being grossly negligent, risking lives, ignoring the science, putting profits over people. Etc. But he held firm. He banked on gaining enough public and media support for Freedom Day. And there was enough support. It's amazing what a difference a bit of support makes. Freedom Day actually happened.

Of course, Johnson was still criticised. For one thing, Freedom Day didn't actually spell a complete end to masks or other coronapanic measures, because his social responsibility fudge meant that organisations could unilaterally mandate those measures. Wherever the furious unions held sway, and wherever the public sector held sway generally, masks and social distancing mandates remained in place, for instance within the NHS, council buildings, dental surgeries, and more. Many major retailers continued to request mask wearing in their stores. The police were still required to wear masks. There was even one instance where the mask mandate remained a legal requirement, and that was on London's public transport system, after the RMT and the TSSA had protested vehemently in the run up to Freedom Day. London's Labour Mayor Sadiq Kahn used his legal powers to back the unions.

Still, on July 19, England was transformed. It became one of the few places in the world with (almost) no legal Covid restrictions. Personally, I have never worn a face mask, apart from once during the first lockdown when I had to go to hospital; I was too ill to put up a fight. Elsewhere, I have very rarely been accosted for being unmasked. Nonetheless, on July 19, I was delighted to be able to go wherever I wanted knowing that legally I was under no obligation to be masked. It felt liberating. Sadly, many lockdown sceptics felt otherwise. Instead of celebrating this victory, they continued to vilify Johnson, because they believed he hadn't gone far enough. They believed he should have banned mask mandates and other coronapanic measures altogether, and told the truth that the whole debacle had been a massive overreaction. Well, yes, I agree, he should have done. In an ideal world. But would telling the truth have still been politically unviable for him? Would he have still faced the risk of being forced out, thus putting Freedom Day itself in jeopardy? I don't know the answer to these questions, but I think Johnson thinks it's 'yes'.

To be fair, lockdown sceptics did have one extremely good reason to criticise Johnson on Freedom Day. On July 19, his public statement contained an absolute bombshell. Here is what he said:

> I should serve notice now that by the end of September – when all over 18s will have had the chance to be double jabbed – we are planning to make full vaccination the condition of entry to nightclubs and other venues where large crowds gather.

Obviously, this is a hideous prospect. If it becomes reality, people who are attending certain types of large gathering will be required to show evidence of vaccination status using the NHS Covid Pass, which is a smart phone app. The specific mention of nightclubs indicated the reason behind the proposed new ruling – nightclubs are mostly attended by young people, and uptake of the vaccine had been relatively low among the young. Fudging, as usual, Johnson said it was matter of 'social responsibility' for nightclubs to require Covid certification over the next few months, but once young people have had the opportunity to take the Covid vaccine, the requirement for certification would become mandatory, at the end of September. Johnson's July 19 announcement meant that the British public were being threatened with future restrictions on their freedom if they didn't take the vaccine. This is blackmail. It's disgusting, especially when you consider that young people, who were the main targets of the blackmail, are virtually invulnerable to Covid-19. Already, many venues are voluntarily requiring certification, including premier league football clubs and some nightclubs. Shame on them.

To understand how it came to this point, you have to understand why this Covid vaccine mania got started in the first place. For Johnson, the vaccines have always been a way to spin his way out of the coronapanic debacle without having to tell the truth. Once enough people were vaccinated, he reckoned, the public panic would die down and Britain could move on. It was herd immunity via a cynical political route. For the pharmaceutical companies and the medical personnel involved in creating or administering the vaccine, there were profits to be made. And for everyone concerned, there was a psychological momentum towards mass vaccination. Once you start vaccinating old and vulnerable people, the momentum spreads to the rest of the population, because no one who has been involved in pushing any of the coronapanic measures will want to admit that there is no justification for vaccinating younger, healthier people; admitting this would be tantamount to admitting that the whole debacle was an overreaction. So Covid vaccination became a mania; everyone must be vaccinated because the alternative was disadvantageous for the politicians, scientists and medical people involved in the debacle.

You can think of the NHS Covid Pass as a sort of bureaucratic power grab. Every bureaucracy wants to increase its fiefdom, and the NHS bureaucracy is no exception. Add in the potential for all vaccines and other health interventions to be linked to the Covid Pass, and there are huge potential profits to made by the NHS and its partners in this project. The burning question is: Why did Johnson suddenly announce on July 19 that the government would collude with the NHS in mandating Covid Passes? Why did he make this announcement on Freedom Day, of all days? Johnson's own view on Covid Passes has been typically equivocal. He has told the press: 'What I don't think we will have in this country is, as it were, vaccination passports to allow you to go to the pub, or something like that'. There are also suggestions that Johnson has privately said he would rather leave the decision to individual businesses. And on July 5 when he announced the forthcoming Freedom Day, he said: 'There will be no Covid certificate required as a condition of entry to any venue or event, although businesses and events can certainly make use of certification.' Yet, in March, when discussing the matter in Parliament he seemed less sure: 'I find myself in this long national conversation thinking very deeply about it'. He added 'the public want me as Prime Minister to take all the action I can to protect them'. Johnson's equivocation is unsurprising. On the one hand, we know he thinks the whole coronapanic debacle has been, in his words, 'bullshit'. And we know he has always been fundamentally against citizen ID cards. But, on the other hand, he now sees mass vaccination as key to his political survival. And he sees his vaccine spin operation as key to Britain reaching herd immunity without inflaming all the mutinous socialists, who were always likely to pressurise him on Covid Passes. In contrast to Johnson's equivocation, other ministers, such as Michael Gove and indeed the vaccines minister Nadhim Zahawi, have outright denied that Covid Passes were under consideration. Zahawi even called them discriminatory. Which makes it all the more important to understand why the government suddenly supported the scheme on July 19.

What's your guess? As usual, it's a case of working out which union applied the decisive pressure. I think the British Medical Association did the job. In the run up to Freedom Day, the BMA was by far the most furious of the unions, going ballistic at the prospect of England reopening. The Chair of the BMA, Chaand Nagpaul, once again was briefing the media about the infection rate and the supposed irresponsibility of restoring people's freedom. Such was the outcry from the BMA, I was a little surprised that Johnson didn't cave in. But then again, perhaps he did cave in; perhaps the announcement of mandatory Covid Passes was a concession to the BMA. We know that GPs have been hiding in their surgeries avoiding normal face-to-face consultations throughout the coronapanic debacle; we know how stubborn and selfish they have been. We know that the BMA supported a strike by junior doctors in 2016. I wouldn't be surprised if there was a threat of unrest from the BMA in July 2021, and Johnson placated the union through mandatory Covid Passes. Let's not forget: doctors stand to make a lot of money not only from completing the mass vaccination programme also from the widespread use of Covid Passes going forwards. Vaccine mania is highly profitable for doctors.

Moreover, the BMA seems to have been pushing the idea of Covid Passes for a while now. In March 2021, the BMA wrote a report into Covid certification.

The report was broadly supportive of the notion, and pre-empted much of the government's July 19 messaging about the Passes. The report argued that mass vaccination was key to unlocking Britain, that groups with low vaccine uptake could be targeted with Covid Pass measures, and that it was only fair that the vaccine should be offered to everyone before Covid Passes were introduced. Tellingly, the report also said that the government should consider whether other vaccines could be added to the Covid Pass, and insisted that the government should promote the NHS as the sole supplier of the technology. The BMA knows where its interests lie.

I think the government announced Covid Passes to keep the BMA and the NHS happy. The Covid Passes, you could say, were a condition of Freedom Day. What a mess. A paradox. However, there are a few glimmers of hope. The Joint Committee on Vaccination and Immunisation has recently recommended against routine Covid jabs for children, on the grounds that the risk far outweighs any negligible benefit. This is significant, because four teaching unions in a joint statement have called for a rollout of Covid vaccinations for pupils. And Patrick Roach, General Secretary of the NASUWT has talked about the 'benefit' of making the Covid vaccine available to schoolchildren. Recently the vaccine has been made available for 16/17 years olds, which has been welcomed by the NEU. There has been an alarming momentum towards vaccinating children, and it seems that this momentum is currently in abeyance. That's cause for hope.

Another cause for hope is the fact that there has been considerable pushback against the government's mandatory Covid Passes plan, from industry leaders, journalists and the public. And in two countries where the Passes were introduced, namely Denmark and Israel, they have now been phased out. It is crucial that lockdown sceptics continue to offer dogged opposition to the plan. I am inclined to believe that Johnson's heart is not in it. Perhaps he even hopes that the public will veto the plan. The phrase he used when he announced the mandatory Passes – 'I should serve notice' – was almost sheepish, apologetic, perhaps even a warning, or a call to arms; a call for the public to finally step in and draw a line in the sand against deranged union demands.

Or maybe I am giving Johnson too much credit. I am aware that I will be accused of 'defending' him by portraying the coronapanic debacle as a battle between the government and the unions. So how guilty is he? Well, personally I am extremely disturbed by anyone who can stand in front of the public and lie for 18 months. But I also realise that if Johnson had been unseated, the alternative could have been worse. We could have had a lockdown hawk in power – someone who wouldn't have fought repeated legal battles trying to keep the country open, someone who wouldn't have pushed Freedom Day over the line. And Brexit might have been thwarted. No leader is a magician. There is a two-way dynamic between the leader and the led. Both influence each other. When virtually the entire apparatus of British government – including millions of public sector workers, and the monopolistic NHS – was driving towards the implementation of draconian Covid measures, perhaps Johnson decided that a true leader would stay at the helm and try to inject some sanity into the proceedings. At the very start, I warned that we were seeing a crime against humanity. My view has not changed. Johnson ostensibly led this crime. But if the alternative to him staying in power was worse, his actions could arguably be justified – just as, for instance, the allied leaders in World War 2 were arguably justified in authorising a nuclear attack on Japan. These are complex issues. My view is that when all the facts are in, the law must decide questions of guilt and innocence.

If Johnson is guilty, I want him punished. I am very much open to that prospect. But here's the crucial point: to reach any sort of legal conclusion, we need to get the truth out there first. We have to talk about the battle that has taken place between the government and the unions, otherwise this insane dynamic of union pressure and government U-turns will go on and on. As I write, the school term is starting, and teachers are running amok already – trying to postpone the start of term, and demanding the same old litany of mad Covid measures in schools. Schoolchildren face the prospect of another year of being tormented by their teachers. And goodness knows what the rest of the unions have got planned this winter. We have to tell the truths that the government itself is too compromised to tell.

In contrast, focusing on a so-called plandemic is futile. Yes, the government has occasionally parroted Great Reset slogans, such as 'Build Back Better'. But there is a big difference between a planned conspiracy to reset the world's economy, and a *post hoc* spin operation by national leaders most of whom are in the same boat, trying to put a positive gloss on the coronapanic debacle. Yes, many international organis-ations and businesses have used the coronapanic debacle to gain power. But there is a big difference between a planned conspiracy to make money from an atrocity, and international organisations and businesses opportunistically exploiting the coronapanic debacle. Yes, the world's borders are now subject to vaccine passport rules. But there is a big difference between a planned conspiracy to create a communist style 'social credit system', and a panicked policy response that culminates in democratic governments being unable to reverse Covid border controls without losing credibility. I might be wrong about all this. But I am also right to warn against paranoia. Plandemic theorists may have succumbed to just as much paranoia as any Covid zealot.

I think all aspects of the debacle have to be taken into consideration, including the global aspect. But in order to get free here in Britain, we need to get our house in order. We need to subdue the socialist unions that have caused chaos here for 18 months. Only then can we reclaim our freedom, like the Texans and Floridians did. In the end, getting our house in order is a precondition of dealing with the global aspect of the problem. Freedom percolates upwards. It has always been this way. Ironically, the more that lockdown sceptics obsess about a global tyranny, and our government's supposed role in that tyranny, the more likely the global tyranny will become, because lockdown sceptics are neglecting to pursue the local actions that will protect us against undemocratic global schemes. In this connection, it's also worth noting that, all around the world, unions may well have played a nefarious role similar to that which they played in Britain. I could say more about this, but here is one relevant contrast: in the USA, where Covid madness is still prevalent, the teaching unions have run amok, whereas in Sweden, which stayed open throughout the coronapanic, the teaching unions have been determined to keep the schools open and protect the welfare of children.

Plandemic theorists aren't the only lockdown sceptics who are reluctant to focus on the role of the unions in the coronapanic debacle. Almost all lockdown sceptics are focusing too much of their anger on the government or on international organisations. I have already intimated the reason for this skewed focus. Unlike myself, and a handful of others, most lockdown sceptics didn't support Johnson on herd immunity; most of them were too busy panicking. To admit that Johnson had almost zero support when he caved in under colossal pressure from the public sector is to admit one's own small role in causing the coronapanic debacle. Lockdown sceptics need to find the inner strength to be honest that they abandoned good sense at the start. They need to start fighting the fight that they didn't fight at the start – against public sector socialists. It's the only path to victory; it's the only path there ever was. Blaming the government alone is like arresting a drugs mule and thinking you've nailed the kingpin. It's barely a victory at all.

There's one final advantage of being honest about one's role in the mass panic that precipitated this disaster. By being honest in this respect, you can extend an olive branch to Covid zealots. Talk to them about the mass panic. Have enough humility and strength to admit that you panicked too. Give them a way out. There is too much stubbornness on all sides. No one wants to admit they made a terrible mistake. Not the government. Not the Covid zealots. Not the unions. And not lockdown sceptics themselves – most of them anyway. We all make mistakes. We're all human. If lockdown sceptics are the enlightened ones in all this, they need to start leading a process of clearing the air. Unleash the awkward truth, and this whole sorry saga will unravel.

August 23, 2021

# The Road to Lockdown:
# How Unions Drove Covid Policy

Recently I've done a lot of research into the role of public sector unions in driving the coronapanic debacle in Britain. I've written a long essay on the topic; 'The Unions and the U-turns'. And I've created two videos; the first was called 'The Unions and the Coronapanic', and the second was called 'The Scandalous Cause of the Third Lockdown'. Since then, I've received a lot of comments and questions, and I've done some more research, uncovering some shocking new information. So I've decided to write another essay on the topic, to fill in a few gaps and provide a few updates.

If you haven't read my other essay, or seen the videos, don't worry. All you need to know is this: unions drove every single escalation of the coronapanic debacle in Britain by making demands or threats to the government, with the government repeatedly caving in. The National Education Union (NEU) played an especially prominent role, driving all three lockdowns. Here's a quick summary of the details I've disclosed in the essay/videos:

The first lockdown happened in March 2020 after

the NEU threatened the government with unilateral schools closures. The masks on public transport mandate in the summer of 2020 happened after the RMT, the rail workers union, threatened to strike. The masks in shops mandate in the summer of 2020 happened after USDAW, the retail workers union, lobbied the government and allegedly threatened industrial unrest. The second lockdown happened in November 2020 after the NEU called for a 'circuit breaker'. Christmas 2020 was heavily restricted after the British Medical Association (BMA) furiously lobbied the government to tighten the Covid rules. The third lockdown happened on January 4, 2021, after the NEU orchestrated a massive teaching mutiny to stop the government from reopening schools; the government panicked and locked the whole country down later that evening, to cover up the mutiny. The first and the third lockdowns lasted as long as they did because teaching unions refused to go back to work as normal. The masks in schools mandates, as well as other deranged measures in schools, including testing, bubbles, isolating, and more, were all driven by teaching unions, with the NEU centrally involved. And Covid vaccines were rolled out in schools, against the advice of the JCVI, because teaching unions demanded the measure.

Overall, the picture is clear, albeit incredible: the whole coronapanic debacle has happened because the government has repeatedly capitulated to demands and threats made by unions. If those demands and threats hadn't been made, Britain would have remained free.

I said that in this essay I want to fill in a few gaps.

The main area I want to look at is the events leading up to the first lockdown.

You will remember that in early March 2020 the government started off pursuing a herd immunity strategy. Johnson stuck to his guns on this for two weeks. As late as March 12, his chief science advisor Patrick Vallance was on TV explaining and defending herd immunity. But the government was on the brink of caving in at that point, under pressure from unions. I now know that the unions were active around Covid-19 earlier than I had previously thought, as far back as February, and they started making threats in the second week of March, also earlier than I thought.

On February 12, the Chief Executives of every local authority in England, Wales and Northern Ireland received a letter signed by the secretaries of GMB, Unite and Unison (three unions with a combined membership of 3.2 million) and the 'Employers Secretary' of the Local Government Association. The letter gives notice of various government agencies that would 'monitor the evolving situation' regarding Covid-19. After a few short paragraphs detailing some further resources, the letter offers a terse reminder of the rules on sick pay: 'An employee who is prevented from attending work because of contact with infectious disease shall be entitled to receive normal pay.' The letter then signs off by saying: 'In the event that an employee is required to self-isolate or is placed in quarantine, the provision above should be applied.' Obviously, this is not inherently unreasonable. But there is something slightly ardent about the letter; it gets to the point a little too eagerly. The message now sounds like a call to arms, given what we know happened: public sector workers developed a maniacal obsession with the spread of an infectious disease, to the point of self-isolating without being ill, and even demanding the right to hide at home on full pay for a year.

I've also unearthed a press release in which the GMB Union talked about 'briefing' its members on Covid-19 'in early February'. I don't know what was said in the briefing. But clearly the unions were waking up to the threat, or perhaps I should say the opportunity, of Covid-19 much earlier than the general public. And no doubt the government will have known that the unions were on the case. I have often wondered why the government was somewhat restrained in its defence of herd immunity. In the first two weeks of March, we saw ministers fall into a pattern that quickly became entrenched: they refused to rule out escalating the Covid response, in case they needed to cave in further down the line. If the government knew that there were rumblings from the unions as early as February, no wonder ministers hedged their bets from the start. The hedging will have included the notorious £119 million advertising contract that the government took out on March 2 for the forthcoming coronavirus campaign. The contract spelled out three potential tiers of messaging, from less severe advice (wash your hands) to more severe advice (stay home). Presumably, ministers knew that they wouldn't be able control how far the coronapanic escalated; it would depend on the reaction of the public and the public sector.

By the second week of March, unions were openly pressuring the government. The first instance may seem trivial, but it had a knock-on effect that was far from trivial. On March 9, Unison started complaining about cleaners being asked to do a 'deep clean' in schools. The issue can be traced back to February, when two schools in England – one in Cheshire, the other in Middlesbrough – were closed after their pupils had returned from a trip to Italy. A few pupils had shown 'flu-like symptoms'; the schools reopened only after a deep clean. On March 9, Unison insisted that any member of staff responsible for 'decontaminating' a school should contact their Unison rep to ensure that the school conducts a 'risk assessment' and provides PPE, including face masks. This intervention from Unison was unhelpful, to say the least. The message coming from the government was that Covid-19 was a mild disease and that the spread of the virus among non-vulnerable people was no bad thing; on the contrary, the spread would help us achieve herd immunity sooner, enabling vulnerable people to come out of hiding sooner. Unfortunately, in schools, a completely different mentality was brewing, according to which the working environment was potentially so contaminated that it couldn't even be cleaned normally. No wonder teaching unions went on to become the most insane Covid lobbyists of all.

The next day, March 10, another union kicked off, along related lines. GMB began complaining that its NHS members were not receiving a lack of adequate protection at work. In a press release, the union declared:

> GMB members working in the NHS say they are being exposed to coronavirus patients but that they have not yet been provided with advice, training, protective clothing or hand sanitisers by NHS trusts.

A 'GMB Organiser', Helen O'Connor, is quoted as saying:

> The anger amongst our NHS members is growing and they are calling for immediate action and resources to deal with the risks they face or they will not come into work.

Needless to say, that last remark is shocking. I don't know how high up this mutiny went within the NHS hierarchy, but medical staff refusing to come to work without adequate PPE was a significant escalation of the coronapanic debacle. PPE for health workers became a *cause célèbre* in the media over the next few weeks, and other unions soon weighed in on the issue, including Unison, which has nearly half a million members working in healthcare. The government was forced onto the back foot very early by the furore over PPE.

And, perhaps most importantly, there was powerful symbolism involved in this early furore. The idea that medical staff urgently needed extreme protection, protection that the government was failing to supply, created the impression of a terrifying plague that ministers weren't taking seriously enough. In turn, the furore over PPE will inevitably have fanned the flames of future union mutinies, providing an implicit justification for them. The episode will also have fed into the 'Protect the NHS' narrative which cowed the public so effectively during the lockdowns. Granted, I am not an expert on infection control in healthcare settings. I do not know what was the appropriate PPE for any medic during any stage of the pandemic. But I do know that socialist unions should not have been dictating the issue.

By March 13, Johnson was starting to crack. That day, he revealed that mass gatherings would be banned. He admitted that there was no scientific reason for the ban; the only reason, he said, was to avoid placing a 'burden' on public services. He specifically mentioned the 'emergency services' being stretched by mass gatherings. But I've now discovered that there was another source of pressure on Johnson at that time. On March 13, the RMT, the rail workers union, issued a threatening press release. (The RMT is the same union that forced the masks on public transport mandate later that summer by threatening to strike.) In their March 13 press release, the RMT complained about what they called a lack of 'leadership' around coronavirus both regionally and nationally. Mick Cash, the RMT's general secretary, said: 'The union will take whatever action is required to protect the well-being and livelihoods of our members.' The press release also spoke of the RMT joining forces with some unnamed London Underground unions. So more than one transport union was kicking off. No doubt the RMT will have been concerned about the 'burden' that mass gatherings would place on the transport system. Given the timing, we can assume that Johnson banned mass gatherings at least in part because he was trying to placate the RMT and other rail unions.

And that was just the start of Johnson's U-turning. From March 13 to March 18, the government's herd immunity strategy crumbled spectacularly, ultimately sending the whole nation into lockdown. Each day, there were important developments leading to that outcome.

On March 14, the NEU wrote an open letter to the government asking why all schools weren't being closed. In this letter, the NEU said to Johnson: 'We now see that you may take legal powers to force schools to remain open even when Heads and teachers think there is good reason to close.' Clearly, there was a battle taking place between the government and the teachers. Johnson wanted to keep schools open, and he said this many times in public over the next few days. And you can appreciate why he held this view. Schools were central to the whole outlook of Britain. Closing them would have a profound effect, not just on the kids but on the parents who would struggle to get out to work if their kids were at home in the daytime.

Bearing this in mind, Johnson's next move was significant. On March 15, the day after the NEU had kicked off, he made a telephone call to someone rather unexpected. A short press release on the government's official website indicates that Johnson telephoned... the Prime Minister of Japan. Now that's a bit weird, isn't it? Why telephone the Japanese PM, of all people? Here's what I think the reason is. In Japan, the government closed all the schools at the start of March, but kept the economy open. This was a very unusual arrangement. I don't know of anywhere else in the world where the schools were shut but there wasn't a full lockdown. Perhaps this arrangement was viable in Japan because gender roles are still quite traditional in Japanese culture; basically, the women are encouraged to stay home and raise the kids. Even so, there are reports that Japanese parents were unhappy about the disruption caused by the schools closures. Presumably Johnson phoned the Japanese PM to find out know how much political damage closing the schools without a lockdown had caused. A similar decision in Britain was bound to cause even more political damage, because British mums are more likely to have high responsibility jobs than their Japanese counterparts.

Whatever happened during that phone call, the prospect of closing schools was obviously on Boris Johnson's mind on March 15, and he was obviously exploring the possibility of keeping the economy open in the face of an ongoing mutiny by the teachers. Alas, Johnson was about to face another forceful ramping up of pressure. What I am about to convey to you is extremely important information that almost no one is aware of.

On March 16, the TUC made a remarkable intervention into the proceedings. The TUC is a federation of unions, representing the majority of unions, 48 in total, with members working throughout the economy but mostly in the public sector. The combined membership of the TUC is 5.5 million people. In other words: a very powerful lobby, especially given its embeddedness within the governing structures of Britain.

On March 16, the TUC held a webinar in which two presenters communicated various demands to the government. Watching the webinar, a few points stand out. First of all, there's the fact that the TUC was making 'demands'. Not suggestions. Not requests. Demands. The unions have been using this kind of bossy menacing language towards the government throughout the coronapanic.

Another thing that stands out is one of the specific demands made by the TUC. They wanted 'full pay for workers affected by schools closures'. This is interesting because among the TUC's affiliated unions, there are nine unions with teaching members. I think it's a fair assumption that all nine teaching unions were pressuring the government to close schools, with the NEU publicly spearheading the campaign, and the TUC acting as a sort of central hub. And note the presumptuousness of the TUC talking about schools closures, when the government was at this point still trying to keep schools open. The teaching unions must have been very determined, indeed confident of getting their way.

Also note the phrasing: full pay for workers affected by schools closures. The TUC wasn't just talking about full pay for people who worked in schools, but for any workers affected by schools closures. This will have resonated with Johnson following his phone call to Japan. He will have known that closing schools would send a shockwave through the whole economy. Parents would face huge inconvenience, and here was the TUC demanding full pay for anyone affected. As one of the presenters explains: 'We don't want anyone to be going without an income during these difficult and uncertain times.'

This point is related to a more general demand made by the TUC. They wanted the government to provide economic subsidies during the pandemic to mitigate any disruption faced by workers and their employers. To this end, the TUC wanted ministers to 'Immediately establish a task force including trade unions, so that we can work together with employers and the government agencies to safeguard jobs and industries'.

Well this is all very interesting, isn't it, because, a

week later, the government announced a furlough scheme which aimed to do exactly what the TUC had demanded. The TUC later described furlough as a 'big win', one which was achieved after 'intensive negotiations' between 'the TUC and other unions' and the government. The Confederation of British Industry was also involved in the negotiations, perhaps helping to crystallise the 'task force' that the TUC had demanded. I don't know if any government-union task force was ever formally established, but I do know that the first mention of government intervention to support working parents and protect jobs and industries came from the TUC. And the TUC got their way.

Of course, you may question why the government would listen to the TUC on this matter. The next revelations from the webinar are even more explosive. When discussing the role of union reps during the pandemic, a presenter suggests 'thinking about industrial action you can take'. Obviously this statement speaks for itself. And it's very damning. What an outrage that the TUC was encouraging its reps to think about industrial action at a time when the nation was supposed to be pulling together. And it gets more damning. Later in the webinar, the presenter specifies exactly what sort of mutiny the TUC has in mind. Speaking about the UCU, the academic union, she says:

Some branches are already talking about using the Health and Safety Act to refuse to carry out duties, and we will post specific advice on that after the webinar. It's quite technical and we want to make sure people are getting things right. Any union could make the same demand on an employer, or organise industrially for a work from home policy.

Wow. There's a lot to take in there. Let's go through it carefully. First of all, note the nature of the mutiny: employees using Health and Safety legislation to refuse to carry out duties. Second, note that this mutiny was already being talked about, and probably already happening, at branch level in at least one union. Third, note that the TUC was proposing a similar mutiny in other unions, albeit using carefully crafted language to avoid responsibility. Fourth, note that the TUC was talking about unions organising industrially for a work from home policy. Later in the seminar, the TUC indicated that even people who can't work from home, e.g. cleaners and security staff, could demand full pay while avoiding the workplace. The presenter uses the phrase 'forcing of the employer's hands' to describe this overall mutiny.

It's shocking, isn't it? Basically the TUC was stoking up a huge unofficial strike, executed by way of unionised workers pressuring their bosses into allowing them to stay at home on full pay, on so-called Health and Safety grounds. And all the while, the TUC had the absolute nerve to demand government financial intervention to mitigate the effects of the mutiny.

Granted, you could argue that the TUC's webinar might not have been that impactful. I don't know how many people watched it live, and it seems that only around 1400 have watched it on YouTube. But then again, you have to remember: many of the people who watched the webinar will have been reps, who then stirred up further trouble at branch level. And the TUC gave the impression that it was talking about events that were already happening, presumably reflecting the general mood among its affiliated unions. Also the TUC probably used other media such as emails to communicate the information presented in the webinar (which included PowerPoint slides). In fact, two days earlier, on March 14, the TUC had issued a newsletter to all its member unions. The newsletter called for the government to set up 'an emergency support package for workers affected by the virus', and to create the government-union task force mentioned in the forthcoming webinar. We can assume that the scale of the TUC work from home mutiny was large.

Indeed, in the webinar, the TUC disclosed that the UCU had 'formally called for universities to close'. The presenter says 'for example' when discussing the UCU demand, which makes you wonder if other unions made similar demands behind the scenes. And let's remember that the RMT had kicked off on March 13, while the NEU and other teaching unions had been agitating since March 14 for schools closures. There's no doubt about it: unions were causing big trouble for the government in mid-March 2020.

So that was the backdrop to the next significant event on Johnson's road to capitulation. At 8pm on March 16, the government held a press conference, five hours after the TUC webinar had finished. With Johnson flanked by his main science advisors Patrick Vallance and Chris Whitty, the press conference was a turning point for the government and the country, featuring a dramatic ramping up of the coronapanic measures. The occasion had an air of unreality about it. Many of us knew something wasn't quite right, but we couldn't quite put our finger on it. Now I think I know exactly what was wrong: the entire press conference was one monumental exercise in spin.

In order to show this, first of all let me run through what was conveyed to us at that crucial press conference on March 16.

The headline message was that the government was now asking us to avoid all non-essential travel and non-essential contact. We were asked to work from home where possible and avoid social venues. This was obviously a huge escalation. But it was also qualified in a couple of ways.

For a start, it wasn't a legal ruling. It was guidance, not a lockdown. Patrick Vallance clearly stated that they were merely 'recommending' the measures. Johnson said he was issuing 'very strong advice'. And the advice was itself caveated. Johnson stated that avoiding unnecessary social contact was 'particularly important' for vulnerable people. In other words: sticking to the guidance was less important for some people than for others. You'd never say that about an actual law, say, the law against arson. The guidance was somewhat flexible.

Taking this into account, the social distancing guidance outlined by the British government on March 16 wasn't substantially different from the guidance that had been issued by the Swedish government. Sweden famously remained open, because its measures around social distancing, avoiding travel, and working from home were all voluntary. Let's also remember that the schools remained open in Sweden, largely because the Swedish teaching unions were compliant. On March 16, Johnson said he wanted to keep the schools open in Britain. I quote: 'We think it's better we can keep schools open for all sorts of reasons.'

Of course, the press conference also contained a lot

of fearmongering. Johnson and his advisors kept talking about the 'fast growth' phase of the virus; we were 'accelerating up the curve' of infections, apparently. We were also told about 'new numbers'. The new numbers had come from a paper published on the same day by Professor Neil Ferguson, who was predicting that half a million people could die from Covid-19. After the Q and A, journalists were ushered into an off-camera briefing where they were shown graphs and statistics about the terrible death toll that was allegedly in prospect if the government didn't take drastic measures to stop the spread of Covid-19. By wheeling out Ferguson's predictions at the March 16 press conference, the government launched him and his work into national prominence.

But curiously, even the fearmongering was qualified that evening. Chris Whitty in particular seemed to go out of his way to downplay the threat from Covid-19. He said that for the 'great majority' of people, it would be a mild illness; many people wouldn't even know they were ill. He said that the great majority of deaths would be among people who were already in poor health. And he talked about the harms that social distancing itself would cause, thus putting the minimal risks of Covid-19 in perspective.

So there were some curious contrasts at the government's March 16 press conference. The measures were being ramped up, but not in any legal sense. And, likewise, the fearmongering was being ramped up, but we were also being told that Covid-19 was generally a mild illness.

And there was another curious contrast. As well as telling us *all* to avoid social contact, Johnson and his advisers rolled out some social distancing measures that were targeted at specific groups. We were told that whole households should isolate if one person had Covid. And we were told that vulnerable people should isolate for the next 12 weeks. It was a bit strange to be presented with these targeted measures when we were all supposed to be social distancing. Again, the drastic message was combined with significant qualifications.

What was going on?

Well Johnson will have known that the unions were up in arms. He will have known about the RMT making threats, the education unions agitating for schools closures, the UCU trying to shut down universities, and the TUC encouraging its 5.5 million members to pressure their employers into allowing home working. Johnson had two options on March 16: he could tell a lot of angry people to stop misbehaving and get on with their jobs, or he could pretend that he was in charge of events. He chose the latter. He was like a bystander who suddenly runs out in front of a parade and pretends to be leading it. He issued the work from home guidance on March 16 because he needed to give the impression of being proactive about something that was going to happen whether he liked it or not. I think he just bolted the work from home guidance onto the more targeted measures that he had originally intended to present that day. At the same time, he could hardly advise working from home if he wasn't consistent about social distancing. There was no point people working from home if they were just going to go out to the pub in the evening; hence Johnson also advised us to avoid social venues. There was a knock-on effect where the measures expanded because he couldn't advocate one without the other.

All in all, the March 16 press conference was an extremely cynical exercise in spin, with the government advising us to avoid all social contact so that the government could avoid confronting the unions.

When you understand this, watching the press conference in hindsight is a creepy experience. You can see Johnson, Vallance and Whitty trying to present a coherent picture, but the overall message has obviously been cobbled together in response to the unions. For example, we've already seen that Johnson said we were all supposed to be social distancing, but that it was 'particularly important' for vulnerable people to do so; the phrase 'particularly important' was like a bridge between the ludicrous bolted-on message and the sensible message that the government had originally intended to convey.

Another example is that Vallance tried to link the advice against attending social venues with the previously announced ban on mass gatherings. You can hear that he's talking like a spin doctor, not a scientist. He says: 'Gatherings are important, big or small, so you get the whole thing together; it's not just the size of the gatherings, it's all gatherings which become important'. They *become* important? What a strange phrase! I guess he meant: they become important when you're being bullied by unions and you're trying to seem coherent.

Above all, you can hear that the three men were obviously very keen to explain their sudden U-turn on herd immunity, to hide the fact that they had caved in to the unions. Johnson asked 'Why now?' as though he was pre-empting the question before journalists asked it. The three men kept talking about the importance of getting the 'timing' right. They told us that the government hadn't acted before now because they didn't want to 'act in advance of need'. Now was the right time to abandon herd immunity, we were told, because now we were accelerating up the curve; there was a 'fast upswing'. A lot of metaphors were flying around that day! Perhaps that's because, beneath all the metaphors, the change in policy made no sense whatsoever. The whole idea behind herd immunity was that Covid would be a mild disease for most people. For this reason, mass infection was to be welcomed; ultimately it would enable the vulnerable to come out of hiding. Abandoning herd immunity because there was an upswing in infections was incoherent.

The men also talked about ventilators, which was obviously another line agreed in advance. We were told that a shortage of ventilators was why the government suddenly had to U-turn. Yet nobody had mentioned ventilators in the previous weeks or months. The government could easily have manufactured all the essential medical equipment during that time. And we haven't heard a peep about ventilators ever since, because you can't keep trotting out an obviously fixable problem every time you cave in to union demands.

Whitty also came up with a couple of even more creative excuses for the U-turn. For instance, he said Covid was now a 'very global disease'; supposedly, we needed to take a different approach now that Britain wasn't one of the first countries affected. But that made no sense either: what difference does it makes to the spread of a disease in Britain if it also happens to be spreading elsewhere, e.g. Peru? The government was already requiring international travellers to self-isolate if they developed symptoms after arriving in Britain. And anyway, when the government first decided to pursue herd immunity, they already knew it was a global pandemic. Or maybe I'm missing the point here: maybe there's an important difference between a global disease and a 'very global disease'.

Whitty also claimed that he was 'proud' of the NHS for 'delaying this', as though herd immunity would have been abandoned sooner if the NHS hadn't done such a great job. But again, the claim made no sense: the whole point of herd immunity was that delaying the spread of the infection was a bad idea, not a good idea.

Watching the press conference back, you get the impression that the three men were neurotically obsessed with justifying the timing of the measures, like naughty little boys trying not to get caught. At one point, Johnson made some remarks about the progress of the disease in London. Let me quote him at length:

It looks as though London is now a few weeks ahead. So, to relieve the pressure on the London health system and to slow the spread in London, it's important that Londoners now pay special attention to what we are saying about avoiding non-essential contact, and to take particularly seriously the advice about working from home, and avoiding confined spaces such as pubs and restaurants.

I hope you are beginning to get a feel for the shiftiness of it all. Consider that phrase 'It looks as though'. It's just ludicrously imprecise, given that all this advice was supposed to be scientific. And again we see that measures that were supposed to apply to everyone were being emphasised for specific people, namely,

Londoners. But most importantly, it's very, very fishy that Johnson chose to emphasise London at this particular time. Remember: three days beforehand, the RMT, the rail workers union, had said they would take whatever action is required to protect their members. In the press release on March 13, the RMT had complained about 'inertia' at regional and national level, but they had noted specifically that they were joining forces with London Underground unions. Clearly London was a hub for the unrest among rail unions. No wonder Johnson told Londoners to pay special attention to the social distancing advice. His comment about the London health system should be taken with a pinch of salt. He was trying to smooth things over with the London rail unions. He urgently wanted to get Londoners off the Tube in case he was faced with industrial action.

And there's more that's creepy about the March 16 press conference, around this issue of timing. Johnson said that the measures he has outlined are the 'right package for this particular moment'. Vallance, similarly, talked about doing things in the 'right combinations' at the 'right time'. Looking back, this is just laughable. The idea that science can tell us the right combinations of draconian restrictions to take at the right times to stop the spread of a cold is just ridiculous. What does the word 'right' even mean in this context? How many right combinations are there? What would a wrong combination look like? What would the right combination look like at the wrong time? Or vice versa?

Looking beneath the spin, it's obvious why this idea of combinations was useful to the government. What measures the government took would depend on what measures the unions were demanding at any particular time. The very randomness of the idea of the right combinations was in fact perfectly designed to reflect the randomness of the demands the unions were inclined to make. Throughout the coronapanic debacle, we've seen the government plucking combinations of measures out of thin air, based on the arbitrary whims of the unions.

So at the March 16 press conference, the government offered many spurious justifications for the sudden U-turn. But there was one justification that trumped all the rest: the idea that half a million people could die from Covid-19, according to new research published by Neil Ferguson that day. This potential death toll was alarming, and it has been credited with driving the government's coronapanic measures in mid-March. But hang on! I hope by now you will be suspicious of the accepted narrative. Given that the government was desperately trying to justify the timing of the new measures, so that nobody would find out that ministers were in fact caving in to the unions, I think it's highly likely that Ferguson's research was wheeled out to supply such a justification. In other words, the conventional narrative is back to front: the government's decision to U-turn caused them to focus on Ferguson, not the other way round. Wheeling out Ferguson was a colossal exercise in spin.

And that's a colossal scandal if true. But it fits the facts. The government knew about Ferguson's results at least a week before March 16. Ferguson himself has admitted it. Let me quote him:

The government were aware of what our results were showing certainly in the previous week, and some of the results in the previous two weeks.

And if that bombshell isn't enough, Ferguson adds an even more damning comment. He says:

The paper came out that day partly because there was pressure on government to be showing the modelling informing policy making.

You can see the smoke billowing from the gun. The pressure was political; the government was trying to appear to be in charge, trying to appear to be rational, when the truth was quite the opposite; they were caving in to the demands of lunatic unions. Ferguson's research was wheeled out to spin the U-turn.

Let's also remember that Whitty and Vallance were the architects of the herd immunity strategy. They too will have known about Ferguson's research in advance, so presumably they were now standing up and promoting his barmy ideas solely because they were under political pressure to do so. Of course, you could argue that Whitty and Vallance had changed their minds, but it doesn't seem likely. As far as I can see, neither of them independently gave any indication around the time of the March 16 press conference that they supported a sudden U-turn into the lunacy of social distancing.

And neither of them looks very comfortable during the press conference. They can't have been very happy about being told to rip up their previous advice and start rationalising lunacy. Whitty seemed especially uncomfortable. At one point he asked: 'You might say why with a disease which the great majority of people are going to recover from, and most will have a mild or non-noticeable disease, would we want to do anything at all?' It's a very good question! Often Whitty seemed contemptuous of the whole idea of supressing a cold through short term draconian restrictions. He said: 'This is going to go on for a very long time, and we should not be under any illusions that if we just do this for a couple of weeks, that will be sufficient'. It's quite poignant hearing those honest words back, isn't it?

Another relevant fact here: there is a BuzzFeed article quoting a 'source' who suggests that both Whitty and Vallance favoured a return to the herd immunity strategy as soon as possible. Interestingly, at the press conference, they both emphasised the need to develop a test to establish how many people had had Covid-19 asymptomatically. Whitty said such a test would be 'transformational'. I think this test was important to he and Vallance, because they will have assumed that as soon as they could get a better insight into how many people had had the disease asymptomatically, they could revert to their original herd immunity strategy. They could potentially show that Britain was already far down the path of herd immunity, and, in doing so, they could put a stop to the nonsense of suppressing a cold through social distancing. Sadly, reason didn't prevail, and the nonsense continued even when the test was available. But the important thing here is that Whitty and Vallance clearly wanted to prove that the March 16 guidance was ludicrous. They were grudgingly backing the guidance, because the government's spin machine required them to do so.

And don't forget about the journalists being ushered aside and shown Ferguson's data after the press conference. This move had all the hallmarks of a spin operation. The government will have wanted the headline writers to be in no doubt that there was a so-called scientific reason for the U-turn. And, indeed, if you want a pseudo-scientific doomsday prediction, Ferguson is the man you want to call on. He has a track record of this sort of thing. During the Swine Flu outbreak, one of his models predicted that 65,000 people could die – the final figure was below 500. During the BSE panic, Ferguson warned the government that 150,000 people could die. Six million animals were slaughtered as a precaution – in the end, 200 people died. And during the Bird Flu outbreak, Ferguson outdid himself and said that 200 million could die – the true number was in the low hundreds. When faced with a massive union mutiny in mid-March 2020, you can imagine Johnson thinking 'We're going to have to U-turn, and we're going to have to spin like crazy, with some scary statistics; let's let Ferguson loose'.

Actually that scenario is probably not even as scandalous as the full truth. The government probably directly influenced the content of Ferguson's paper. This might sound fanciful but in fact it's normal procedure, judging by a recent exchange on Twitter between the journalist Fraser Nelson and Graham Medley, who is a Professor of Infectious Disease. Referring to the prospect of restrictions over the Christmas period in 2021, Nelson asked Medley why modellers hadn't considered the possibility that the Omicron variant is mild. Medley replied: 'We generally model what we are asked to model. There is a dialogue in which policy teams discuss with the modellers what they need to inform their policy'.

That's a jaw-dropping statement. Having heard it, we're entitled to wonder if such a 'dialogue' took place in March 2020 between the government and Ferguson. We're entitled to wonder if Ferguson was asked to produce doomsday predictions because this was what the policy teams needed to inform their policy.

That's speculation. But there is evidence strongly suggesting that the government influenced Ferguson's paper in at least one way. The evidence concerns the issue of schools closures. At the March 16 press conference, Johnson, Whitty and Vallance all kept emphasising that schools closures may be necessary at the right time. Johnson said closing the schools was something the government was keeping 'under review'. Remember that the NEU had been openly agitating for schools closures since March 14, probably with the support of the other eight teaching unions. The NEU had even alleged that the government was exploring legal action to keep the schools open. So when Johnson talked about schools closures as something that was under review on March 16, he was being shifty; keeping schools open depended on whether or not the teaching unions backed down.

Here's why this issue points towards a strong likelihood that Ferguson's research was influenced by the government. Astonishingly, in Ferguson's paper, he too endorsed the shifty idea that the government 'may' need to close schools. Indeed, the claim can be found in the paper's abstract – the part of the paper that journalists were most likely to read. Ferguson notes that suppressing the virus would involve social distancing and whole households isolating, to which he adds: 'This may need to be supplemented by school and university closures'. Oh, fancy that! Exactly the sort of message you would want to hear if you were a politician readying yourself for a possible capitulation to mutinous teaching unions. And let's also not forget that the UCU, the academic union, was trying to shut down universities at that time. Ferguson's message was right on cue there too.

This matter is so grave, I won't rely on sarcasm to make the point. Ferguson's paper was supposed to be a serious scientific document modelling a pandemic. We were entitled to expect rigour and precision, especially when we were being asked to participate in the nightmare of social distancing for an unspecified period of time. Yet when it came to schools and universities, the most that Ferguson's paper was able to say was that they 'may' need to close. Where was the precision? And if the whole point of social distancing was to prevent mass death, wouldn't closing schools and universities have been an essential precaution? Granted, Ferguson did try to quantify the potential effects of closing schools and universities, arguing that the closures may not be necessary because the NHS might be able to cope without the closures. But, still, the argument is a little too convenient. Apparently, Ferguson's modelling just couldn't quite say for sure whether the NHS would be tipped over the edge if schools and universities remained open. And nor did he address the most obvious objection: if the hospitals had started filling up with 80-year-olds, no scientist in their right mind would have blamed it on the virus spreading among young people. I cannot see any way to make sense of Ferguson's equivocation over closing schools and universities other than by assuming that the government required him to include the equivocation in his paper.

It's not as if Ferguson wasn't capable of making confident assertions about schools closures. Later in the paper, he declares 'school closure is predicted to be insufficient to mitigate (never mind supress) an epidemic in isolation'. In other words: closing schools while leaving the economy open – the Japan option – would be insufficient, according to Ferguson. Exactly the line that the British government ended up taking. We're entitled to wonder if Ferguson was instructed to include this point too, given the obvious whiff of collusion around the idea that schools 'may' need to close.

And it wasn't just schools closures where Ferguson opened the door to a government climbdown. Several times in the paper, including in the abstract, we find Ferguson peddling the idea of 'combined' measures – the same idea the politicians kept peddling. Granted, there is an element of truth behind the idea. Obviously the more stuff you shut down, the fewer opportunities people will have to mix socially. But it would be more accurate to speak of 'cumulative measures'. The word 'combinations' seems to suggest some extra property that individual measures acquire when joined together, like a flurry of different punches that floors a boxer. And it's very telling that the new measures Ferguson discussed as potential combinations just happened to tally up with the measures that were on the government's radar at the time: possible schools and universities closures, to placate the unions, and a social distancing policy, again to placate the unions, along with whole household isolation and shielding the vulnerable. If Ferguson had thrown in some analyses of other specific measures – for instance, shutting down cinemas or sports clubs or dating apps – his concept of combinations might have seemed less fishy. We're entitled to ask if the government instructed him to talk about combinations because the concept was useful to the government.

All in all, the Ferguson episode reminds me of the so-called sexed-up dossier that led to Britain's participation in the Iraq war. BBC reporter Andrew Gilligan famously alleged that the intelligence officers who had compiled the dossier had been pressured by the government to include scary claims, including the infamous claim that Saddam Hussain could unleash weapons of mass destruction in 45 minutes. Politicians wheeled out the dossier to support the decision to invade Iraq, a decision that had in fact been made on other grounds. Likewise, Ferguson's paper may have been sexed up to justify the government's decision to mandate social distancing and (possibly) schools and universities closures, while all those decisions would in fact made on other grounds, namely, caving in to the unions.

Anyway, whether or not the government sexed up Ferguson's paper, his research was almost certainly wheeled out on March 16 in order to spin a U-turn that was based on massive union unrest. There is one more piece of evidence that suggests this. It comes inadvertently from the testimony of Dominic Cummings who was involved in the decision-making process at that time. In interviews, Cummings has claimed that he and two data scientists, the brothers Ben and Marc Warner, persuaded Johnson to change his mind about herd immunity. Cummings says: 'It was like a scene from *Independence Day* with Jeff Goldblum saying the aliens are here and your plan is broken, you're going to need a new plan'. This interaction is supposed to have happened on March 14.

Do you believe that Cummings was the one who changed Johnson's mind? Well, glossing over the fact that Cummings uses an example from science *fiction* to illustrate the scene, I'm not even convinced that Cummings believes his own account, because he admits that Johnson was still sceptical in the days that followed. In my opinion, Cummings is telling an obvious lie. But then if Cummings is lying, why didn't Johnson correct him publicly? Presumably, the reason is that Johnson wasn't keen to have any sort of public discussion of the events leading up to March 16, because any retrospective scrutiny of that period could place him in very hot water. The awkward truth, which neither man will have wanted to admit, was that unions drove the government into the measures on March 16. Cummings felt emboldened to claim that he was the hero of the hour because he knew Johnson wasn't going to dare contradict him.

As well as claiming that Johnson remained sceptical after March 16, Cummings has also claimed that there was no government plan to lockdown on March 16. This seems plausible: no indication of a forthcoming lockdown was given at the press conference. Johnson certainly gave the impression of not favouring legal enforcement. He said: 'Most people would accept that we are a mature and grown up and liberal democracy where people understand very clearly the advice that is being given to them'. At one point, a journalist basically came out and asked Johnson if there would be a lockdown. Johnson didn't say yes. But he did say 'we're keeping all measures under review'. He then immediately added 'particularly, people will be thinking about schools closures'. That's interesting because we know that closing schools was another thing which the government said was under review. And we know that Johnson was trying to avoid closing schools, so we can assume that keeping lockdown 'under review' likewise meant trying to avoid lockdown. Tellingly, Johnson then added: 'there is an argument about schools closures'. That's also a revealing choice of phrase, because there was indeed an argument taking place – between the government and the teaching unions.

And we now know that the government lost that argument. The very next day, March 17, the mutinous teachers upped the ante. The NEU wrote another open letter to the government, this time explicitly demanding the closure of all schools, and threatening to support any Heads who unilaterally closed schools. Furthermore, it is reasonable to wonder if some teachers were handing in Section 44 letters to Heads that day, in line with the wider work from home mutiny being stoked by the TUC. Certainly, on March 17 a petition from parents and teachers calling for schools closures reached almost 640,000 signatories. (I have also discovered that PCS Union – the civil service union – reported that they 'met the Cabinet Office' on March 17, 'to raise concerns about the impact the coronavirus outbreak is having on our members'. More pressure on Johnson.) On March 18, the day after the NEU had openly threatened unilateral schools closures, the government caved in, announcing that all schools would close. On Friday March 20, the same day the schools shut their gates, the government announced that the rest of the economy was closing too. Looking back at the March 16 press conference, we can see clearly why Johnson immediately mentioned the prospect of schools closures after he was asked about the prospect of a lockdown. Both prospects were 'under review' because they were, in practice, equivalent. Following his phone call to Japan on March 15, Johnson had obviously concluded that trying to keep the economy open without schools would cause too much chaos. The schools closures plunged Britain into lockdown.

So there you have it. March 13 to March 18: five decisive days leading to a manmade catastrophe. And of those five days, March 16 was especially pivotal. It was an inflection point. On one hand, Johnson announced drastic measures that day, in order to hide a massive union mutiny that was already taking place. The RMT was making threats, the UCU was trying to shut universities, and the TUC – a federation of 48 unions – was stoking a work from home mutiny. On the other hand, Johnson was also trying to hold back the tide that day, trying to prevent schools closures, to avoid a full lockdown. The guidance he issued on March 16 was his last throw of the dice. If he could get the country on board with voluntary social distancing, maybe the teachers would be less anxious about the spread of Covid; maybe they would agree to keep the schools open. It didn't work. Within 48 hours of saying that the schools 'may' need to close, the government had decided that schools definitely did need to close, thanks to the NEU's determination to force the issue.

Britain's coronapanic debacle was caused by a union mutiny in March 2020. If you still doubt this, imagine a parallel universe in which the unions didn't mutiny. Imagine if the unions had recognised that

Johnson's herd immunity policy was both wise and humane. Imagine if the unions had understood that young and healthy people had an obligation to keep the economy going, to protect the vulnerable. Imagine if the unions had accepted that they had no right to demand special treatment when the virus was infecting people indiscriminately. Imagine if the unions had pledged to do everything within their power to keep Britain open and protect children from harm. Do you really think the government would have abandoned herd immunity in those circumstances, after holding firm for two weeks? Yes, the media was stoking fears, and there was widespread panic throughout Britain, but it wasn't until the unions started kicking off in mid-March that the government started caving in, in eerie synchrony with the specific demands being made by the unions.

And, of course, as I have showed in my previous essay and my videos, the government has carried on caving in to specific union demands – masks on public transport, masks in shops, masks in schools, the second lockdown, the third lockdown, last year's ruined Christmas, and vaccines in schools. All were union driven. And the government is still caving in to the unions. This winter, we've seen the RMT demand masks on trains again and USDAW demand masks in shops again; we've seen the government cave in. We've seen the BMA and NHS Confederation pressuring the government to enact a 'Plan B', including mandatory Covid passes; we've seen the government cave in. In the process, we've seen Johnson claim that a new variant of Covid necessitated the new measures, the same mendacious excuse he used for the third lockdown. There always seems to a new variant ready to hand when a capitulation is in progress. Needless to say, no one involved in the sham has bothered to emphasise that the latest variant – 'Omicron' – is particularly mild.

Recently I've discovered that NHS Confederation has been 'working closely' with NHSX, the organisation that built and designed the Covid Passes. By way of this partnership, the NHS has lobbied the government to mandate Covid passes, because the new technology will boost vaccine uptake, and vaccines are highly profitable for the NHS. The BMA has also been heavily involved in lobbying for Covid Passes. The whole damn scheme is extortion, pure and simple. At the same time, we've seen Johnson himself calling for a national vaccination campaign to supress the Omicron variant. Having spun his way into the coronapanic debacle, he's still trying to spin his way out, using vaccines as an exit strategy. No wonder a PM who places so much emphasis on vaccination hasn't been able to resist the pressure from the NHS over Covid passes. Meanwhile, with Covid vaccine propaganda emanating from both the government and the NHS, and with both sides ignoring evidence of the adverse effects of the vaccines, the public is stuck in the middle, being jabbed up to the eyeballs and treated like collateral. Horrifyingly, Johnson has even called for a national conversation about mandatory Covid vaccination.

Let me tell you now: I will never submit. I will not be forced into taking a vaccine for a cold.

Finally, we've seen the despicable teaching unions kicking off again, demanding the return of cruel and deranged Covid measures in schools, including masks in corridors. The teachers are still callously disregarding the welfare of the kids, and the government has capitulated again. As I write, the teachers are rearing up for a showdown with the government in the New Year, just like last January, when Johnson sent the whole country into lockdown to cover up the fact that the teaching unions were refusing to return to work. Whether the schools reopen properly this January is anyone's guess.

It's all an unrelenting shambles, an unspeakable disgrace. The fundamental problem is that the government won't confront all these insane union demands. To confront the unions properly, Johnson would have to say: 'We don't need to take any new measures'. But then the socialist lunatics in the unions would start calling him a 'butcher' again. He'd have to start defending herd immunity. And he's not going to do that, because if he defended herd immunity now, he'd be confessing that he should never have abandoned the policy in the first place; he'd be confessing that the whole coronapanic debacle was a monstrous overreaction. He's in far too deep to come clean. That's why it's so crucial that the public understands what really happened in mid-March 2020, and what has been happening ever since. Those of us who understand that the whole debacle has been union-driven need to educate the rest of the public. When the public understands that none of this madness was ever necessary, they will demand that ALL the Covid rules are discarded. Democratic pressure is our only hope of escape. And telling the truth about the unions is the only way to generate the required democratic pressure.

People often say that Johnson has failed to stand up to the unions because he is weak. I don't know. Maybe he is, maybe he isn't. What I *do* know is that you can't decide one way or another without taking into account the parliamentary arithmetic Johnson has faced since the start. Let us remember that a British PM is 'first among equals'. No PM can exercise power without parliamentary support. A PM can try to generate that support, but there are no guarantees of it. And let's also remember that the Labour Party has consistently advocated restrictions, as have many members of Johnson's own party. All it would have taken was around 40 Conservative MPs withdrawing their support for Johnson at any point and he would no longer have had the support of a majority of MPs. It's also worth noting that on March 13, 2020, Jeremy Hunt, Johnson's former leadership rival, was openly calling for schools closures and social distancing. Johnson would surely have faced a serious leadership challenge if he had lost the support of Parliament in the early stages, or indeed at any point since. Hunt went on to back the NEU in October 2020 over the union's demand for a circuit breaker – a demand which very likely caused the second lockdown. Then, on January 2, 2021, Hunt said 'It is massively risky to open schools when so many parts of the NHS are teetering on the brink'. And on January 4, the day that the NEU was mutinying, he directly called for schools closures. After the government caved in and closed the schools, the NEU went as far as thanking Hunt for his support. Bearing all this in mind, parliamentary arithmetic has probably been another reason the coronapanic debacle has dragged on for so long. The PM has been hemmed in by Covid zealous MPs as well as Covid zealous unions.

Actually, it's possible that Parliament undermined Johnson in the most palpable way at the start of the coronapanic. During the March 16 press conference, a journalist asked Johnson 'Do you think Westminster can stay open till July?' Johnson's response was intriguing. He said the 'The speaker and all parties and the leader of the House of Commons are working together to find a way forward', adding: 'There may be more to come on this'. I wonder what went on behind the scenes. Whenever the PM has declared that a course of action 'may' happen during the corona-panic, it's usually because he's fending off pressure in the background. Were MPs trying to force through a work from home policy? If they were, it would certainly have added significantly to the pressure that drove Johnson into his U-turn. Notably, 80 MPs are members of GMB, which has recently been trying to force MPs to wear masks. I think we are entitled to wonder if GMB played a role in closing down Parliament in March 2020.

You might argue that Johnson was right to cave in to all the pressure at the start because it was better for him to stay in power and try to turn things round than be unseated by a Covid zealot such as Hunt. But the longer the whole debacle has gone on, the harder it has become to make that argument; Johnson's lies have become more and more farcical (we're facing a 'tidal wave of Omicron'), and more and more repellent. Indeed, you might also argue that Johnson should have walked away from power and fought back from the sidelines rather than collude in any of this lunacy. I personally would have walked away. But in a way, the issue of what Johnson should or shouldn't have done isn't that important. Far more important is the issue of what *we should do now*. If Johnson won't tell the truth about caving in to the unions, the onus is on us to tell that truth. Unless we the public supply the democratic pressure, the PM and his colleagues will just carry on covering their backsides, refusing to talk about the immense crime that has been inflicted on the British public since March 2020.

And the problem is not just the PM and his colleagues. All MPs have supported this madness at one point or another, and all are still keeping their heads down. I don't know of a single MP who has ever openly said 'The entire coronapanic debacle was unnecessary and wrong; the government should have stuck to herd immunity instead of caving in to the unions'. As things stand, we still have a democratic mountain to climb to get out of this mess. Indeed, we haven't even reached base camp yet, because, never mind the MPs, I hardly know of any *journalists* who openly say that the government should have stuck to herd immunity. Even the anti-lockdown journalists generally don't say it. The vast majority of anti-lockdown journalists didn't support Johnson on herd immunity at the time, so now they don't want to talk about this sensible policy and why Johnson abandoned it. The whole topic of the government caving in to the unions is awkward for any journalist who failed to stick up for freedom when it mattered. Most anti-lockdown journalists are still insisting that the original lockdown was justified. Their main complaints seem to be that the lockdown shouldn't have lasted so long and the government has been too heavy-handed ever since. I think this is an abject stance to take. The journalists are quibbling about how much mistreatment the British public deserves. None of this Covid madness was ever justified or necessary, and all journalists should come out and say it.

Other anti-lockdown journalists take a different approach to ignoring Johnson's herd immunity phase. These journalists think that the pandemic, and the world's pandemic response, was in fact *planned* by way of an international conspiracy – the whole thing was a 'plandemic', so the theory goes. According to the most popular version of the theory, there was a single mastermind behind the plandemic, a German academic called Klaus Schwab. The Chairman of the World Economic Forum, Schwab has long advocated shutting down the global economy and restarting it in a greener fashion – he calls this proposal a 'Great Reset'. Supposedly, Schwab conspired in secret with politicians and officials around the world to make his Great Reset happen in March 2020. Supposedly, Covid-19 was deliberately released, then the world's countries locked down by way of a prior agreement.

I'm sorry, but I don't buy it. Yes, I know that in the summer of 2020, politicians rallied round Schwab's Great Reset concept, because it offered them a chance to put a positive spin on their Covid crimes. Yes, I know there has been *opportunism* on a global scale, for example from pharmaceutical companies, international organisations, the Chinese Communist Party and no doubt Klaus Schwab himself; we certainly need to investigate all this opportunism. And yes, I know that the panic about Covid-19 was global, leading to similar policies being enacted all round the world. But similar does not mean the same. Covid policymaking hasn't been the same everywhere. Some places didn't lockdown; other places locked down then admitted it was a mistake. And there was blatantly no plan to lockdown in Britain. Johnson pursued herd immunity for two weeks, before caving in to the unions. You could hardly imagine anything that looked less planned than those chaotic five days in mid-March when the government U-turned.

In fact, when it comes to the relationship between Britain and the global picture, the plandemic theory probably gets things back to front. Despite not planning any Covid measures at all, Britain ended up helping to drag the whole world into Covid lunacy. On March 16, the British government issued a joint statement with the other G7 leaders announcing that they'd all work together on a 'coordinated international approach' to Covid-19. In his press conference that day, Johnson even claimed that Britain was leading this international effort. The G7 is a group of countries comprising Canada, France, Germany, Italy, Japan, the UK and the USA, seven of the world's most powerful economies. In their March 16 statement, the G7 countries declared that they were committed to taking the 'necessary public health measures to protect people at risk from Covid-19', and to ensuring 'the stability of the global economy'. The statement added: 'We call on the International Monetary Fund and the World Bank Group and other International Organisations to further support countries worldwide as part of a coordinated global response'.

At first sight, a coordinated global response may sound very much like a plandemic. But the comparison is superficial. The key point is this: the G7 venture wouldn't have happened without the buy-in of Britain and the USA, and both of these countries tried to resist imposing any Covid restrictions at home, never mind abroad. Johnson originally thought the best thing to do about Covid-19 was just to wash your hands. And Trump was no less nonchalant. When asked by a reporter on February 29 how Americans should 'prepare' for the virus, Trump replied: 'I hope they don't change their routine'. He declined to impose a national lockdown in the USA; states ended up in lockdown only because of decisions made at state level. If Johnson and Trump had got their way, Britain and the USA would have remained free, which means that the G7 intervention was *ad hoc*, not planned. Also, it's important to note that the G7 statement on March 16 made no mention of lockdowns. We know that Johnson was still trying to avoid lockdown at that point; he was calling for voluntary social distancing, nothing further. And Japan never locked down. The G7 countries, including Britain and the USA, ended up playing a significant role in exporting Covid restrictions around the world, including lockdowns. But this was far from being a planned global lockdown.

So why did the G7 leaders work together? A major part of it was probably safety in numbers. The leaders will have known that the stakes were extremely high and that their decisions around Covid would be heavily scrutinised. Although the G7 statement made no mention of lockdowns, the leaders were clearly moving towards greater intervention, be it voluntary measures or legal measures. Either way, there would be a lot of disruption for the G7 countries. By moving together, and bringing other countries along too, the G7 leaders wouldn't be so exposed. In addition, global coordination will have had economic advantages for the G7 countries. 'Financial stability' was probably a euphemism for not being economically outcompeted during the pandemic. Perhaps the G7 countries, working with the IMF and the World Bank, offered other governments incentives to impose Covid restrictions; the incentives might have included debt relief or cheap credit.

I am speculating. But the speculation can be taken a step further, based on other factors. We know that the March 16 press conference in Britain was a spin operation. We know that Johnson escalated Britain's pandemic response to hide a union mutiny. We can assume that he joined forces with the other G7 countries to add further credibility to his bogus policymaking around Covid. But all this points to an intriguing possibility. What if the G7 countries were all facing union mutinies? What if the G7 countries joined together because they were all trying to hide these mutinies? What if the G7's pandemic response statement was essentially just a bigger version of the spin operation that Johnson was undertaking in Britain?

I can't prove any of this, because I don't know how much trouble unions have caused in other G7 countries, or the timelines involved. There has definitely been union unrest in Canada and the USA, especially from the teaching unions, but I don't know if this was a factor at the start of the pandemic. More research is needed; I call on lockdown sceptics worldwide to investigate the role of the unions in their own countries and get in touch with me.

However, at this point, I do have one more bombshell revelation to make, and it's on the topic of union unrest in the G7. Remember the TUC webinar I mentioned earlier? In that webinar, the presenters talked about trade union members handing in Section 44 notices to force through working from home. But the presenters didn't just talk about this kind of mutiny happening in Britain. They said it had happened somewhere else too: *in Italy.*

Italy! Italy was the second country to lockdown, and, according to the TUC, in early March there was industrial unrest among Italian trade unions. You cannot help but wonder if the Italian lockdown was a spin lockdown, just like Britain's lockdowns. You also cannot help but wonder if the Italian teaching unions played a decisive role, just like in Britain. The schools closed in Italy four days before the national lockdown was announced.

Let me propose a theory. It may prove true. It may not. I call it the 'coagulation theory'. Coagulation means blood clotting; I am using this as an analogy for economic shutdown. We know that in Britain unions were trying to unilaterally shut down workplaces before the government went out front and pretended to lead the process. We know that there was similar unrest in Italy. Let's speculate that union unrest happened in all the G7 countries. Let's speculate that the G7 countries all decided not to confront the unrest but to mould Covid policy to fit the union demands. And let's speculate that the G7 countries all decided to back each other up in doing so. Let's also speculate that they then marshalled the various mechanisms of international cooperation, especially financial powers, to make sure that other countries around the world fell into line. If I'm right about this, then the global Covid response led by the G7 was the biggest political spin operation in history. Naturally, none of the leaders and officials who were involved in all this terrible corruption would have wanted to talk about it. And in turn, their reticence would explain why the global coronapanic has been so difficult to reverse.

You could summarise my 'coagulation theory' as

follows: trade unions coagulated individual G7 countries, then individual G7 governments accelerated the process, then the G7 countries joined forces to coagulate the rest of the world, and the world hasn't uncoagulated yet because the leaders are still covering each other's backsides.

However, a caveat: I am always telling people not to assume that all the Covid madness had a single cause, so I should take my own advice. Maybe some of the G7 governments didn't require a union mutiny to push them into their Covid policies. Maybe, worldwide, there were governments that didn't require a push from the G7 countries. Maybe there was simply a lot of mimicry happening between governments worldwide, in keeping with the global panic that was also spreading by mimicry. Maybe the G20 countries played a significant role too; at the March 16 press conference, Johnson said he was working with the G20 as well as the G7, although there was no formal joint statement made by the G20 countries on that day. Finally, there's evidence that the Chinese Communist Party has been pushing lockdown policies worldwide. The global picture is complex, naturally.

And, anyway, I don't want to dwell too long on the global dimension of the whole debacle; there's a risk of getting bogged down in speculation. One of my main gripes with the plandemic theory is that it's so dismal. I'm not even convinced that the plandemic theory is all that different from Covid lunacy itself – they both involve paranoia about a hidden global threat. Endless unsubstantiated speculation about an overwhelming global plandemic just demoralises people. And in their demoralised state, they become flippant, and passive. Plandemic speculation has become a form of virtue signalling, as though people are saying: 'I care so much about this gigantic global problem, but it's so gigantic, and it's all planned out, so there's nothing I can possibly do about it'. I also think many of the people who support the plandemic theory are trying to exonerate themselves for tamely surrendering their freedom at the start; much easier to tell themselves that they were swept up in a global plan. I think they're still surrendering. They're surrendering to the unionised socialists who have driven all this lunacy in Britain.

One of my followers on Twitter made a perceptive comment about this. She said blaming the coronapanic debacle on a plandemic is much less awkward than confronting your fellow countrymen who have participated in the debacle – your friends, your colleagues, your boss, your child's teachers, your doctor, and maybe even your family... the list is likely to be long. Whether we like it nor not, we will need to have these sorts of confrontations if we want to get free, because Britain's coronapanic debacle began domestically, and it is being perpetuated domestically.

No country has ever freed itself from communism by banging on about the international aspect of communism. The same goes for any country that wants to free itself from all this Covid lunacy: each country needs to get its own house in order. That's why I generally focus on my country, Britain. Indeed, I think the British lockdown sceptics who ignore what's happening in this country are being especially remiss. In Britain, we have a unique opportunity to demonstrate that the whole coronapanic debacle was corrupt from the start. We know that the leading scientists in Britain favoured herd immunity, and that they did so for good reason. We know that the government followed their advice faithfully until there was a potent union mutiny, whereupon the government caved in. We know that the only reason the government escalated the coronapanic measures in mid-March 2020 was because of pressure from unions. We know that the road to lockdown should never have been taken.

Let's recap the main events on that road. First, on March 10, medical staff from GMB threatened to mutiny, citing inadequate PPE for NHS workers. Other unions soon waded in on the issue, and the scene was set; the government was accused of not taking the pandemic seriously. Gradually the government caved in under pressure from unions. Mass gatherings were banned on March 13, following threats from the RMT, the rail workers union. Meanwhile, a huge work from home mutiny was being stoked by the TUC, a federation of 48 unions. At the same time, the UCU was trying to shut down universities, and the teaching unions were agitating for schools closures. There were probably other mutinies too, behind the scenes. Faced with this situation, the government went into spin overdrive, holding a press conference on March 16 in which Johnson, Whitty and Vallance desperately tried to justify a U-turn on herd immunity. To this end, they wheeled out Neil Ferguson's preposterous paper with its doomsday predictions and its advice on 'combinations' of measures. Moreover, the paper itself was likely influenced by the government, including Ferguson's claim that schools 'may' need to shut. The next day, March 17, the NEU threatened unilateral schools closures and, the day after that, March 18, the government caved in, announcing that schools did indeed need to shut. This was the decisive capitulation, and it plunged Britain into lockdown. On March 20, the day that the schools shut their gates, the government announced that the rest of the economy was shutting too. The result: nearly two years of lunacy and spin. Unions have been making demands and threats ever since mid-March 2020, and the government has kept on caving in, while the public has been dragged into hell.

There is a repeating pattern, and it's happening in plain sight. A union pressures the government to implement a certain measure, then the government says the measure is under review, then, more often than not, the government caves in and implements the measure because the union won't back down. We cannot go on like this. We cannot keep watching all this lunacy unfold while hardly anyone will talk about what is actually happening. Politicians and journalists are still skirting around the truth: that the entire coronapanic debacle has been union-driven and pointless. Lockdowns, social distancing, masks, mass testing, test and trace, mass vaccination, Covid passes, and children being subjected to unbelievable cruelty: it has all been pointless and wrong. Herd immunity was the right policy, and it was abandoned because of mutinous unions. It's high time we put these facts front and centre of the national conversation about Covid-19.

It's also high time that lockdown sceptics stopped pretending that all this was planned. There was no plandemic. Quite the opposite: Britain's original plan was sensible, and the lockdown was unplanned. People who support the plandemic theory often call me 'parochial'. They say 'Yes, Ben, but who is *behind* the unions?' My reply is: sure, we need to consider that question. But we mustn't lose track of our priorities. When you're witnessing a crime, you don't sit around speculating about who is 'behind' the culprits. You deal with the culprits, and you investigate possible collusion in the process. When we properly confront the unions that have driven the coronapanic debacle in Britain, I have no doubt that their crimes will be shown to have a global dimension, and this will need to be dealt with in turn. But obsessing about the whole world while British unions continue to run amok is only making things worse for us in Britain. Moreover, if we don't get our own house in order, we will leave ourselves prone to the opportunism of the globalists. The plandemic theorists who believe that this whole nightmare unfolded by way of a global plan are in fact creating a self-fulfilling prophecy; the globalists will prevail if we keep assuming that they have already defeated us.

In Britain we can show that none of this Covid madness was ever necessary. Let us seize the opportunity. Let us talk about herd immunity, the sensible policy that the government abandoned. Let us talk about the government capitulating to the unions, and capitulating repeatedly, spinning every time. Let us break the vicious cycle, rip this entire thing apart, so that nothing is left of the coronapanic debacle in this country. Let us put it all behind us. Britain could be the first country to fully free itself from Covid lunacy. The first domino to fall. Let us apply the democratic pressure that will make it happen.

January 1, 2022

# Boris versus the NEU: The Second Lockdown Explained

> History doesn't repeat itself, but it rhymes.
>
> — Mark Twain

## I

The more that Britain's coronapanic debacle dragged on, the more outraged I was at the impact it was having on my life, on the public generally, and on children especially. I was also outraged at the complete lack of journalistic investigation into why Boris Johnson kept overseeing Covid restrictions that he clearly didn't believe in. It didn't take the 'Partygate' scandal – all those illicit lockdown gatherings in 10 Downing Street – to know that every single restriction has been pointless and dishonest from the start. Covid-19 was a cold with an average age of death of 82. There was never any prospect of the NHS being 'overwhelmed'. And the lockdowns and the mask mandates and the social distancing rules were all ineffectual, and they would have been wrong even if they weren't ineffectual, and wrong no matter how dangerous Covid-19 was or how overwhelmed the NHS was. During the last 18 months, I've taken it upon myself to do the missing journalism, to unearth the real reason behind the restrictions. My research has pointed to a recurring theme: threats and demands made by public sector unions. From the first lockdown to the masks on public transport to the masks in shops to the masks in workplaces to the second lockdown to the Christmas restrictions to the third lockdown to the masks in schools to the vaccines in schools and the vaccine passes... all these measures were driven by unions, with the government repeatedly caving in.

More recently, I have broadened my research to look at the global picture, going right back to where it all started. I discovered, to my amazement, that the Wuhan lockdown was driven primarily by mass panic and civil unrest, probably with a union element to the unrest. As I have explained in my book 'The Truth About the Wuhan Lockdown', China's president Xi Jinping gave the hysterical Chinese public what they wanted, then he lashed out at the world with a shock-and-awe pro-lockdown campaign.

But throughout my research, one question has nagged at me: what exactly happened with England's second lockdown? The whole episode is shrouded in mystery. Why did Johnson shout 'no more fucking lockdowns' but then do a lockdown anyway? Was he 'bounced' into the measure by a press leak? Who leaked the information? What exactly was the role of the National Education Union? The NEU was demanding a 'circuit breaker lockdown', basically an extended half term holiday for the teachers. Johnson obliged with the lockdown but he kept the schools open. Why this paradoxical combination? And when the NEU continued demanding schools closures during the second lockdown, why didn't Johnson cave in again?

I looked long and hard at these events and I couldn't make sense of them. But then I realised my mistake. The second lockdown is not a puzzle. It is a puzzle piece. And a puzzle piece only makes sense when you slot it correctly into the surrounding picture. You can only understand the second lockdown when you see it as a battle in a longer war: Boris versus the NEU. If this war hadn't happened, I believe Britain would never have gone into lockdown, not once. From March 2020 onwards, the NEU relentlessly attacked both the British government and the British public, especially schoolchildren. Johnson fought back with his hands tied behind his back and his mouth taped up. But I think history will record that he did try, in a fashion, to defend freedom. History may even record that he won.


II


Johnson's war against the NEU consisted of three major battles. The first battle must be understood in detail before the second makes any sense. Later, we will see that the third battle also sheds light on the second.

Britain's coronapanic debacle began in mid-March 2020. Throughout February and the first half of March, Johnson had pursued a 'herd immunity' strategy, as advised by the government's chief scientists. The idea was that old and vulnerable people would stay out of harm's way for a while and then emerge as soon as the virus had spread harmlessly through the young and healthy population. Johnson was well aware that locking Britain down would be counterproductive and wrong. Privately he was saying that 'the real danger here is the measures that we take to deal with the disease and the economic destruction that that will cause'. He and his science advisors reassured the public that the virus would be mild for the great majority, and, accordingly, that the great majority should continue going about their business.

Unfortunately, the government's sensible approach wasn't met with a sensible response. The world was descending into panic, and, after Italy locked down on March 9, the atmosphere in Britain became rabid. The media was fearmongering mercilessly, and there were growing calls for a lockdown. Most of the calls came from politicians and journalists on the left, but the right played a part too. Britain's leading right-wing newspaper, the *Telegraph*, spewed out pro-lockdown propaganda. From February to April 2020, the paper is alleged to have published more than 50 articles paid for by the Chinese Communist Party (many of the articles subsequently being deleted). Amid almost zero support for herd immunity, the government made a half-hearted attempt to defend the policy, whereupon the socialists decided to force the issue.

In mid-March 2020, there was an escalating series of demands and threats by large unions. Health unions demanded better PPE in hospitals, with the GMB Union threatening a staff mutiny. The RMT, the leading rail union, promised to take 'whatever action was required' to protect its members. The academic union, the UCU, called for universities to close. The NEU began agitating for schools closures. The legal union, the LSWU, called for the government to 'shut down the courts'. The TUC – a federation of 48 unions – stoked a work-from-home mutiny and demanded a furlough scheme to protect people's incomes. PCS union – the civil service union – lobbied the cabinet. There was probably also a union-driven campaign to shut Parliament. The government gradually caved in. The capitulation began on March 13 with the banning of mass gatherings, a measure that Johnson admitted was not based on scientific advice; rather, he explained, he wanted to relieve a 'burden' on the public sector. On March 16, the herd immunity strategy was consigned to history, as the PM held a press conference at which he announced that from now on the public should work from home and practice social distancing. These measures were happening whether Johnson liked it or not: he got out in front of the parade and pretended to lead it, justifying the U-turn by wheeling out Professor Neil Ferguson's preposterous doomsday predictions of mass death. From herd immunity… to a herd mutiny… to herd lunacy… in a matter of days.

But note: there was still no legally enforced lockdown on March 16. At the press conference, Johnson explicitly said he was issuing 'advice'; he insisted that Britain was 'a mature and grown up and liberal democracy', the implication being that no legal curbs on freedom were required. A journalist asked the PM explicitly if there would be a lockdown. Johnson hedged, saying 'We're keeping all measures under review', then he added, ominously: 'Particularly, people will be thinking about schools closures'. Behind these words lay an iceberg of hidden truth.

An iceberg into which British democracy was about to crash.

III

On March 17, the NEU wrote an open letter calling for
the government to shut all the schools. The letter
warned that headteachers would unilaterally shut
schools if there were staff shortages caused by self-
isolation. On the face of it, this warning might sound
reasonable. But it wasn't. It was extremely unreasonable. The official government position was to keep
schools open, because there was very little danger in
doing so, and very much danger in not doing so. The
unions should have promised to do everything within
their power to keep children in education. Warning of
unilateral schools closures *while also calling for all
schools to close* was clearly a threat, an attempt to
force the issue.

The same goes for all the unions that were agitating
at this time. All the demands and threats made by
unions in mid-March 2020 were an attempt to until-
aterally shut Britain down.

People often ask me – why did the unions do it?
Well, fear was certainly a factor. Britain's major
unions are run by socialists, and in general socialists
have been frantic about Covid-19 since the start of the
outbreak. While Johnson was pursuing herd immunity,
they called him a 'butcher', a 'murderer', even a
'fascist'. They accused him of 'culling the weak',
which was a brazen lie; the entire point of the herd
immunity strategy was for the strong to bear the
burden. The unions became a battering ram by which
socialists inflicted their anxiety on the country.

However, there was more to the union agitation
than an irrational fear of the virus. Socialism itself is
an irrational ideology, indeed an ideology that contra-

dicts everything good in human nature. Socialists demonise anyone who believes in freedom and individual responsibility. Socialists disparage the idea that voluntary shared projects, such as businesses, real communities and charities, are the building blocks of a good society. Socialists are blasé or hostile towards family values. Socialists claim that the only way to create a better society is for the state to exert control over people's lives. And, above all, socialists insist that the state has a monopoly on compassion. Of course, what the socialists don't tell you is that they themselves are the main beneficiaries of state control. All the opprobrium heaped on Johnson in March 2020 was standard fare, as far as socialism is concerned. The furious demands to shut down the country and abolish all natural human relations so that socialists could have a quieter time at work or luxuriate at home on full pay while pretending to care about people... it was pure socialism.

And, as for the people who did manual or service work during the pandemic, they were, in effect, enslaved by the socialists. I myself worked most evenings as a delivery driver. The lockdown shifts were exhausting, expensive and dangerous: I burned through several cars and crashed into a signpost in the snow. I felt like one of those Cambodian political prisoners who were forced to dig ditches while the Khmer Rouge stood around barking instructions and shrieking about equality. My experience left me in no doubt whatsoever that socialists are hypocrites and liars. The common interest isn't served by socialism. The common interest is served by the conservative ideology of individual autonomy, small government and real human fellowship. Indeed, this was *especially* true during a pandemic. The right thing for healthy people to do was to carry on as normal, to stay strong for each other, to keep working for each other, to care for each other. The idea of an entire population abandoning each other and confiscating each other's rights was utter madness.

There were further reasons why socialists were ideologically disposed to support lockdowns. For one thing, there was an assumption on the left that locking Britain down must have been a good idea if communist China thought so. But also, socialists were well aware that the policy would be destructive. With their absurd belief that profit is exploitation, socialists reckoned that destroying the economy would be a virtuous thing to do. They waxed lyrical about the supposed upsides of the lockdowns: the 'egalitarian' furlough scheme, the environment having a chance to 'recover', and people having a chance to 'slow down' (try telling that to the delivery drivers). Socialists considered unilateral economic destruction to be a legitimate rebuke to capitalism.

And there was something even darker in the souls of socialists: an awareness that the damage caused by the lockdowns would damage the government. Vladimir Lenin, who became the world's first communist head of state after the Russian revolution in 1917, once remarked: 'The worse, the better'. What Lenin was getting at is that the more the Russian people suffered under the Czar, the more they would support a communist revolution. A century later, at the start of the Covid outbreak, British socialists agitated for a lockdown because they knew that the hardship caused by the policy would be blamed on the Conservative government, leading to more support for socialism. The socialists even had the nerve to suggest that there would have been less hardship if the government had locked down quicker and harder. Apparently, the only way to mitigate the lockdown policy was for the government to administer the severest possible lock-down without hesitation! Either way, the socialists would hold the Conservatives responsible for the ensuing devastation.

Moreover, socialists had a specific motivation for damaging the government in March 2020. In July 2019, Johnson became Conservative leader on the promise of delivering Brexit – that is, leading Britain out of the European Union – three years after the public had voted for the policy in a referendum. During those three years, the most ardent Remainers had waged a disgusting campaign to thwart the 2016 vote. These 'Remoaners', as they were aptly dubbed, relentlessly tried to delegitimise the referendum decision. They claimed that Leavers were nothing but stupid racists, that the entire leave campaign was based on lies, that Brexit would be followed by apocalyptic consequences, and that a second referendum was required to confirm the first, otherwise the process supposedly wouldn't be democratic. Meanwhile, in Parliament, MPs passed a statute that prevented Britain from leaving the EU without a trade deal. The statute gave the EU no incentive to offer a reasonable deal. Bad deal after bad deal was offered, with Parliament repeatedly voting down the bad deals, whereupon Remoaners blamed the gridlock on the Brexit vote, rather than their own manipulativeness. Throughout this disgraceful period, there was a significant Remoaner lobby among conservatives, but the main anti-Brexit impetus came from Britain's socialists. The socialists were motivated partly by Leninist principles – the gridlock in Parliament would potentially harm the hated Tories – but also by a genuine desire for Britain stay in the EU; the EU is a fundamentally left-wing project.

Even after the public elected Johnson as Prime Minister on a resounding Brexit mandate, the socialists didn't let up. The day that Johnson had become Conservative leader, one of Britain's most prominent left-wing campaigners, Owen Jones, had tweeted: 'OK, team. Let's bring him down'. When Britain formally left the EU on January 31, 2020, there was a transition period of 11 months. The Covid outbreak came at exactly the right time for the socialists. They saw Covid-19 as a golden opportunity to reverse Brexit, insofar as lockdowns could disrupt the practical process of leaving the EU, or at least cause economic disruption that would be blamed on Brexit – all those apocalyptic predictions coming true.

Fear, hatred, self-interest, phony compassion, economic vandalism, Leninist opportunism, anti-Brexit manipulation: the left had many reasons to agitate for lockdowns in March 2020. Socialists live by ideology, and the British public had given them a reality check by voting for Brexit and the Tories. Lockdowns were the revenge of the ideologues. And foremost among the ideologues were militant teachers.

IV

When the NEU threatened unilateral schools closures on March 17, Mary Bousted and Kevin Courtney, the union's co-leaders, knew exactly what they were doing. They were attacking freedom, attacking the Tories, and trying to secure the easiest possible ride for teachers during the Covid-19 outbreak. The government also understood exactly what was going on. The March 17 threat will not have come as a shock to the PM. Trouble was brewing very early in schools: on February 26, the *Guardian* reported that 13 schools had unilaterally shut because of coronavirus, and a further 25 had been sending kids home to 'quarantine'. On March 12, Johnson was compelled to say publicly: 'We are not – repeat not – closing schools now. The scientific advice is it will do more harm than good at this time'. However, two days later, on March 14, the NEU penned an open letter which, although not explicitly calling for schools closures, was agitating for the policy; the letter demanded to know why schools were being kept open while mass gatherings were banned. The March 14 letter also contained a shocking revelation. Addressing the government, the NEU leadership noted: 'We now see that you may take legal powers to force schools to remain open even when Heads and teachers think there is good reason to close'. Clearly, if the government was threatening to sue the NEU at this point, then the NEU's threat to unilaterally close schools had already been made behind the scenes. As far as I know, no British journalist has ever even *mentioned* what was happening here: in mid-March 2020, a game of brinksmanship between the NEU leadership and Johnson had begun. The NEU wanted to close schools. Johnson wanted to keep them open. The NEU was threatening to force the issue. Johnson was threatening to fight back, at least covertly. The only question was which side would cave in first.

Both the NEU and the government knew that this type of confrontation was not without precedent. Going back to the early nineteenth century, Britain has a long history of unions using collective bargaining to further the interests of their members. Much of this lobbying has been justifiable, and constructive, as unions have gradually secured vital improvements in workplace conditions. But, at the same time, there has always been an inherent tension between the requirements of unions and employers; the interests of the two sides aren't completely aligned and, naturally, both sides want the best deal. Ever since Karl Marx wrote *The Communist Manifesto* in 1848, socialists have hijacked the legitimate function of unions by using collective bargaining as a cover for blackmailing employers. Instead of seeking a reasonable accommodation with employers, socialist-led unions have made uncompromising demands, so as to provoke employers into standing firmly against the demands, which in turn has served as a recruiting tool for socialism. Socialists have also used union unrest as a means of damaging capitalist governments, along Leninist lines. This strategy has proved especially effective when the government itself has been the employer. What better way of discrediting a government than by sowing discord and chaos within the apparatus of the state, thereby showing that the government is incapable of overseeing even its own affairs?

In 1926 in Britain, the TUC arranged a 'general strike' in sympathy with coal miners who were involved in a pay dispute with the government. Railwaymen, transport workers, dockers, printers, steelworkers and ironworkers all participated in a nationwide walkout. The action lasted 9 days. In many places, there were clashes between crowds and the police. Some 4,000 strikers were arrested. The following year, the government passed sweeping anti-union legislation. Mass picketing and 'sympathetic' strikes were banned, which, in effect, made any future general strikes illegal. Additionally, civil service unions were banned from affiliating to the TUC.

Some commentators have argued that the government's 1927 crackdown on the unions simply drove more working class people into the arms of socialism. By 1945, the socialists were in the ascendant, as Britain's war-battered electorate handed Clement Atlee's Labour Party a landslide general election victory. Labour MPs sang the 'Red Flag' in Parliament and proceeded to nationalise education, housing, health, welfare and the railways, plus a raft of major industries. Atlee's government also repealed the anti-union legislation of 1927, prompting an increase in union membership over the next few decades. For a while, the unions were relatively cooperative, especially as the Labour Party was generally against radicalism at that point, and the Conservative Party was making an effort to reach out to the working man. Nobody had much of an appetite for aggravation after the war; re-building was everyone's priority. But in the 1960s, when radical left politics re-emerged in Britain, the relationship between unions and the government deteriorated. By the 1970s, when union membership peaked, there was open warfare.

Between 1970 and 1974, there were strikes by coal miners, dockers, rail workers, postmen, NHS staff, and more. The strikes by the National Union of Mineworkers were the most disruptive. The first was in 1972. Led by Arthur Scargill, a Marxist, the NUM blackmailed the government into giving miners a pay rise. The strikers blockaded not just pits but power stations and coal depots; the aim was to completely cut off Britain's power supply. NUM members and socialist agitators from other trade unions were bussed around the country to take part; these military-style deployments became known as 'flying pickets'. With electricity output reduced to 25%, there were widespread power cuts. There were even stories of cabinet meetings held by candlelight. Prime Minister Edward Heath was reluctant to confront the strikers, for fear of provoking violence; he capitulated, agreeing to give them a 30% pay rise.

Alas, when inflation promptly wiped out the pay rise, the unrest surged back. In 1973, the NUM voted to ban overtime. Coal production halved overnight. Heath announced a three-day week, and soon shops were running short of goods, but the NUM didn't let up. In 1974, they voted to wage another strike. Heath responded by calling a snap election, asking the public 'Who governs Britain?'. The public delivered their verdict, ridding Heath of his parliamentary majority. The Labour party took power as part of a coalition and agreed to give the miner's a 35% pay rise.

But still it wasn't over. The union unrest continued under Labour, reaching a crescendo during the infamous winter of 1978/79. Amid freezing weather, unions staged more than 2000 strikes across the country, the largest industrial action since 1926. Again the trigger was the issue of pay. Factory workers, truckers, dockers, railwaymen, ambulance drivers, doctors, nurses, waste collectors, gravediggers and other public sector workers withdrew their labour at various stages, in what became known as the 'Winter of Discontent'. With rubbish bags piled high in the streets, bodies lying unburied in mortuaries, and cancer patients going untreated, the national mood was captured by the famous *Sun* headline 'Crisis? What Crisis?', the phrase being a sarcastic reference to Prime Minster Jim Callaghan's mulish denial that there was 'chaos' in Britain. On May 3, 1979, the electorate took their revenge again, this time awarding a majority to a new Conservative leader who promised to confront the unions once and for all. Her name was Margaret Thatcher.

What followed has become the stuff of legend. But throughout her career, Thatcher wasn't always as robust with the unions as her reputation suggests. She was a politician, and all politicians will compromise sometimes. In 1960, when Thatcher was a back-bencher, she became fleetingly famous for persuading Parliament to pass a statute that would stop councils from excluding the press from committee meetings. In fact, Thatcher ended up proposing a watered-down version of the statute, after government ministers had asked her not to upset the councils and unions. Later, when she was Education Minister in the early 1970s, Thatcher publicly leant support to a series of union-driven policy U-turns by Edward Heath. And in the same role, she herself was regularly frustrated by the education unions that were driving the agenda in schools and universities. Thatcher was able to 'covert-ly obstruct but not overtly initiate', as her biographer Robin Harris explains, adding: 'Even her powers to prevent changes she deplored were weak'.

Everything changed when Thatcher became Prime Minister. She had long been itching for a fightback against the unions. During the industrial unrest in the

1970s, Thatcher had declared that walkouts by mono-poly groups were 'not strikes against the government, but strikes against the people'. She was elected in 1979 to defend the people, and that is what she did, announcing that she was 'not for turning'. Her gov-ernment passed a series of statutes designed to constrain the activities of unions. For instance, pickets were restricted in size, 'closed shops' were curtailed (a closed shop is when union membership is mandated for new employees of a company), sympathy strikes were banned (again), all strikes were made illegal without a ballot, and unions were made liable for damages from illegal strikes. The success of these reforms is indicated by the fact that, in 1990, industrial action caused less disruption than in any year since 1935. Only 2 million working days were lost in 1990 compared to an average of almost 13 million a year during the 1970s. Meanwhile, union membership fell under Thatcher – from half of the workforce to a third.

However, the reforms were not without pain. Thatcher's stance brought her into confrontation with the government's old adversary, the National Union of Mineworkers, still led by Scargill. In 1984/85, the NUM conducted a year of strikes. Pay was a factor in the dispute, but the main issue was the government's decision to close a series of unprofitable pits. Parad-oxically, the striking miners were trying to prevent the pit closures by temporarily shutting as many pits as possible, so as to cause power shortages that would hold the government hostage, thus forcing ministers to back down and keep the unprofitable pits open. Scargill's stance was utterly uncompromising. When asked what amount of loss-making he was willing to tolerate at any given pit, his response was 'As far as I am concerned, the loss is without limit'.

The government's announcement of the first pit closure, in Yorkshire, triggered a strike that succeeded in shutting almost every mine in the county. Other local strikes followed, all endorsed by the national executive of the NUM. Scargill wanted a national strike, but he knew he wouldn't win a national ballot. His strategy was to foment as many local strikes as possible. Wherever there was reluctance to hold a ballot, or wherever he feared that the ballot might go the wrong way, he sent in thugs to intimidate the local unionists. He also sent in thugs to bolster the picket lines during strikes. The tactic was a continuation of the 'flying pickets' seen in the 1970s.

Thatcher, for her part, sent in riot police wherever Scargill used flying pickets. Violent clashes ensued, the most infamous of which took place at Orgreave in South Yorkshire. 5,000 miners and troublemakers threw rocks and darts at the police, who responded by charging on horseback into the crowd. Law and order prevailed on that day, but it didn't on every occasion. The thugs also attempted to intimidate non-striking miners behind the front lines. Even wives and children were considered fair game. One Yorkshire miner was beaten up in his home by 15 men. A Welsh taxi driver was killed when a concrete block was dropped onto his car while he was driving a miner to work. History has portrayed the striking miners as the victims; this couldn't be further from the truth. Scargill's campaign was an act of pure socialist aggression, designed to extort money from the government and the British public while also causing as much Leninist disruption as possible.

Ultimately, Scargill was defeated, by a combination

of factors – the non-striking miners' refusal to be intimidated, Thatcher's principled stance, and the use of the new anti-union laws to prosecute the NUM. In the end, the NUM itself voted to discontinue the strikes, against Scargill's exhortations. Buoyed by the victory, Thatcher conducted firm but fair negotiations with other unions – unions that could have caused major national disruption should they have felt emboldened to do so. Robin Harris concludes his discussion of the era by noting that, thanks to Scargill's defeat, 'no union or group of unions could ever again make the country ungovernable'.

Sadly, Harris's prediction was inaccurate, as the events of March 2020 demonstrate. One of the reasons I have compiled this brief history of British union unrest is that I'm aware that not everyone is convinced by my claim that unions were the driving force behind this country's Covid-19 restrictions. Many people are doubtful that unions would ever attempt to shut down the national economy, let alone succeed in doing so. History shows that these doubts are misplaced. On multiple occasions, unions have deliberately inflicted catastrophic damage on Britain. Moreover, on multiple occasions, unions have worked together, waging their campaigns in parallel or in sequence. This is true whether there was an overarching plan (such as when the TUC arranged the general strike in 1926) or whether the campaigns were largely based on shared goals (such as in the 1970s). When unions started trying to force through a work-from-home policy in mid-March 2020, egged on by the TUC, both types of coordination were involved.

Most importantly, the history of union unrest in Britain enables us to better understand the decisive role played by the NEU at the start of the coronapanic. The NEU leadership adopted a strategy similar to that which Scargill adopted in 1984/5. Scargill wanted a national walkout but without a national ballot, so he intended to cause as much disruption as possible by shutting as many individual pits as possible. Similarly, the NEU wanted a national walkout but without a national ballot, so the NEU's leaders Mary Bousted and Kevin Courtney intended to shut as many individual schools as possible. (Presumably the NEU didn't hold a national ballot because they were too impatient – the process would take five weeks – or didn't believe they would win the vote). Both the NUM and the NEU wanted to cause economic chaos by knocking out a crucial pillar of the economy. Without power, the economy must falter. Without schools to supervise the children of working parents, the economy must falter. Above all, both unions were utterly uncompromising. Both the NUM and the NEU were unwilling to countenance any sort of sacrifice on the part of their members. Scargill declared that the loss-making at the unprofitable pits was 'without limit'. The NEU insisted that the safety of teachers was without limit; the idea of teachers being exposed to a mild virus in schools was deemed unconscionable.

Of course, there were differences. In the 1980s, the NUM sought to shut down mines as a means of blackmailing Thatcher into abandoning further pit closures, whereas during the coronapanic the NEU sought to shut down schools as an end in itself, not just a means of causing economic disruption. There was also a difference in the way Thatcher and Johnson responded to the two crises. Thatcher refused to be blackmailed, whereas Johnson caved in.

Or perhaps that's putting it too starkly. Johnson caved in, but arguably it was a tactical retreat; he lived to fight another day, and he learned lessons from the defeat. Let's take a closer look at what happened in March 2020. If we are to understand how Johnson responded to future NEU threats – including the threats that led to the second lockdown – we need to analyse the rationale behind the decisions Johnson made in the lead up to the first lockdown.

V

Put yourself in Johnson's shoes in mid-March 2020. You've recently been elected to deliver Brexit after Remoaners have spent three years trying to undermine British democracy. China has sent 60 million of its citizens into a deranged lockdown over a virus that is harmless to almost everyone. Italy has followed suit. With the virus spreading worldwide, your chief science advisors have wisely suggested that you keep Britain open. You have pursued this policy amid a growing public panic and a media outcry. There isn't a single journalist publicly defending you (not yet). Suddenly a bunch of huge unions are making demands and threats, agitating for a lockdown. Each of the mutinying unions has the capacity to inflict major economic damage on Britain. One union in particular could inflict catastrophic damage: the National Education Union, with 450,000 members. There are 10.3 million schoolchildren in the UK, with around 13 million working parents, including almost 3 million single parents. The total working population of the UK is 32.8 million, but, of these people, millions will be sidelined by sickness or self-isolation. If the NEU succeeds in closing a significant number of schools, parents will face massive disruption. If all the schools are closed, the economy would lose around a quarter of an already depleted workforce. An exodus on this scale could wreck some businesses, which would have a knock-on effect on other businesses. The schools closures will cause havoc, added to the havoc that the other unions are unleashing.

Faced with this situation, Johnson seems to have readied himself to back down, while keeping his options open for as long as possible. On March 14, the Health Secretary Matt Hancock wrote an article for the *Telegraph*. In the article, Hancock announced meekly that the government wasn't pursuing herd immunity, contrary to what the chief science advisor Patrick Vallance had indicated 48 hours earlier; the aim in fact was to 'protect life'. There was an ominous warning from the Health Secretary:

> Next week we will publish our emergency bill, to give the Government the temporary powers we will need to help everyone get through this. The measures in it allow for the worst case scenario. I hope many of them won't be needed. But we will ask Parliament for these powers in case they are.

However, despite preparing for the worst, the government wasn't actually assuming the worst. Ministers may have abandoned the phrase 'herd immunity' but they hadn't abandoned the policy. Hancock only made two specific policy announcements in his March 14 article; that people should stay at home for a week if they developed a high temperature or a cough, and that 'in the near future' there would be measures to shield old and medically vulnerable people. 'Everyone will need to help to ensure they get the support they need to stay at home', Hancock warned. In other words: the government wasn't proposing to lock the country down. Quite the opposite; healthy people would be out and about supporting the people who were shielding. That was how to 'protect life'. 'We can all keep doing our bit by continuing to wash our hands more often, for 20 seconds or more and having plenty of tissues around', Hancock enthused. The government was passing an emergency bill that would cover for every eventuality, including a lockdown, but, for the time being, almost everyone should carry on as normal.

The reason Johnson was making preparations for the 'worst case scenario' is easy to understand when you consider what was likely to happen if the NEU didn't back down. Imagine if the NEU had started closing schools unilaterally. There would have been chaos, and Johnson would have been blamed for it. The state education system is supposed to be government-run. Johnson would have been accused of losing his grip on the situation. While he was telling people to carry on working, the unilateral schools closures would have meant workplaces gradually emptying, as parents were forced to stay home and look after their children. In turn, employers would have called for certainty, trying to continue running their businesses without knowing when or whether their staff would return; Johnson would have been unable to provide the certainty because the decisions would have been in the teachers' hands, not his. Meanwhile, teachers would have been telling parents that Covid posed a major threat to schools, while

Johnson was denying this fact, even though he was powerless to keep all the schools open. The media would have started saying 'Crisis, what crisis?', as the chaos mounted and Johnson's authority ebbed away.

What about the government's alleged threat of using legal action to keep the schools open? We can assume that Johnson didn't place much faith in this option. Legal processes take time, and the mutinous teachers wouldn't have waited. Moreover, amid the chaos of unilateral schools closures, Johnson's authority would have been further undermined if he'd resorted to legal action. Everyone would have known that the teachers were defying him; that he'd lost control of the schools; that he couldn't execute his decisions without legal backup. Perhaps that's why the NEU went public about the government's threat of legal action, warning the PM how embarrassing such a recourse would be. Johnson might even have been advised that the legal action would fail. He may simply have been bluffing when he threatened to sue the NEU. I am reminded of Robin Harris's comment about the difficulties Thatcher faced as Education Secretary: 'Her powers to prevent changes she deplored were weak.'

Still, whether or not he was bluffing, Johnson was clearly trying to hold back the tide, to keep the schools open. Even when the unrest from other unions pushed the government into a U-turn on social distancing, Johnson used the occasion as an opportunity to place further pressure on the NEU. During the March 16 press conference, at which Johnson started advising working from home, he publicly reiterated that the government wanted to keep the schools open. Bear in mind: *he didn't need to draw this line*. This fact is extremely important. He could have capitulated more thoroughly on March 16; he could have announced that children and teachers should 'work from home' just like everybody else. But he didn't. He remained hopeful that he could outmanoeuvre the teachers. Perhaps he was hopeful that the NEU would back down if the government was taking steps to reduce the transmission rate throughout the country. Also, the more people who were working from home, the less impact the unilateral schools closures would have, because more working parents would be at home where they could look after their kids. It's as though the PM was implicitly saying to Bousted and Courtney: 'The virus will now be less prevalent in schools, so teachers needn't be concerned. And if you start shutting individual schools, the government will now be protected against the fallout, so we won't be bullied into shutting all the schools.'

Unfortunately, Johnson's limp last stand for sanity didn't last long. The *Independent* reported that he was facing 'mounting anger over [his] decision not to close schools'. On the day after the press conference, March 17, which was a Monday, there must have been a febrile atmosphere in the schools. The NEU probably stirred up the atmosphere, and, on March 16, the TUC had advised its constituent union members to hand in Section 44 letters; possibly a few teachers followed the advice. With the hashtags #Covid19Walkout and #CloseTheSchoolsNow trending on Twitter, March 17 was the day the NEU wrote to the government to publicly threaten unilateral schools closures. Johnson promptly caved in. On March 18, he announced that all schools would shut their gates at the end of the week. 'Looking at the curve of the disease and looking at where we are now, we think now that we must apply downward pressure, further downward pressure on that upward curve by closing the schools' was his bogus explanation. On March 20, the Friday evening, the PM gave another press conference. With the schools shutting their gates earlier that day, he declared, no less bogusly: 'We need now to push down further on that curve of transmission', hence 'We are strengthening the measures announced on Monday [March 16]'. Specifically, he explained: 'We are collectively telling cafes, pubs, bars, restaurants to close tonight… and not to open tomorrow'. He added: 'We are also telling nightclubs, theatres, cinemas, gyms and leisure centres to close on the same timescale'. In other words: the shutdown of the schools had instantly triggered a near-complete shutdown of Britain. Three days later, on the evening of Monday 23, the government announced a legally enforced lockdown.

Based on this timeline, you can see clearly that the NEU caused Britain's first lockdown. The delay between the announcement of the schools closures and the schools actually closing, followed by the delay between the schools closures and the lockdown announcement, can be attributed to the time required to prepare the legislation – the 'emergency bill' that Hancock had promised. The overall timeline indicates a battle of wills between the NEU and Johnson. A battle that Johnson lost, whereupon he sent the country into lockdown.

But *why*? Why did Johnson decide that the closure of all the schools necessitated a lockdown? Why did he give the NEU (and the other unions) the lockdown they wanted? Why didn't he (partially) confound the NEU by shutting down the schools while leaving everyone else alone?

Well, one factor is obvious. If Johnson feared that the NEU's campaign of unilateral schools closures would cause economic disruption, he will have been maximally concerned by the prospect of every school in the country closing. If he'd tried to keep the economy open with all the schools closed, employers and employees would have berated him mercilessly for the disruption. Many sectors simply wouldn't have been able to function at all; imagine an airport trying to operate with 1 in 4 employees missing, or any other complex workplace. Later in the year, Conservative MP Tobias Elwood gave an insight into the hidden reality behind the government's policy decisions when he said: 'The impact of closing schools is huge. The collateral damage caused from that, with parents not being able to go to work, is phenomenal.'

Tellingly, on March 15, Johnson made a telephone call to the Japanese PM, Shinzo Abe. Johnson will have been interested to discuss a pertinent fact: on March 2, Abe had closed every school in Japan, but he had kept the Japanese economy open. During the pandemic, this combination was very unusual world-wide. Abe had faced a lot of domestic criticism for his policy. No doubt he communicated this to Johnson, who must have been alarmed.

Johnson was probably also aware that the disrupt-tion caused by Abe's policy was being mitigated by Japan's relatively traditional gender roles; if Johnson were to pursue the same policy in the UK, the disruption would be even greater. For one thing, there are slightly fewer working mums in Japan compared to the UK (70% versus 75%). But that doesn't tell the whole story. In Japan, women are less likely to have high responsibility jobs, and the men notoriously work long hours; inevitably, it would have been mostly the mothers who were encouraged to go home and look after the kids, an exodus that would have had less of an economic impact in Japan than in the UK. Another relevant factor is that Japanese husbands do less housework than their western counterparts; consequently, an expectation that women would go home and supervise the children would have caused less controversy in Japan than in the UK. In a politically correct country like ours, there would have been a furious debate about whether mothers or fathers should quit work during the schools closures. Mothers in high-powered jobs would (understandably) have been outraged at the prospect, and feminists would (less understandably) have cried 'sexist', as many fathers encouraged mothers to go home and look after the kids. There would also have been feminist outrage at single mums having to quit their workplaces. Johnson surely will have wanted to avoid being caught up in all the controversy.

And that was the least of his worries. In March 2020, Japan and Britain differed not just in terms of gender expectations but in a much more fundamental respect: *the schools closures in Japan weren't driven by teaching unions.* The decision to close Japan's schools seems to have originated with Abe himself. This meant that Abe knew he wouldn't face opposition from the teachers when he tried to reopen the schools. Johnson, in contrast, knew he probably would face opposition from the teachers, which meant he had no guarantee of being able to get Britain's schools open again. Indeed, Johnson was right to be wary: the teaching unions *didn't* cooperate with him; they refused to return to normal working conditions until over two years later. Given the real prospect of a long-term teaching mutiny, Johnson will have known that copying Abe's policy in Britain was fraught with risk.

Imagine how things would have panned out if Johnson had closed all the schools without doing a lockdown. Cafés, pubs, etc, would have stayed open, as would many workplaces, but there would have been a lot of people working from home, a lot of parents off work, a lot of disruption, and a lot of complaints. The public would have noticed the inconsistency between the schools closing and the rest of the economy staying open. Some people would have continued raging at Johnson to shut everything down. Other people would have started asking probing questions about why the schools were shut. And the questions would have grown more numerous with time. Gradually, as the mass panic subsided, and as immunity accumulated in the population, people would have started returning to their workplaces and to social venues. Johnson would have found himself under pressure to explain why the schools were still shut. And he would have had no credible answer. He'd have had to say 'because the teachers are refusing to work'. This admission would have undermined his authority. Indeed, his authority would have been doubly undermined when people realised that the only reason he had shut the schools in the first place was that the teaching unions had bullied him into it.

When you look at the situation like this, you can see clearly the problem that Johnson had. Keeping the economy open *with or without the schools* was a political minefield for him. In both scenarios, he would have been humiliated by the NEU. If he had tried to keep all the schools open while keeping the country open, the NEU would have waged a Scargillesque campaign to unilaterally shut schools, and Johnson would have been humiliated. Alternatively, if he had agreed to shut all the schools while keeping the country open, the NEU would have refused to return to work amid growing public scrutiny of the schools closures, and Johnson would have been humiliated. He shut down the entire economy because he calculated that this was the only way to stop the NEU from undermining his leadership.

The NEU leadership will have been aware that they had placed Johnson in this position. They will also have been aware that if Britain locked down, they were likely to escape responsibility themselves, because Johnson would never want to publicly admit that he had been bullied by the NEU. There would have been no point in him doing a lockdown to avoid being humiliated if he had then admitted that the NEU had bullied him into the policy. In effect, the NEU had forced the government into the perfect capitulation. Johnson was blackmailed into pretending that he wasn't blackmailed. He and his scientists portrayed themselves as the impetus behind the lockdown, proactively taking the lead, so as to hide the fact that they had backed down. Similarly, locking down was also a way for Johnson to emphatically grab hold of the news agenda. The lockdown would ensure that any trouble with the NEU would remain under the radar, because the news would be dominated by the announcement of the restrictions.

For all these reasons, the lockdown was essentially a spin operation. Johnson embarked upon a lockdown spin operation to protect himself and the government.

The government's real policy was: *we need to avoid being humiliated by the NEU.* The spin operation was: *we need to lockdown to protect everyone from Covid-19.* The entire aim of the lockdown was to spin a political manoeuvre into a so-called health measure.

No, that still doesn't quite capture the astonishing reality of what happened. Let me put it another way. Johnson passed an emergency bill through Parliament, enabling the government to legally confiscate the freedom of 66 million people, because the alternative meant the government getting into a humiliating confrontation with the NEU. The bill would enable the government to avoid such a confrontation for the foreseeable future. The legal enforcement of the lockdown would boost the chances that the public would abide by the policy, thus making the lockdown a viable policy option for as long as possible, thus maximising the government's chances of spinning away from a confrontation, should Bousted and Courtney continue blackmailing the government.

Obviously, the fact that the government pursued such a strategy is mind-blowing. In any normal situation, no government would give a moment's consideration to the idea of committing a crime against humanity in order to avoid confronting a teaching union. But March 2020 was not a normal situation; or rather, the public were not behaving normally. For one thing, there was a petition calling for the government to 'Close Schools/Colleges down for an appropriate amount of time', which gained 685,394 signatures in March 2020. There was also, inexplicably, a growing clamour for Johnson to close the entire country down. While the government was pursuing herd immunity, much of the population was already beginning to self-isolate. On March 15, MP Robin Millar noted that 'Anecdotally, people are already changing their behaviours – public transport in London is half full this evening'. By the time Britain went into lockdown on March 24, 76% of the public were 'strongly supportive' of the measure. A further 17% were 'somewhat supportive'. The lockdown was a viable option for the government because of the level of public support: 93% in total. Granted, that's not the same as saying the public directly caused the lockdown. They didn't. On March 16, Johnson tried to keep the schools and the economy open *even when he knew there was massive public demand for the lockdown.* The NEU's blackmail on March 17 was decisive.

Public support for the lockdown was also boosted by the furlough scheme, which was essentially a means of bribing people; it was easier for ministers to dole out free money to the public than to survive a confrontation with the NEU. At the same time, furlough was a concession to the TUC; the union later described the scheme as a 'big win' that resulted from 'intensive negotiations' with the government. From the government's perspective, throwing furlough money around killed two birds with one stone – shutting the unions up, and consolidating the already strong public support for shutting Britain down.

The situation in March 2020 was abnormal in another key respect: the Brexit factor. Remoaners had spent three years trying to reverse the 2016 referendum decision. Against this backdrop, Johnson will have known that if he faced a serious loss of authority, there was a risk of a remain coup. Johnson's main leadership rival Jeremy Hunt was a Remainer. Hunt had been mooting the idea of schools closures since as early as February 28. On March 13, he said the government's lack of action over Covid-19 was 'concerning'; he urged Britain to 'move faster to social distancing'. On the day the lockdown was announced, he called it 'absolutely the right decision'. Hunt was accompanied in Parliament by 144 Remainer conservative MPs – 40% of the 2019 intake of Conservatives. The other main parties, Labour and the Lib Dems, were overwhelmingly in favour of remain. Many Remainer MPs were talking about diluting Johnson's electoral mandate, supposedly in the name of the pandemic. Lisa Nandy, a Labour Remainer who was standing to replace Jeremy Corbyn as leader, was urging the government to create a 'National COBRA that formally brings together Government, Opposition, trade union and business leaders with devolved governments, charities and community leaders to build a common national action plan'. George Freeman, a conservative Remainer, similarly proposed the idea of a 'government of national unity' – a 'Covid coalition'. Furthermore, according to Dominic Cummings, some of Johnson's 'closest aides' had been plotting to oust the PM since weeks after his 2019 general election victory. If Johnson had been forced out of office in March 2020, his usurpers would have locked Britain down anyway and tried to reverse Brexit in the process. Johnson must have calculated that if a lockdown was going to happen *even if he tried to avoid locking down*, the least bad option was for him to lockdown and try to save Brexit.

At the root of this dreadful dilemma was the NEU's Scargillesque threat to unilaterally close schools. For as long as that threat remained credible, Johnson felt compelled to lock Britain down. Alas, Bousted and

Courtney didn't let up. As the weeks and months unfolded, there were further exchanges between the NEU and the government, and these exchanges further demonstrate the NEU's role in driving the lockdown. Every official speech given by the government during the first lockdown contained a coded message to the NEU. And, every time, the NEU responded by slapping the government down. The NEU caused the first lockdown, in two senses. First, by triggering it. Then by perpetuating it.

## VI

When announcing the lockdown, Johnson said 'I can assure you that we will keep these restrictions under constant review. We will look again in three weeks, and relax them if the evidence shows we are able to'. Three weeks after March 23 was... April 13, which was in the middle of the school Easter holidays. The government had bought themselves three weeks plus a little more time, to try to get the NEU to cooperate.

The NEU refused to cooperate. On April 14, Bousted and Courtney wrote another open letter to the government, saying 'Our members are disturbed... by increasing media speculation that schools will soon be reopened'. (In fact, the schools were already open – but only to the children of key workers. In what follows, I will gloss over this fact, as did the NEU in the previous quote; 'reopening' the schools meant opening them to *all* the children.) The NEU's letter noted that before the schools reopened it 'seems essential' for there to be 'extensive testing, contact tracing and quarantine in society as a whole'. With the

NHS's 'test and trace' app still six weeks away, and months away from being in widespread use, the NEU was in effect refusing to countenance going back to normal working.

The letter also listed a bunch of manipulative questions the NEU wanted the government to answer. One of the questions was 'whether the Scottish Parliament, the devolved assemblies in Wales and Northern Ireland and our neighbours in the government of the Republic of Ireland agree with your plans [to reopen schools]'. The NEU was harnessing the pro-lockdown positions of England's neighbouring administrations to heap pressure on Johnson. Even more manipulatively, the letter noted that the media speculation about the schools reopening was 'seemingly being stimulated by unnamed Government ministers'. Note what was happening here. Johnson wanted to reopen the schools but he was reluctant to go public about it, because if the NEU didn't cooperate he would be humiliated. He was trying to crank up the pressure on the NEU by planting 'speculation' in the press. In response, the NEU was imperiously contradicting the speculation and insinuating that the government was behind it, as though Bousted and Courtney were reminding ministers that getting into a confrontation with the NEU was politically unwise.

The government backed down again. Boris Johnson himself was ill with Covid, so this time Dominic Raab fronted up the capitulation, announcing on April 16 that 'the government has determined that current measures must remain in place for at least the next 3 weeks'. Along with the usual nauseating lies about 'stopping the spread', Raab gave the following justification for continuing the lockdown:

If we rush to relax the measures in place, we would risk wasting all the sacrifices and all the progress we have made. And that would risk a quick return to another lockdown.

In other words: Britain was doing a lockdown to avoid a lockdown. Now the government was not only capitulating to the socialists but borrowing their insane rationalisations. The lockdown had to be based on insane rationalisations because the entire policy was a con trick, a political manoeuvre masquerading as a health measure. The government's real agenda was unchanged: to avoid a humiliating confrontation with the NEU. Raab tried to sound upbeat about the situation, promising a 'review in just a few weeks', but he also laid the foundations for the next capitulation, warning that 'it would not be responsible to pre-judge the evidence'.

Raab's speech did however contain an intriguing hint that the government was taking steps to mitigate the next capitulation. He explained that the government was looking to 'adjust the measures to make them as effective as possible', and this 'could involve relaxing measures in some areas, while strengthening measures in other areas'. Varying the measures between areas was a strategic move against the NEU's Scargillesque tactics. If there were areas of the country where the NEU didn't have much support, the government could reopen those areas and maintain the lockdown in the areas where the teachers were causing trouble. A finer-grained capitulation, but also a fightback of sorts. The more areas that remained open, the more pressure the government could potentially exert on the mutinying teachers.

On Friday May 8, at the end of the latest three-week interval, the NEU again warned the government not to end the lockdown. By now, the TUC and six other teaching unions had joined in. They issued a joint statement citing various 'tests' that must be met before the schools reopened. The tests included a 'full rollout of a national test and trace scheme'– the same unmet demand as last time. The teachers were also making the same old threat, now masquerading as a demand: they required 'Local autonomy to close schools'. This was like saying: 'The condition of reopening the schools is that teaching unions will close them at will'. The NEU backed up these demands/threats with a new petition which called for schools to reopen 'only when safe to do so'. There were nearly 350,000 signatories, including 150,000 teachers and 10,000 headteachers.

On May 10, Johnson popped up with the inevitable capitulation, in his most bizarre and rambling statement yet. After a splurge of dishonest waffle about the 'science', he finally got to the point: 'And so no, this is not the time simply to end the lockdown this week.' Surprise, surprise. Actually, it was somewhat surprising because, on April 30, Johnson had been telling everyone that we were 'past the peak' of the outbreak. Now he was backpedalling furiously, saying 'We have been through the initial peak, but it is coming down the mountain that is often more dangerous' – possibly the most ludicrous analogy any British PM has ever uttered. Johnson's sole aim remained the same: to cover up the fact that the teaching unions were refusing to reopen the schools. However, he did have some encouraging words: 'We are taking the first careful steps to modify our measures'. There was definitely a fightback in the offing.

'The first step is a change of emphasis', Johnson explained. 'We now need to stress that anyone who can't work from home, for instance those in construction or manufacturing, should be actively encouraged to go to work'. Reading between the lines: most of the people going back to work would be men, so there wouldn't be too many angry debates about who would look after the kids while the schools were shut; hopefully no one would notice the gendered policy. The teachers were still refusing to reopen the schools, but Johnson was now trying to minimise the economic damage without causing too much controversy. He then issued a warning to those who were returning to work: 'You should avoid public transport if at all possible − because we must and will maintain social distancing, and capacity will therefore be limited'. The timing of this comment is notable, because, on May 4, Britain's three rail unions had written to the PM urging him not to lift the lockdown and not to run more trains. Johnson was trying to salvage something of the economy while also trying to appease the rail unions, and presumably other transport unions too.

He issued another warning about the return to work: 'To ensure you are safe at work we have been working to establish new guidance for employers to make workplaces COVID-secure'. The timing of this comment is notable too, because on May 5, the union Unite had issued a statement about workplace safety. Addressing Unite's 1.3 million members, General Secretary Len McCluskey said: 'Your union is at the table with governments across the UK and Ireland, and with our sister unions, on talks over what a safe and effective back to work programme looks like'. The phrase 'sister unions' was a reference to the fact that Unison, USDAW, GMB and the TUC were all involved too. Together they wrote to the *Observer* on May 10 to say: 'The trade union movement wants to be able to recommend the government's back-to-work plans. But for us to do that we need to ensure that ministers have listened and that we stay safe.' The *Guardian* headline put it more succinctly: 'Trades unions tell Johnson: no return to work until we feel safe'. Similarly, the TUC barked that Unite was 'laying down conditions'. Unite and the other unions drove the ridiculous workplace Covid measures that Britain was subjected to during the coronapanic debacle.

For the people who weren't returning to work, Johnson issued a somewhat pathetic call to action: 'We want to encourage people to take more and even unlimited amounts of outdoor exercise'. You get the impression that Johnson was goading the British public into ending the lockdown themselves. This was a risky strategy, because a less fearful public might start demanding that the schools reopened, whereupon the teaching unions might not back down. But there was always a hope that the teaching unions might be swayed by public opinion. Johnson was getting braver.

Indeed, he was brave enough to announce a plan to try reopening some schools: 'In step two – at the earliest by June 1 – after half term – we believe we may be in a position to get primary pupils back into schools'. Johnson was issuing a challenge to the teaching unions. He was emboldened by the prospect of being able to impose local restrictions. 'We will be monitoring our progress locally, regionally, and nationally', he declared, 'and if there are outbreaks, if there are problems, we will not hesitate to put on the brakes'. If the teaching unions caused 'problems', the government could cover up the controversy by imposing new restrictions in the areas affected, or even a national lockdown if necessary.

Five days later, on May 13, the NEU and – now – *eight* other teaching unions responded by confirming that they had every intention of causing problems. In a joint statement with the TUC, the unions reiterated the demands they made on May 8. The new statement declared: 'We call on the government to step back from the 1st June.' Step back? This was clearly the language of brinksmanship, and it was a direct response to Johnson's plan to reopen primary schools. Johnson had upped the ante, and so had the NEU, enlisting an additional three teaching unions, meaning that *all* the teaching unions were now publicly against reopening schools.

Johnson did not step back. In a newspaper article on May 17, he said he still 'hoped' that primary schools would reopen on June 1. The next day, the *Times Education Supplement* published an article in which 22 academy leaders called for schools to reopen; perhaps there was government support for this statement behind the scenes. A week later, on May 24, Johnson confirmed the plan: Year 1 and Year 6 schoolchildren would be returning to school on June 1 (there was also a plan to get some reception kids back in classes). There would be a 'phased reopening' of primary schools, with all the children returning before the end of the term. In addition, from June 15 onwards, secondary schools would 'provide some contact for Year 10 and Year 12 students'. Johnson admitted that this was a 'deliberately cautious approach', explaining that it came 'after a constructive period of consultation with schools, teachers and unions'. He seems to have thought that the unions would cooperate with him at this point. But he obviously wasn't fully confident, because he acknowledged that 'a 1 June opening may not be possible for all schools'. He also warned that the 'progress' Britain was making was 'conditional, provisional'.

On May 28, Johnson gave another statement to the nation. After the usual dishonest waffle about the 'science', he declared that the government would 'move forward with adjusting the lockdown in England'. He insisted that the government's plans for June 1 and June 15 were going ahead, but he also hedged again, saying that the 'steps we have taken, and will take, are conditional'; he was merely 'hopeful' that there would be 'progress' in the coming weeks. Johnson was still nervous.

But then again, he was unlikely to be humiliated. For one thing, most people in England were still under lockdown, aside from the few people who had been permitted to return to work; so if the teachers were obstructive, there wouldn't be too much fallout. Moreover, only a small percentage of children would be returning to school anyway; so most of the parents' childcare arrangements would be unchanged. Plus, the entire plan was still shrouded in the dishonest idea that whether or not schools reopened would depend on the virus. Johnson had already warned parents that reopening wouldn't be 'possible' for some schools, and he could always fall back on local lockdowns if he needed to cover up any serious disruption from teaching mutinies. He issued a warning:

There will be further local outbreaks. So we will

monitor carefully, we will put on the brakes as required, and where necessary, we will re-impose measures. It's important to be clear about that up front.

Johnson also unveiled his trump card: the NHS's 'test and trace' scheme, which had been launched the previous day. Maybe now the teaching unions would back down. Armed with the ongoing national restrictions, an embryonic test and trace scheme, and the prospect of local lockdowns, Johnson was nervous but battle-ready.

Johnson was nervous because his opponents were battle-ready too. The NEU leadership had spent weeks tubthumping. They declared that 'the government must accept it is simply not yet safe for the wider opening of schools'. They cautioned (in the words of the *Mirror* newspaper) that 'parents should not send their children back to school until it is absolutely safe'. They complained that the test and trace scheme was not in fact 'in place'. They cited a report by Independent SAGE that called for schools to remain closed. They cited a survey suggesting that 80 per cent of parents didn't want schools to reopen. They enlisted the support of the TUC and other unions. They observed that 'Every day more English councils are joining Scotland, Wales and Northern Ireland in pushing back against the UK Government's June 1st target date'. They warned that many schools 'say they will not open more widely on 1 June as they do not believe it is safe'. They held a Zoom call, which some 20,000 members viewed; it was the 'biggest trade union meeting in history', the leadership claimed. They wrote to all primary Heads to convey the message that 'we believe that it is not safe to open schools more widely on 1 June'. Finally, according to one exchange on Twitter, the NEU issued advice on 'using Section 44 to protect members from having to work in dangerous workplaces' – the advice was sent out to 'primary members and reps'. From what I can gather, the advice was issued behind the scenes, but the leadership did write an open letter, published in the *Mirror* on 12 May, saying 'Our strong advice is that... you should currently not engage with any planning based on a wider reopening of schools'. To support teachers who didn't want to return to work, the NEU also supplied a 'model letter' for members to hand in to their headteachers; the letter can be read online. Unison issued its members with a similar letter.

What was about to happen was clear; in many places the schools wouldn't reopen, because many teachers would refuse to return to work, their refusal possibly backed by local authorities. On May 29, which was a Friday, the government suffered one last bout of the jitters. A spokesperson for the PM clarified that teachers were not 'obliged' to go back on Monday; they would not be 'in breach' of their contracts if they didn't. Johnson's administration was bracing itself.

When June came, the outcome was a victory for the NEU, but not quite a crushing victory. Around a quarter or a half – estimates vary – of the Year 1 and Year 6 children went back to the classroom at the start of June, with some schools reopening and others not. Some local authorities emailed every school in the area and advised them not to reopen. In the schools that did reopen, the children were subjected to social distancing rules and kept in mutually isolated groups throughout the day, supposedly to control the spread of the virus. In fact, these creepy, prison-like conditions were to placate the teachers. The NEU was triumphant, crowing about 'what a very long way the Government has to go to convince the nation's parents and teachers that a wider opening of schools is safe'. Kevin Courtney noted that 'many schools intend to delay wider opening', and this 'will make our communities safer'. He added: 'It was always reckless of Boris Johnson to set an arbitrary date and expect schools to fall in line'. Mary Bousted agreed, saying 'schools were never going to be able to accommodate all their students with the current Government guidelines'. Above all, the NEU had succeeded in keeping the government on the back foot. Britain remained under lockdown, amid an ongoing national effort to 'control the virus', all because the government was still spinning the teaching unrest into a health policy. The NEU was continuing to cause massive economic harm to Britain.

As for the government, they abandoned their plans for all primary schoolchildren to return before the end of term. September was the new target. Gavin Williamson, the Education Secretary, tried to put a positive spin on the situation, exaggerating that 'the majority' of primary schools had reopened to Year 1 and Year 6 pupils. He also tried to deflect away from the fact that teachers and local authorities had kept many schools closed. The government would never hesitate to close 'clusters' of schools where Covid-19 outbreaks occurred, he insisted. A spokesperson for the PM said, similarly: 'Our approach to schools throughout has been that we need to be cautious'. Most importantly, from the government's point of view, there was no major political scandal resulting from the June 1 defeat. Although the media reported that teaching unions, councils and parents had exerted an influence on the government, Johnson wasn't humiliated. Wherever the schools remained closed, he had succeeded in spinning the local policy variation and the economic disruption as some sort of prudent epidemiological approach.

It seems there was only one place where the situation got out of hand: Leicester. You may recall that Leicester was the first place in Britain to be sent into a 'local lockdown'. Before I investigated, my expectation was that the NEU would be central to what happened in Leicester. That was indeed what I found.

Nearly all of the 112 primary schools in Leicester reopened as planned at the start of June. But by June 19, the BBC was warning of a 'Covid surge' in the city. The same day, Leicester's secretary for the NEU, a man called Joseph Wyglendacz, is reported to have 'asked the council whether schools could close'. He noted that some education workers were 'absolutely terrified'. It seems however that the council wasn't keen to close any schools. When five schools unilaterally shut their gates on June 23, Leicester's Director of Education responded forthrightly, declaring that 'The number of positive cases in schools remains very, very low' and that 'There is no evidence that we have seen of transmission within schools'. He added, even more unequivocally: 'The schools that are shut have actually gone further than the advice given to them. They didn't need to close the whole school'.

Alas, the local NEU branch grew more determined. In an article published a few weeks later, a man called Simon Robinson, the President of Leicester NEU, explained what unfolded. The city saw 'outbreaks in schools during June, many in east Leicester', and this 'led Leicester NEU to call for a temporary closure of all schools while the outbreak was investigated'. Robinson also disclosed that an organisation called 'Safety First' had 'linked up with Leicester NEU' to 'put pressure on headteachers and the council'. He added that 'the call was ignored by the city Mayor, Labour's Peter Soulsby, and the local public health officials, until the government declared the current lockdown'.

So there you have it. With the national media spotlighting the situation, the government had stepped in and caved in to the NEU's demands, shutting all the schools in Leicester and then locking the whole city down on June 30 to cover up the union unrest. Tellingly, when Matt Hancock spoke to the BBC about the Leicester lockdown, he claimed that there was an 'unusually high incidence' of Covid-19 in children in Leicester. Similarly, when explaining to Parliament the decision to impose harsher restrictions on the city, he said: 'As children have been particularly impacted by this outbreak, schools will also need to close'. He was lying, spinning like crazy, obliquely acknowledging the centrality of the schools to the unfolding situation in Leicester without acknowledging the centrality of the NEU.

Another thing Robinson noted in his article was that there was an 'online meeting' on July 11, 'attended by members from at least eight different unions and campaign groups, and supported by Leicester and District Trades Council, which coordinates across unions in the area'. One of the attendees, a bus driver from Unite, spoke about how he helped 'organise bus workers in London to gain vital safety measures'. Another attendee, from BFAWU, spoke about a 'campaign to unionise workers in many of the 1,500 sweatshop textile factories in east Leicester'. With all these unions seemingly piling in to support the NEU, the government was clearly facing significant unrest in Leicester. Furthermore, ministers may have been spooked by a racial element to the developing story. The BBC's report on June 19 was headlined: 'BAME community fearful over Leicester Covid surge'. Reports of Covid-19 ravaging the 'sweatshops' where many BAME people worked would have been terrible PR for the government. Perhaps all this explains why Leicester stayed in lockdown for several months after the rest of England had reopened.

England gradually reopened its economy throughout May and June, but the government didn't start easing the work from home guidance until July 17, the day after the schools had shut for the summer. Johnson didn't want all the people who could work from home to start returning to the office until he was sure that he wouldn't get into a confrontation with the NEU; he didn't want to end up sending all the working parents home again, in the event that there were further 'problems' with the teachers.

What a relentless pantomime it all was.

From March 14 to July 17, the NEU drove the Covid policy of the British government by threatening to shut as many schools as possible, and acting on those threats; a Scargillesque campaign of economic disruption. The details I have supplied in this section leave little doubt.

However, there is a risk that the details will swamp the key facts, so let me recap:

At some point before March 14, behind the scenes, the NEU threatened unilateral schools closures. Johnson countered by privately threatening legal action to keep the schools open. On March 14, the NEU hit back, publicly agitating for school closures and implicitly threatening to close schools unilaterally. Johnson didn't cave in immediately. On March 16, when other unions had forced him into a U-turn over social distancing, he used the occasion to publicly reiterate his desire to keep the schools open. However, on March 17, the NEU upped the ante, explicitly threatening to close schools. Now the PM caved in. On March 18, he announced that all schools would close. Two days later, on March 20, the schools shut their gates. On the same evening, Johnson shut what was left of Britain's economy, amid huge public support. Three days later, on March 23, by which time the legislation was ready, he announced a legally enforced national lockdown, to be reviewed after three weeks. The entire point of the lockdown was to hide the fact that the NEU was defying the government. In the meantime, the government planted stories in the press suggesting that the schools would reopen. But after three weeks, the NEU wrote an open letter, basically refusing to reopen the schools. The government capitulated again; Dominic Raab announced that the lockdown would continue for another three weeks. Three weeks after that, the NEU plus five other teaching unions again refused to reopen the schools. Johnson caved in again, announcing that the lockdown would continue, albeit in an 'adjusted' form. The PM's aim was to reopen some sectors of the economy, while carefully ensuring that the reopening would be immune to any further threats by the NEU. At the same time, Johnson declared that the Covid measures would now vary by region, thus enabling him to cover up any future teaching mutinies with local lockdowns. With these protections in place, he announced that Year 1 and Year 6 primary school pupils would return on June 1. But, on May 10, the NEU and eight other teaching unions issued a press release opposing the scheduled return of the primary school pupils. When June came around, the teaching unions succeeded in keeping most of the returning pupils away from school. However, the ongoing national restrictions plus variations between local areas ensured that Johnson wasn't humiliated; the whole shambles was portrayed as a carefully crafted health policy, a new iteration of the same ridiculous lie that the government had peddled since day 1 of the lockdown.

Looking back at the press conferences the government gave during the first lockdown, what stands out is Johnson's mind-boggling deception. When you know that he didn't believe in any of these measures, that all the measures were merely a spin operation, a strategic response to the NEU's attack on Britain, Johnson can be seen as a breathtakingly skilful liar. The same goes for his science advisors. Everyone involved descended into the deepest depths of dishonesty by pretending that any of the lockdown lunacy was in any way scientific or justified.

As you behold all this dishonesty, knowing that it enveloped the whole country, a swirling miasma of lies penetrating into almost every corner and every soul, you find yourself asking… *Was it worth it? Was it worth all the dishonesty, just so that Johnson could maybe avoid a possible coup and thereby maybe save Brexit from a possible threat?* My view is that Johnson made the wrong decision – and I say this as a staunch Leaver. I readily admit that, in the circumstances, there were no black and white decisions available to him. If he thought he was saving Brexit, and if he thought he could quickly cajole the teachers back to work, I can understand why he chose to lock Britain down. But my judgment is that he shouldn't have done it. He should have publicly confronted the NEU from the start and tried a lot harder to quell the mass panic in Britain. Ultimately, if he had been humiliated and unseated, he could have walked away with his head held high. He could have spoken out from the sidelines; he could have been a voice of truth, helping to end Britain's coronapanic debacle sooner. Indeed, as the first lockdown dragged on, and the lies deepened, and the suffering of the public deepened, I believe that Johnson himself knew with increasing clarity that he had made the wrong decision. According to Dominic Cummings, Johnson expressed regret about the lockdown, saying 'I should have been the Mayor of Jaws and kept the beaches open'.

Yes, he should have been. And I believe he wanted to prove to himself and others that he still could be. However, Johnson never came clean. He never admitted that the entire coronapanic debacle was pointless and dishonest from the start. Perhaps he feared the legal consequences of admitting that he had lied. Or perhaps he believed there was still a risk that he would be unseated by Covid zealots if he admitted that his heart wasn't in the restrictions. Whatever the reason for Johnson's continuing insistence that the first lockdown was necessary, his failure to come clean undermined his efforts to reinvent himself as the Mayor of Jaws. He was soon manoeuvred into further lockdowns.

VII

The NEU was far from being the only union running amok throughout the coronapanic debacle. I don't know of *any* publicly funded sector where there wasn't at least one union at some stage exerting pressure on the government to impose restrictions on Britain. Pressure also came from unions representing the private sector. For example, the shop workers union, USDAW, demanded the masks in shops rule that came into force in July 2020. From summer 2020 onwards, every enclosed public space in Britain required mask wearing and social distancing, thanks to the combined campaigns of USDAW, the RMT and Unite/the TUC.

Further lobbying came from local authorities, including lobbying for schools closures. In the previous section, I mentioned that the NEU cited some English councils that were opposed to the June 1 schools reopening. The NEU provided direct quotes from council leaders in Bury, Rochdale, Knowlsey, Hartlepool and the London Borough of Barking and Dagenham. Numerous councils 'voiced concerns' at this time, the *Guardian* reported, and Bousted spoke similarly of 'a widespread revolt among councils'. The Local Government Association weighed in too, insisting that councils should be given access to testing data in order to reopen schools safely. Throughout the coronapanic debacle, there was a constant interplay between local authorities and the government, with both sides trying to dictate Covid policies; regional officials wanted 'more power in shaping the rules that affect their communities', as one report put it. Sometimes the regional officials demanded more restrictions; sometimes the government did the same.

The six-month period between the first and third lockdowns was peppered with 'local lockdowns', most of which seem to have been driven by the government. Although the policy was brought in to deal with the NEU – and that was how things played out in Leicester – the local lockdowns during the school summer holidays came about for other reasons. Of course, the official 'scientific' reason was always that there was a local spike in Covid-19 cases. But this reason can be discounted in every instance. Wherever the government issued restrictions at any point in Britain, the virus was a pretext. One councillor in Manchester complained that local health officials had been overruled in what he called a 'nakedly political approach'.

On July 31, the government announced that there would be local lockdowns in Greater Manchester and parts of East Lancashire and West Yorkshire. The announcement came just a few hours before the start of the Islamic religious festival of Eid al Adha, which began at sunset that evening and ran until August 3. Muslims in the affected areas were furious that the festival had been cancelled, and furious at the late notice. Understandably so. People had bought gifts for their relatives, prepared food, erected marquees and even set up bouncy castles. Events were scheduled to take place in homes, mosques and parks. In Blackburn alone, up to 5000 people were likely to participate. Muslims vented their dismay online by sharing a meme of a green-faced Boris Johnson, captioned as 'The Grinch who stole Eid'.

On July 31, Craig Whittaker, the Conservative MP for Calder Valley, one of the areas that was locked down, went on the radio to offer an explanation for the new measures. 'There are sections of the community that are just not taking the pandemic seriously', he told the DJ, who responded 'So it is the Muslim community?', to which Whittaker replied 'Of course'. Everybody suspected as much, even if the government wasn't explicitly saying it: that many of the local lockdowns were designed to stop Muslims from breaking social distancing rules. At the time, there were many anecdotal reports of Muslims 'not taking the pandemic seriously'. I myself noticed that the Bengali lads at the takeaway where I worked were generally quite nonchalant about Covid-19, although, being a sceptic, naturally I was relieved that my colleagues weren't being lunatics.

Throughout the summer, there were other local lockdowns that gave the impression of Muslims being singled out. Leicester remained in lockdown – Muslims may have been a factor there too – and Luton and Blackburn went the same way on July 24. On August 5, lockdowns were issued in Stockport, Wigan and Burnley, with Preston added to the list the next day. On August 26, more areas of Lancashire and West Yorkshire went into lockdown. On September 2, Batley and Dewsbury followed. On September 15, Birmingham, Sandwell and Solihull succumbed, with Leeds and Blackpool next on September 26. The summer also saw many examples of local areas going in and out of lockdown then back in again. Whether areas remained in lockdown depended on whether they 'followed the guidance', the PM confirmed. Matt Hancock talked of councils 'doing excellent work with their local communities to address an increase in coronavirus cases and we continue to work collectively with them' – the implication being that keeping the virus down by following government guidelines would keep people out of lockdown.

However, when assessing these 'Muslim lockdowns', you have to be careful again not to fall into the trap of taking the government's explanations at face value. Health officials had long warned of the Islamic community being particularly 'at risk' because Muslims tend to live in 'multi-generational' households. But remember: *all* the Covid-19 measures deployed up to and including summer 2020, from the lockdowns to the mask mandates and the two-metre social distancing rule, were union-driven and completely pointless. Whether or not Muslims followed the guidelines made no difference to anything, because the guidelines were scientifically meaningless. Moreover, corralling Muslims in their multi-generational households was hardly likely to protect the older members of the community. And with the transmission rate of Covid-19 tanking during the summer of 2020, the threat was miniscule anyway. The reason Muslim communities were locked down was not because of Covid-19. The government's entire Covid strategy was a spin operation. If Muslim communities were targeted with lockdowns, there must have been a subtext.

A clue to what was really going on can be seen in events that took place earlier in the summer. From May 31 to June 21, there were widespread protests in

Britain over the murder of a black man called George Floyd. Floyd was an American criminal who was asphyxiated by police officers while being arrested in Minneapolis. His death led to worldwide protests, many of which were organised by Black Lives Matter, a Marxist campaign group that accuses white people of being inherently racist. In the UK, as elsewhere, some of the BLM protests descended into disorder. There were attacks on property and on the police. There was also a spate of vandalism against historic statues. Notoriously, the Winston Churchill statue in Parliament Square was daubed with the words 'was a racist'. In response, a series of counter protests materialised, aiming to protect towns and cities from further vandalism. Tommy Robinson, the founder and former leader of the English Defence League, attended a counter protest in London on June 13 and called for his supporters to defend statues across Britain. EDL members and sympathisers were out in force during the following week, leading to clashes with BLM protestors. On some occasions, the BLM protests were cancelled on the advice of the police.

By the end of June, the unrest surrounding Floyd's murder had fizzled out. However, there was a lingering sense of grievance that the BLM protests had been allowed to go ahead. Many people who had been diligently obeying the government's Covid rules were dismayed at the double standard. And lockdown sceptics were rightly pointing out that the virus can't have been much of a threat if the BLM protestors weren't required to follow the rules. Against this backdrop, the government was faced with the prospect of Muslims celebrating Eid in a very public way. The festival was a potential flashpoint, and therefore a potential source of embarrassment to Johnson.

The fact that Luton was one of the first towns to go into a Muslim lockdown is telling. Luton is Tommy Robinson's hometown, where he founded the EDL in 2009, the movement's founding mission being to protect England against Islamic extremism. The EDL rapidly grew in popularity over the next decade, amid a series of Islamic terrorist attacks and the 'grooming gang' scandals that rocked towns and cities across England. With Muslim men overrepresented in grooming gangs, there were (correct) accusations that local authorities had turned a blind eye to the crime for fear of being called racist. In many parts of the country, there was a feeling that Muslims were being given special treatment by the authorities, while the Muslims themselves claimed the opposite – that they were under unfair suspicion. In 2020, Luton was a place where tensions persisted between the Islamic and non-Islamic communities. On July 28, two days before Eid, the media reported that Robinson had 'fled abroad' after an arson attack on his wife's home near the town. It seems likely that the unrest over the BLM protests had not died down in Luton. It also seems likely that the longstanding tensions between the locals and the Muslim community had ignited.

And perhaps similar tensions were igniting across the country, or at least at risk of igniting. Almost every area that went into a local lockdown is an area where an EDL demo has taken place in the past. Scouring Twitter for clues as to what went on in summer 2020, I found an intriguing tweet that spoke of 'EDL idiots who won't wear face-coverings in shops (in Bradford and elsewhere)'. These maskless EDL members no doubt resented the idea that Muslims were being exempted from Covid rules that the natives were expected to follow. There may also have been some lockdown zealots within the EDL, who would have been no less resentful. And many other locals, whatever their opinion on the restrictions, may have felt the same. Some people may have called for restrictions purely to stop Muslims from breaking the rules. The summer local lockdowns were probably designed to quell any further resentment surrounding the issue. A strong hint to this effect can be found in the words of Qari Asim, who was a government 'Islamophobia' adviser at the time and a senior Imam in Leeds. After entreating Muslims to 'stay home' during Eid, Asim explained that he did not want the festival 'to give rise to Islamophobia, hateful narratives that some groups will try to exploit when Eid celebrations commence'. Clearly, the prospect of intercommunal strife was on the government's mind.

In the weeks preceding Eid, the authorities in Blackburn made 'an urgent effort to avoid a centrally imposed lockdown', according to a *Guardian* report. Masks were mandated in the town's shops in advance of the national mandate, and the local population was advised to avoid social contact. Mohammed Khan, the Council's leader, warned that 'life cannot go back to normal just yet, and we must all make sacrifices to avoid a local lockdown'. Blackburn didn't avoid a local lockdown. And, throughout the summer, nor did many other areas with large Muslim populations. The reason, I believe, was that the Muslims who weren't following the government's guidelines would have faced an angry backlash in the aftermath of the BLM protests. The government's authority would have been undermined by the backlash and any ensuing unrest.

The government may even have feared that the unrest would lead to an uprising against the whole idea of Covid restrictions.

Granted, it's possible that I'm exaggerating the role of the EDL and generally the potential for resentment towards rule-breaking Muslims. Even without inter-communal tensions, the spectacle of Muslims brazenly disobeying the Covid rules may have been enough to spook the government into issuing local lockdowns. But I'm not so sure. After all, the government had already allowed the BLM protests to go ahead. The politicians were too afraid of being called racist to ban the protests in May and June. Even when the protesters turned violent, the police responded with kid gloves. When the protests were finally discouraged by the authorities, it was because of the counter protests. Accordingly, I think the government would have pursued the politically correct option of turning a blind eye to Muslim rule-breaking if it weren't for the prospect of resentment and unrest among Britain's native population. Indeed, not all areas with a large Muslim population were locked down; perhaps in some of these areas there was no risk of resentment among the natives.

Hearing all this, you may be thinking: Why didn't the government just allow the Muslims *and* everyone else to do whatever they wanted? If Johnson's agenda was to reopen Britain, why didn't he just let everybody start socialising normally again, to turbocharge the reopening? Well, one reason was that the government had already caved in to USDAW, the RMT and Unite/the TUC on mandatory masks and social distancing. Johnson couldn't encourage everyone to socialise normally while he was being blackmailed into imposing rules in other contexts. The rules governing socialising were a necessary adjunct to the rules governing shops, public transport and workplaces.

Of course, Johnson could have confronted USDAW and the other unions in the summer of 2020. But then again... he faced the looming threat of a second wave of the virus in the winter, along with the inevitability of further Scargillesque aggravation from the NEU. Confronting the other unions in the summer must have felt like a pointless risk, from a political perspective. If the NEU tried to shut schools again in the winter, any successes in the summer would have been for nought. Indeed, the successes would become liabilities because the more that life went back to normal in Britain, the more abrupt would be the government's climbdown when the teachers started unilaterally shutting schools again. Ongoing restrictions in shops, on public transport and in workplaces, combined with restrictions on socialising, would create a more coherent political framework for a winter lockdown if/when the NEU tried to force the issue.

Throughout September and October, there were some local lockdowns that I can't say with confidence were 'Muslim lockdowns'. On September 17, the North East went under heavier restrictions (apart from Middlesborough and Hartlepool, which followed on October 1). Included in the North East restrictions were the counties of Northumberland and Durham; these are areas with few Muslims. Maybe the government didn't want the public to ask awkward questions about why some areas were included in the lockdown and some weren't, so the whole region was locked down. Or maybe other factors were involved.

Subsequent events, in the North West, may shed

some light. On September 22, heavier restrictions were imposed on Liverpool and some surrounding areas. A week later, the city's Labour Mayor Steve Rotheram called for even tougher restrictions in the region – a 'circuit breaker lockdown'. A Labour councillor in the borough of Knowsley said much the same, while a newspaper survey at that time found that 57% of Liverpool's residents wanted tougher restrictions. The unfolding story even reached the national media. Shortly afterwards, a 'government source' was reported as saying that 'if there is somewhere that additional measures are brought in it is likely to be in that area'. And so it transpired. Liverpool went into lockdown on October 12. I don't know what exactly caused the Liverpool lockdown. Perhaps it was a Muslim lockdown. But another possibility is that the government was spooked into the measure by the pro-restrictions outcry from the local leaders and the local/national media. The same could have been true of many other local lockdowns.

On the day that the Liverpool lockdown began, Mayor Rotheram went on Channel 4 and dismissed the idea that the decision to lock the city down had been made locally: 'It wasn't local leaders', he insisted; 'it was the government and it's disingenuous of them to suggest otherwise'. He added that he would refuse to endorse the new restrictions unless the city received a 'package of support'. On the face of it, you may think the Mayor's demand for funding was noble. But don't be fooled! Endorsing the local measures on the proviso of receiving money from the government was equivalent to putting a price on freedom. *Selling people's freedom is not noble.* And let's not forget that the Mayor had agitated for the restrictions; he himself was being disingenuous. Calling for restrictions then blaming those restrictions on the government then demanding money to cooperate with the government – I can hardly imagine how anyone could behave more disingenuously. In partnership with the Mayor, Liverpool's six local authorities issued a joint statement demanding financial compensation for a lockdown that they themselves supported. Needless to say, the local authorities would have had their cut of any funding received.

At the same time, another large Northern city, Manchester, was facing the prospect of heavier restrictions. Unlike in Liverpool, the local leaders in Manchester didn't support the proposed escalation. Well, not exactly. On October 14, the city's Mayor Andy Burnham and the region's ten local authorities issued a joint statement in which they confirmed that 'our primary focus continues to be on driving down the rates of Covid infection'. They noted that 'back in July, we took the difficult decision to agree with the Government's request for additional restrictions'. And now the local leaders were in support of 'building on' the existing measures... but just not with measures as severe as the ones being proposed by the government. One reason Manchester's leaders were hesitant was that 'the financial package' the government was offering was 'nowhere near sufficient to prevent severe hardship'. Once again, freedom was being haggled over. And once again, the local authorities would take their cut of the funding.

When the government placed Manchester into lockdown on October 17, the local leaders issued another statement. Again they complained that 'the government is not giving city-regions like ours and the

Liverpool City Region the necessary financial backing for full lockdowns'. The leaders added that they had spoken to the Deputy Chief Medical Officer and he had told them that the 'only thing certain to work... is a national lockdown'. A burden shared, and all that! Meanwhile, Andy Burnham went on TV to rage about Manchester's forthcoming restrictions – or rather the government's unwillingness to pay enough money for the restrictions. He informed the media that 'we put forward a costed package of measures'. He noted that in 'negotiations with the government we were prepared to reduce our request... we even were prepared to go even lower'. And he protested that the government had 'walked away from negotiations'. For this outburst, Burnham was hailed as some sort of freedom fighter. A more accurate phrase would have been 'freedom salesman'.

As with Liverpool, I'm not sure why the government wanted to put Manchester under further restrictions, although the councils' October 17 statement mentioned that 'some of the poorest parts of England' would be going under lockdown, which makes you wonder if it was another Muslim lockdown. There may also have been involvement from the NEU in Manchester, and in Liverpool too; I will return to this possibility in the next section. As a general point, there were so many local lockdowns in the summer of 2020, and the government's edicts were so numerous and baroque and dishonest, and the local authorities were so shifty, and the media reports were so vague, it is impossible to know for certain what happened in every part of the country. Indeed, in mid-October, as complaints grew about the government's labyrinthine Covid policies, ministers tried to 'simplify' the rules.

From now on, there would be a 'tier system' – three tiers of restrictions, each more severe than the other. Manchester and Liverpool went into the third (the strictest) tier.

The tier system was not so much a simplification of the labyrinthine Covid rules as a codification of them. The government was trying to make the constant stream of *ad hoc* rule changes seem rational. Of course, the real rationale behind all the rule changes was the same as ever: the PM wanted to maintain an appearance of being in charge while the country roiled and rebelled during the pandemic. With different factions of the public endlessly pushing for or against Covid restrictions, the government was spinning the variegation into policy.

Way back at the March 16 press conference, Johnson and his chief science advisors all mentioned a phrase that remained central to the government's strategy: imposing 'the right combinations of measures at the right time'. The phrase was scientifically meaningless (what would the wrong combination of measures look like at the right time, or vice versa?). But it was a canny way of allowing the government to steer its Covid policies in whatever direction the unions or other factions were driving. Whatever combinations of demands or threats the government faced, ministers could spin the pressure into a combination of policies. The tier system was the apotheosis of this strategy. Measures could now be imposed in different combinations in different combinations of places, at different times, depending on the political exigencies. This was the government's 'war game', an attempt to prevent a second lockdown by playing a national game of whack-a-moles. A hammer of spin-

restrictions would descend on every Covid controversy, so that the PM wouldn't have to squash the whole country every time he was forced to intervene anywhere.

Such was the summer of 2020, the backdrop to the second national lockdown. It was a summer of local lockdowns, protests, counter protests, and constant wrangling between the government and councils. It was a summer in which the public was legally required to wear masks in shops, on public transport, and in other enclosed public spaces, including most workplaces, at the behest of the unions. It was a summer of pointless arbitrary Covid rules, the rules gradually evolving into the tier system, a nationwide patchwork of lies. And it was a summer capped off by a most unexpected development: the teaching unions agreed to reopen the schools.

## VIII

To understand the chain of events that led to the second lockdown, you first need to understand why the teachers went back to school. The second lockdown happened because the NEU changed strategies in response to a change in the circumstances. An opportunity arose that wasn't there at the start of September.

On the face of it, the fact that the NEU to agree to reopen the schools in September is surprising. Bousted and Courtney had already waged a largely successful campaign to hamper the government's efforts to re-open schools on June 1. Why didn't the NEU likewise try to disrupt the autumn reopening?

There were several reasons. For one thing, the

'science' wasn't providing much support for keeping schools closed at that point. Of course, I am not suggesting that there was ever a period during the Covid pandemic when the science supported the schools closures or any of the restrictions. Rather, the point is: the science didn't even provide a plausible *pretext* for closing the schools in September 2020. The number of Covid inpatients in England's hospitals had bottomed out during August; the figure was in the mere *hundreds* on any day across the whole of England. That meant fewer than one Covid inpatient per hospital per day. Even a lunatic socialist would be hard pressed to say the NHS was in danger of being 'overwhelmed' in those circumstances. Moreover, the estimated 'R rate' was low in August – below 1 – which meant that the outbreak had been shrinking; by the end of the month the estimate was nudging around 1, which suggested minimal growth at the most. Minimal growth of a minimal problem.

Meanwhile, the government's chief scientists were going out of their way to emphasise that the problem was especially minimal in schools. On August 23, the Chief Medical Officers of England, Scotland, Northern Ireland and Wales issued a joint statement to reassure parents and teachers that reopening schools was safe. The statement declared that 'compared to adults, children may have a lower risk of catching COVID-19 (lowest in younger children), definitely have a much lower rate of hospitalisation and severe disease, and an exceptionally low risk of dying from COVID-19'. The statement also declared that 'teachers are not at increased risk of dying from COVID-19 compared to the general working-age population'. And the statement added that 'ONS data identifies teaching as a lower risk profession (no profession is zero risk). International data support this.' The statement even claimed, almost cheekily, that the spread of Covid-19 in schools 'may largely be staff to staff (like other workplaces) rather than pupil to staff'. Finally, the statement pointed out that 'The international real-world evidence suggests that reopening of schools has usually not been followed by a surge of COVID-19 in a timescale that implies schools are the principal reason for the surge'. Granted, as well as all these fairly forthright assertions, the Chief Medical Officers invoked the government's usual get-out clause, noting that 'It is possible that opening schools will provide enough upward pressure on R that it goes above 1 having previously been below it, at least in some local areas. This will require local action.' But overall, the message was clear. The Chief Medical Officers had pulled the rug out from under the NEU. The NEU would receive no scientific backing for keeping the schools closed.

A final reason why in September 2020 the NEU didn't agitate to keep the schools closed is there was hardly any public support for the policy at that point. Since June, a petition had been circulating entitled 'Keep schools closed until Covid-19 is no longer a threat'. By the end of August, the petition had received a paltry 1030 signatures. Compare that number to the 685,394 people who signed a petition to close the schools in March. British parents in general wanted their kids to go back to school in September. The shops were open, the pubs were open, most work-places were open. Working parents had made their usual childcare arrangements for the summer, but now they would need the schools to reopen for the autumn term as usual. If the teaching unions tried to obstruct the reopening, the move would not receive popular support. We can also assume that the move wouldn't have received much support from teachers, given the low number of signatories to the petition.

As for the government, they were more determined than ever for all the schools to reopen. The policy was announced on July 2, and ministers never deviated from it. On August 1, all shielding advice for adults and children was 'paused'; clearly this was an effort to circumvent any prospect of the NEU using staff shortages as a pretext for closing schools. On August 5, the Schools Minister Nick Gibb told the BBC's today programme: 'All children will be returning to school in September, including in those areas that are currently subject to a local lockdown – Manchester, Greater Manchester, Leicester and so on – because it is important children are back in school'. Granted, as was customary, Gibb left the door open for local U-turns, noting that the government 'can't decree this for every single case, and it will depend on the circum-stances of a local increase in the infection rate'. But then again, the government was obviously quite blasé about the R rate if they were willing to open schools in areas where there were local lockdowns. Gibb left little doubt as to the government's position: 'We want all children back in school'.

Boris Johnson himself weighed in. On August 8, he made his most unequivocal defence yet of reopening the schools. Writing in the *Daily Mail*, he said 'it is a national priority to get all pupils back into school'. He gushed 'we can do it – and we will do it', adding: 'Now that we know enough to reopen schools to all pupils safely, we have a moral duty to do so'. And note: the phrase 'moral duty' was not a rhetorical flourish. Johnson emphasised the point: 'Keeping our schools closed a moment longer than absolutely necessary is socially intolerable, economically unsustainable and morally indefensible'. The PM was committed to reopening the schools, and no doubt he had solicited the support of the Chief Medical Officers to back him up. The *Mail* summed up Johnson's article with a phrase that offered a rare hint as to the reality behind the scenes: 'Boris Johnson today throws down the gauntlet to union leaders'.

The phrase also revealed something about the NEU: just because the NEU's leaders didn't disrupt the start of the autumn term, doesn't mean they didn't ideally want to. On August 6, the *Telegraph* reported some comments made by Mary Bousted at the NEU Councillors Network, a meeting between local councillors and the union. Bousted opined that 'Local authorities and schools should take the confidence to do what they can do and that will mean for many schools that they cannot have all children fully back in September'. She warned that ministers 'won't be able to carry out their threats' to reopen schools. Threats! You have to pinch yourself that teachers would feel threatened by the idea that they should continue providing children with an education while a cold was going round. The phony victim mentality, the narcissism, was astounding. Such narcissism was the basis of two years of callousness towards millions of children. However, even a narcissist understands when to hang back, when to wait for maximum impact. Bousted's comments came before Johnson threw down the gauntlet. The NEU decided not to pick it up. Not yet.

Instead of disrupting the September reopening, the

NEU settled for a series of 'safety' measures in schools, a 'system of controls', as agreed with the government. Just like in June, the schoolchildren would be expected to follow social distancing rules throughout the day and would remain in groups – known as 'bubbles' – to keep mixing to a minimum. There would be 'strict hygiene and cleaning protocols', and, in areas where there were local lockdowns, the children would now be required to wear masks in 'communal areas' such as corridors and canteens.

Although the government was clearly pandering to anxious teachers in an effort to keep the schools open, both the government and the NEU also had cynical reasons for supporting these measures. Both sides were doubling down on their previous stance, keeping up the pretence that a proactive response to Covid-19 was necessary in schools, as elsewhere. Moreover, both sides knew that the safety measures would create an ongoing context in which schools closures could be justified in future. Saying 'we tried to control the virus in schools but it wasn't enough' would give the NEU an excuse for forcing the closures, and the government an excuse for caving in. Finally, there was an even more malign reason why the NEU supported the safety measures: from the start, socialist unions saw the pandemic as an opportunity to exert control over the population. Socialism is inherently an exercise in control, and the Covid paranoia only added to the control freakery of the socialists, for whom the kids were easy prey. Schools became mad madrassas of hypochondria.

It was a dismal prospect for the returning schoolchildren. The masks in communal areas policy was especially abominable, and it would soon open the door to further, even crueller, mask mandates in schools. Yet, on September 1, there was a faint trace of hope in the air, as the children turned up to their classrooms, advised by the government to 'walk, cycle or scoot to school'. For many of the kids, it was the first time they had seen their friends in six months. Meanwhile, the economy was spluttering back to life, and the government was planning to end the furlough scheme on November 1. Britain was returning to a semblance of normality.

Alas, the unions, including the NEU, had other ideas.


IX


The schools had barely been open a week before the NEU reared up. On September 8, the NEU's Assistant General Secretary Nansi Ellis intoned that 'Our government needs to ensure teachers, school staff and students have the facilities and funding to get through this period'. She added: 'The NEU calls for government to ensure that track trace and test [sic] is fully operational and effective across the country'. The NHS's test and trace scheme had been operating for three months by this point, yet the NEU was not satisfied; the scheme was only as effective as the number of people who used it, and not everyone in Britain had downloaded the voluntary app; not everyone wanted to pointlessly stay at home for a fortnight because their phone had beeped.

On September 11, the NEU published another open letter, this time complaining that the current measures in schools were insufficient. Bousted and Courtney were writing to the PM to 'underline urgent safety measures that must be in place to ensure education continues for all pupils'. Needless to say, the required new measures were all neurotic and unreasonable. For example, the letter stated that the government must 'carry out regular asymptomatic testing of school staff and older secondary students', 'monitor ventilation in schools', 'make emergency efforts to reduce class sizes', 'source new spaces for schools to enable them to be less crowded' and 'report to trade unions of all school outbreaks... and what can be learned from them'. The PM had displayed 'blind optimism' and 'wilful disregard for advice offered to him', Bousted and Courtney raged, before concluding that 'It is vital government does everything in its power to permit schools... to remain open'.

Once again, the NEU was making demands and thinly veiled threats. The cogs were turning, cranking up the pressure on the government, and cranking the country towards a second lockdown. Meanwhile, another gigantic system of cogs was about to be activated. Three days after Bousted and Courtney's statement, the TUC – a federation of 48 unions – held its annual conference, on Zoom. The conference comprised two sessions, on September 14/15, with speeches from scores of union leaders and other union representatives. On the second day, Kier Starmer, the Labour leader, gave a speech supporting the union movement. I have watched the conference in full (for which I deserve a medal). The sessions contained a wealth of incriminating disclosures about the activities of unions before and during the first lockdown, and also in the run up to the second lockdown. I will share these disclosures in detail, to show exactly what sort of situation the government was facing in autumn 2020.

The conference kicked off with a speech by the Chair, Ged Nichols. In his opening remarks, he made a reference to Brexit. The government was in the process of wrangling with the EU over a trade deal, and Nichols felt compelled to say: 'What happens in the next few weeks will be absolutely critical. The risk of a catastrophic No Deal departure is alarmingly real and our movement must fight tooth and nail.' That said, Brexit was rarely more than an implicit theme of the TUC's 2020 conference. The most prominent theme was the role of unions in shaping the government's Covid policies. All the speakers agreed that unions should be proud of the campaign they had waged so far; Starmer himself crowed that 'Trade unions have always been the unsung heroes of our national story, and through this crisis you've helped write another proud chapter'. And all the speakers agreed that unions should continue the campaign. Dave Ward, the General Secretary of the Communication Workers Union, summed up the mood when he said: 'Throughout this pandemic, we've seen the [union] movement reassert our voice, our values, our role in society, and I honestly believe that we are on the brink of the rebirth of collectivism'. Socialists had aimed at nothing less since day 1 of the coronapanic debacle.

At the TUC conference there were several disclosures that confirmed some of the examples of union influence that I have mentioned in my other essays. Dave McCrossen, the Deputy General Secretary of USDAW, confirmed that mandatory masks in shops was a policy 'we fought for, and won'. It's worth dwelling a moment on that word 'fought'. On May 1, the *Telegraph* reported that USDAW and the British Retail Consortium had made recommendations to the government about how to reopen the retail sector 'without any threat of industrial unrest'. By the sounds of it, USDAW 'fought' for measures in shops by threatening to be disruptive.

On a similar note, the video of the conference featured a montage in which a voiceover confirmed that, regarding 'health and safety' at work, 'only union pressure made the government change its guidance'. The word 'only' speaks for itself, while the word 'pressure' was presumably a reference to Unite leader Len McCluskey who had led a joint union campaign to make workplaces 'Covid safe' in summer 2020. McCluskey didn't speak at the TUC conference. But James Anthony, the vice president of Unison, one of the unions that participated in the summer campaign, did. In his speech, Anthony indicated one way in which Unison had exerted pressure: workers were joining the union 'in droves', he said, and the leadership was encouraging them to 'get active', which 'has meant boosting the number of vital health and safety reps to help us through the pandemic and beyond'.

Mary Bousted, in her speech, made a torrent of similar remarks regarding the NEU's ongoing attempts to shape government policy. She spoke of NEU members writing '70,000 letters to their MPs'. She spoke of how the NEU, Unison, GMB and Unite had created a 'digital health and safety checklist app' when the government was trying to reopen schools in June; hundreds of members who weren't reps became 'checklist monitors' and are 'now reps in all but name'. She recounted how the union 'rang all our reps' in the week before the September reopening to make sure they had filled the checklist in; as a result, she said, the NEU is 'creating real time information about the Covid readiness or unreadiness of our members' workplaces' and is 'using this information to put pressure on the government to keep our members safe'. She boasted that 'we've recruited over 50,000 new members' and that '100,000 members have joined our Zoom calls'. She reported that 'We've hosted regular Zoom calls with officers and reps, explaining to them what they should be doing at each stage of the pandemic'. She noted that 'the NEU rep density has increased by 12%', and that '700 reps attended our new online health and safety course, 1,000 reps attended our 90-minute new reps briefing… and 2,000 reps have attended our regional online training'. She declared that 'our trained reps have acted decisively', that '72% of them have held formal meetings with school and college management', and, perhaps most significantly of all, '85% have set up virtual communication platforms such as WhatsApp, to speak to their members during the pandemic'.

Bousted's litany of self-incrimination demonstrates what the government was up against during the pandemic. Beneath all the threats and demands that the NEU made in public, there was also a groundswell of agitation at grassroots level. Orchestrated and stirred up by the NEU leadership, unionised teachers were furiously beavering away on Zoom and WhatsApp, collectively blackmailing the government into inflicting ridiculous, unscientific, malevolent Covid policies on children. Bousted concluded her speech by proclaiming: 'We've stepped up. We've not left a terrible crisis to go to waste. We've used it to show our members, and potential members, the power of the union'.

Another monumental example of 'the power of the union' was celebrated at the TUC conference. Many of the attendees waxed lyrical about the role that unions had played in securing the furlough scheme – also known as the 'job retention scheme'. Francis O'Grady, the TUC's General Secretary, led the self-plaudits, saying 'I'm proud that we helped to win the job retention scheme', adding: 'It's no coincidence that the scheme that paid the wages of over nine million workers was the one that unions had pushed for'. Dave Ward from the CWU spoke about 'pushing the government to actually act and introduce the furlough scheme, the job retention scheme, that we called for', and Steve Turner, the Assistant General Secretary of Unite, likewise praised 'the role our movement played in securing furlough'. Kier Starmer himself echoed the message. Addressing the 'union movement', he said: 'Without you, there would not have been a furlough scheme. That's where the idea came from'. He emphasised: 'If it had been just down to the government, it would have been a case of sink or swim'. There was also a mention of the furlough scheme in one of the conference's montages. The voiceover crowed: 'This movement should be proud. We forced a Conservative government to protect the livelihoods of over 12 million through the job retention scheme and self-employed scheme.'

Forced! Let us the recall the circumstances in which the government introduced the furlough scheme. In the middle of March 2020, the TUC stoked a work-from-home mutiny, openly defying the government's herd immunity strategy. Union reps were encouraging employees to hand in Section 44 letters, that is, letters arguing that the workplace was unsafe and that employers had a right to stay home on full pay. Many employees were able to work from home. But many weren't – for instance people like cleaners and porters. The TUC proposed that even people who couldn't work from home during the pandemic had a right to receive full pay while avoiding the workplace, and that they should be supported in this by their working-from-home colleagues. Indeed, for many workplaces, there would have been no point in cleaners or porters showing up; they'd have been the only staff there.

To appreciate why ministers caved in on furlough, you have to appreciate the position the government was in. The national workplace exodus was primarily driven by people who could work from home but who didn't usually do so – around 4 million people. Let's call them 'laptop workers'. Laptop workers believed that they were being reasonable in abandoning the workplace. In fact, they were being very unreasonable: they were sending a shockwave of destruction through the economy. Not only did they nullify the jobs of their nonlaptop colleagues, but they also jeopardised the incomes of the surrounding businesses that serve a thriving workplace; shops, cafes, transport providers, factories, and so on. The economy is an eco-system; if millions of workers suddenly stop leaving the house, stop operating in a physical world, revenue streams dry up and the entire ecosystem is at risk.

Against this backdrop, the TUC agitated for the government to step in and pay people's wages where necessary, to avoid mass redundancies. In turn, many employers no doubt made the same demand. With the economy screeching to a halt, employers couldn't afford to pay cleaners and porters to sit at home doing nothing. There were also workplace mutinies that were driven predominantly by nonlaptop workers. In those situations, employers will have looked searchingly towards the government to bail them out. Indeed, many employers will have taken the side of the mutinying workers, calculating that outsourcing the wage bill to the government was a better bet than trying to navigate the impending economic turbulence. As a general rule, any employer who was worried about their economic survival will have preferred the certainty of furlough to the uncertainty that was ravaging the economy in March 2020.

When you understand all this, you can appreciate why the TUC said they had 'forced' the government into furlough. The whole episode was an exercise in blackmail. By unilaterally shutting down workplaces, the unions placed countless employers and employees in jeopardy, driving them into economic peril which for many people would have dire consequences. At the same time, the unions, echoed by the lockdown-mongering media, would blame the government for the economic havoc that followed. If people had starved, the government would have been held responsible. Caving in on furlough was a matter of political survival for the PM. Like a hostage who commits a crime under duress from his captors, Johnson agreed to the furlough scheme because the unions were going to destroy him if he didn't commit the crime.

To really drive the point home, let me provide a few examples of the kinds of workplace mutinies that took place in mid-March 2020 (and beyond). The examples come from an essay entitled 'Covid-19: the battle in the workplace', which was published in July 2020 in a Journal called *International Socialism*. The author was a man called Mark L Thomas, who calls himself a 'workplace and trade union organiser for the Socialist Workers Party' – a man who had his ear to the ground in March 2020, unlike the British media.

Thomas is under no illusions about the mass panic and union unrest that drove the government into the lockdown. In his essay he notes that before the ban on mass gatherings, a slew of public events were cancelled by the organisers, for example pop concerts, Premier League football matches, rugby's six nations tournament, the London Book Fair, the NEU's annual conference, and a Stand up to Racism national demonstration. Thomas summarises: 'Faced with government inaction and growing fear about the threat to health and life, civil society gave a lead'. He then explains that 'In workplaces, in response to government foot-dragging, there was an upsurge of battles to protect workers'. In some cases, this meant sending the 'vulnerable' home on sick pay. In other cases, 'demands went beyond this and focused on shifting the maximum number of people to working from home or even stopping non-essential work regardless of whether people could work from home or not'.

Thomas quotes a 'council worker' as saying: 'As a union branch, we raised concerns about the threat of the virus in mid-February... In March, after Johnson declared that many would die as part of a herd immunity policy, we passed an emergency motion through our branch the next day'. That was March 12-13. Thomas also quotes a 'civil servant in a government department' as saying: 'The coronavirus crisis began to really hit home over the weekend of 14-15 March. The reps in my office discussed the potential impact...and planned PCS members' meetings for the

Monday lunchtime'. The Monday evening – March 16 – was when Johnson started advising social distancing. With the TUC now in open revolt, the PM was spinning the work-from-home migration as a government policy. However, despite Johnson insisting that he was offering 'advice' and that Britain was 'a mature and grown up and liberal democracy' – in other words, despite him favouring Sweden-style voluntary arrangements during the pandemic – unions intended to push the advice as far as possible, to 'push for more control over the lockdown process', as Thomas puts it. He explains: 'The government's U-turns put employers on the back foot, making them more vulnerable to pressure'. He continues: 'Overall the impression is of a sudden upsurge in workplace fights, especially where a rep or another activist pulled together a meeting, formulated demands and put them to management'. He adds: 'In report after report, the picture is one of management retreats'.

The aforementioned 'council worker' recounted:

We issued guidance to all union members. All places that could not maintain distancing should close. All staff, except those in refuse services, children's residential services and emergency social work, should work from home. If staff thought it was unsafe, we organised immediate union meetings and then informed managers that staff were removing themselves from potentially dangerous situations.

A bank worker recounted:

In the big centres, the union pushed the bank into

moving staff to work from home, and the bank did this very quickly. The numbers working from home have increased tenfold. But in the high street branches, staff were unhappy and felt not enough was being done to protect them. This has improved but nothing like as quickly as the move to home working. In general though, whatever the union has pushed for, the bank has conceded.

A PCS rep in the Department of Work and Pensions recounted:

In my office, about 50 percent of workers have gone home. And they are on full pay, not sick pay. We have forced management to enforce the advice from the government.

Thomas himself relays numerous examples:

At a large college in Scotland... lecturers lodged a request in mid-March to work from home if they didn't have classes to teach. Management answered by saying that they 'were not minded' to allow this. The response was a mass walkout. By the end of the week the college was closed.

At London's School of Oriental and African Studies (SOAS), support staff forced managers to close the site by threatening to walk out after a student was diagnosed with the virus.

Workers across ten libraries in the London borough of Lambeth walked out citing Section 44 of the 1996 Employment Rights Act, which allows workers to refuse to attend an unsafe workplace – the local council's 'gold command' had insisted that the libraries remain open despite those in neighbouring boroughs closing.

Staff in library hubs in Tower Hamlets in east London forced their closure after managers ignored health advice.

Hundreds of warehouse workers in Barnsley in South Yorkshire employed by fashion retailer ASOS walked out at the end of March over unsafe conditions.

There were further walkouts by postal workers at delivery offices in Bridgwater in Somerset and in Southwark over unsafe working conditions.

In the latter example, the enforced closure seems to have been temporary; Thomas cites some other examples of temporary closures. In each such case, workers protested what they saw as inadequate safety measures which were soon rectified, albeit with a loss of workplace efficiency as a result. Unions forced a tsunami of economic disruption in March 2020.

What happened was obvious to anyone who was paying attention at the time: 'The government began to see an erosion of its authority', as Thomas puts it. And no less obvious was the result of all the union agitation: the lockdown was 'more extensive than the government had intended'. Staggeringly, Thomas even claims that 'The lockdown did not go as far as many trade union activists were pushing for'. And of course, there was another source of pressure on the government at that time, as explained by a *Financial Times* article that Thomas cites:

> Ministers never intended to close quite so much of the British economy... Some employers said they closed their businesses during the lockdown not because of government prohibition but rather due to 'societal pressure' as people had not understood why they were still open.

The British economy was crushed in March 2020 by a mass panic and a massive union mutiny. One of the major initiating events was the RMT's threat of unrest, on March 13. But you cannot help but wonder if there was union agitation earlier than March 13. The furlough scheme was backdated to March 1, suggesting that the government was picking up the tab for a public sector workplace exodus that had been going on for weeks. Moreover, the unrest didn't end when the country went into lockdown. I have already mentioned the agitation from USDAW, Unison, the RMT and the NEU during the first lockdown. Thomas gives other examples. There was a campaign by 'construction activists' to shut non-essential building sites – 'Shut the Sites'. There was a campaign by Unite to ensure that the door next to the driver's cabin on buses was kept shut. There was a 'string' of walkouts by postal workers, which escalated into a national-level dispute between Royal Mail and the CWU. Under pressure from the union's members, Dave Ward made an announcement on April 1: 'Have you got the right PPE in place – gloves, sanitisers – and is social distancing strictly enforced in your office? If no, you should not be working and we will back you.' Royal Mail responded by going on the offensive. The organisation's Chief Executive, Rico Back, cancelled Saturday shifts – which was a longstanding objective of the board. CWU promptly threatened to strike, actioning an affirmative ballot that had been passed before the pandemic. The government summoned Ward and Back for a meeting, which resulted in Royal Mail backing down.

On April 28, the TUC called for a minute's silence to mark 'Workers Memorial Day'. There was participation across the country. Many workers staged walkouts and protests, waving banners and demanding Covid workplace measures such as PPE and hand sanitiser.

Overall, the impression you get from Thomas's essay is of a bubbling cauldron of union unrest both before and during the first lockdown. However, surveying all this unrest, an important question emerges: *Would the first lockdown have happened even without the schools closures?* Have I exaggerated the role of the NEU? Thomas, for his part, is well aware that the government caved in to the NEU's demand to close all the schools. He asks: 'Who was leading who here? It appeared that the government was being driven by pressures from below'. Indeed! But as far as Thomas is concerned, the NEU was just one of many unions that pushed the government into the lockdown.

I do not think so. The NEU was uniquely dangerous to the government, due to the scale of the economic disruption that the schools closures would cause, and the reputational damage that the government would sustain if the NEU's mutiny came to light. A government that can't even run one of its main state sectors can hardly be considered competent to run a country.

Covering up the schools closures by locking up the whole country was, in the PM's estimation, the only way to neutralise the threat from the NEU. The lockdown was the strongest possible measure to allow a big enough cover up on a long enough timeframe. A drastic enough gesture to seize control of the narrative and keep control of it. Contrast this with the government's response to the other union mutinies. Johnson could deal with them, it seems, within the framework of 'advising' social distancing, or by occasionally issuing *ad hoc* measures like masks or workplace Covid restrictions. The cauldron could bubble away, with the country opening or reopening as the unions saw fit, and the government intervening only occasionally, without the PM ever being vulnerable to an economy-wrecking mutiny within his own orbit of power.

Let me put it another way: Johnson couldn't say 'I advise schools to stay open'. That would be equivalent to advising himself. He had to make a decision on a national level. And if the schools were going to shut (and stay shut) whether he liked it or not, and if there was going to be a huge economic shockwave whether he liked it or not, the only way he could cover up the mutiny and the damage was by 'deciding' to do a lockdown. Moreover, at the start of the coronapanic debacle, Johnson didn't have the option of fighting back against the NEU by doing local lockdowns. With mass testing still to be rolled out, and barely a handful of cases in hospitals, there was no data on which local lockdowns could be spun.

Of course, there were other sectors of the state that were being convulsed by union unrest. The civil service, led by the PCS union, almost certainly pushed for a work from home policy in March 2020, and there was agitation from local authorities throughout the first lockdown. But if civil servants and council bureaucrats were permitted to work from home, this wasn't going to automatically extract a quarter of the working population from the economy, as the schools closures would. The UK has around 500,000 civil servants and around 1.4 million local government employees, including front line staff who carried on working (around 20% of the total). Civil servants and council bureaucrats working from home was an economic shock, but not an earthquake. The school closures should be understood as a huge exacerbation of the ongoing union unrest. Not so much the last straw – more a bale of straw.

There was also the fact that the NEU leadership was exceptionally 'combative' during the pandemic, as Thomas notes. He cites a post made by Kevin Courtney (at some unspecified time) on an 'unofficial union Facebook page':

> If your Head says they have to be in, tell them no. Tell them it's your union's advice. Tell them you will work from home. Tell them we will see them in court. Tell them if they mess you about there will be trouble.

Courtney added: 'This is your union's advice: follow it, fight for it.' The threat from the NEU was not only large in scale but in intent.

Putting all this together, we can conclude that the TUC-driven mutiny in March 2020 undoubtedly forced the government into the furlough scheme, but, without the NEU mutiny, the government probably wouldn't have imposed a legally enforced lockdown on Britain. I say 'probably' because I think that's a fair appraisal of the evidence. The general union mutiny that caused the furlough scheme could be compared to a body shot. The shot wasn't fatal, not immediately, but it may well have become fatal. In contrast, the NEU mutiny that caused the schools closures could be compared to a head shot. Johnson locked Britain down to spin a fatal economic blow into a health policy.

Granted, there couldn't have been a lockdown without the furlough scheme. But that's not the same as saying there couldn't have been a furlough scheme without the lockdown. In Sweden, there was a furlough scheme despite the country staying legally open. Indeed, in Sweden, the schools stayed open too, because the teaching unions cooperated with the government. Social distancing remained voluntary in Sweden throughout the pandemic, because teaching unions didn't crowbar the Swedish government into a lockdown. The moral is: if you don't want a lockdown, get the teaching unions onside. And if you don't want a furlough scheme, get the rest of the unions onside.

Alas, during the coronapanic debacle, neither the teaching unions nor the rest of Britain's unions were on the British government's side, as the TUC conference in September 2020 amply demonstrated. For five gruelling hours, the speakers parroted the same pathetic socialist slogans about solidarity and safety. Kier Starmer threw his weight behind the madness, proclaiming that the Labour Party 'was born out of the trade unions. We are one family. One movement. And under my leadership we will always stay that way'. Everybody at the conference agreed that the 'workers' could only be protected by demanding that the hated Tories provide the protection. By way of a fierce campaign of blackmail, unions had 'forced' the government into adopting the furlough scheme and imposing lunatic Covid restrictions on workplaces and other venues. Now the unions were bragging about the achievement. And, what's worse, they were bragging about their up-coming plans.

Two more shots were about to be fired at Britain.


# X

Let us pause to recap the situation that Boris Johnson was in in September 2020. The government had re-opened all the schools, while reassuring parents and teachers that it was safe to do so. The government had reopened the economy, albeit an economy that was defaced by the abhorrent mask mandates and social distancing rules that the unions had demanded. The government had 'paused' all shielding advice, meaning that there was no reason for anyone not to go back to work. And the government had announced that the furlough scheme would end on November 1.

The TUC and the NEU intended to thwart all these policies, with a new campaign of disruption.

First, the TUC took aim. I must say, even after spending 18 months researching the role of the unions in driving Britain's Covid restrictions, I was stunned watching the TUC's September 2020 conference and discovering what they were up to at this point. As well as boasting about 'forcing' the government into the furlough scheme in March 2020, the TUC announced a new aim: *to force the government into continuing the scheme*. I suppose I shouldn't have been surprised, because I already knew that there was never any justification for any of the union lunacy in March 2020. I already knew that socialists are merciless. I already knew that the sole business of socialists is collective predation. But still! The mass panic had largely subsided, and the harms that the unions had inflicted on Britain were now a concrete reality. The country was waking up to the aftermath of a hurricane, the destruction plain to see, yet in the cold light of day the TUC was planning to do it all again.

Francis O'Grady, the TUC's General Secretary, laid out the plan across two speeches she made to the conference. Preparing the ground, she took a swipe at Margaret Thatcher, the arch enemy of the union movement: 'If there's one lesson we have learned from this terrible pandemic, it's that there is such a thing as society', O'Grady intoned, adding: 'It takes a whole community to beat a pandemic.' She issued a warning to the conference: 'From Thursday this week, it will be just 45 days before the job retention scheme is due to end.' She outlined the TUC's position: 'The pandemic isn't scheduled to end in October, so neither should state support for jobs.' She made an offer to the government: 'We worked together once before; we are ready to work with you again', to 'build on the job retention scheme'. And she made a threat: 'Whatever happens, we won't give up: unions will fight for every job, even more so with the clock ticking down on Brexit.'

O'Grady's offer to 'work with' the government was premised on the idea that state intervention was needed to prevent job losses during the pandemic. The TUC had peddled the same idea when blackmailing the government into the furlough scheme in the first place. At the September conference, O'Grady formally proposed a new 'jobs protection and skills deal' supposedly to prevent mass unemployment. The alternative, she insisted, was 'economic masochism on an epic scale'; jobs were 'on the line, for one reason only: the global pandemic'. Needless to say, the entire premise was profoundly dishonest. The pandemic didn't cause economic disruption in Britain in March 2020; unions caused the disruption by unilaterally shutting down workplaces. The herd immunity policy would have meant hardly any job losses at all. Similarly, the government's plan to send everyone back to work in the autumn and end the furlough scheme would have meant minimal economic disrupttion going forward. The TUC intended to keep causing disruption, keep blaming it on the government, and keep demanding that the government fix the problem.

Of course, the TUC didn't describe their plan in quite that way. In an online summary posted on the organisation's website, their stated aim was to 'bring people back to work and save jobs'. At the conference, O'Grady explained that this could be achieved using 'using short time working, wages subsidies and training incentives'. The idea was that cash-strapped employers could retain employers on shorter hours while the government met part of the wage bill and also paid for some training. That might all sound reasonable. But it wasn't. The economy would be in better shape if employers were simply left alone – at last! – rather than being crowbarred by unions into another labyrinthine bureaucratic scheme that would only increase the tax burden and cost jobs long term.

And that wasn't the biggest problem with the 'jobs protection and skills deal'. The biggest problem was that the deal was a Trojan horse for continuing the furlough scheme in its present form and thereby giving unions an ongoing basis for creating havoc. O'Grady complained that 'too many workplaces still aren't safe', because of the 'pursuit of profit over safety'. She carped 'So thank you Prime Minister, but we don't need another pep talk about returning to work'. The online summary of the TUC's new plan included the following recommendation: 'Workers should continue to receive at least 80 per cent of their pay for time they are not working'. Another recommendation was that 'The scheme should support workers who cannot work because they are in the group previously told to shield'. In other words: as long as the pandemic continued, the TUC wanted ongoing support for the people whom the government had recently said *didn't need to shield*, and ongoing support for anyone else who wasn't working. Far from trying to 'bring people back to work' the TUC was contemptuously ignoring everything the government had said, and demanding the continuation of the furlough scheme while calling it something different and adding in a few extra clauses about wage subsidies and training. There was even a condition about the government providing support for workers who have 'caring responsibilities that mean they cannot work' – an alarming hint that the NEU might be about to run amok again.

Dave Ward indicated the TUC's real intentions, almost comically, when he stumbled over his words, talking about 'continuing to pressurise the government to extend the furlough scheme, er, and also introduce something similar as the TUC have put forward'. You can see that he had hastily bolted on the part about 'something similar', that is, the window-dressing proposals about training and wage subsidies. He had already blurted out the real aim: continuing to press-urise the government to extend the furlough scheme.

Francis O'Grady explained how she wanted the pressure to be exerted:

> Starting today we must fight back. Organising, campaigning, lobbying—doing what our movement does best together. So to our brilliant activists and reps, I say this – lead the way. Get around the table with your employer. Lobby your constituency MP. Ask all your members to do the same. Let's get organised and fight for every job, just as our friends in the trade union movement in France, in Austria, in Germany, lots of other countries, are doing exactly the same.

Steve Turner, the Assistant General Secretary of Unite, spoke of 'the actions now required of government' and reiterated O'Grady's call to arms:

> Congress, none of this week's fears or demands will be won passing a motion, sending a clever tweet to Johnson, or a meeting with the Chancellor. We've got six weeks now to win the ongoing supp-ort we demand. And it's going to take every ounce of our strength to do it. We're going to have to win it, in our workplaces, our communities, on street corners, buses, and the march to confront our MPs in every UK constituency. It's our responsibility, our duty, to raise a call to arms and to inspire and mobilise our members, our families and our comm-unities to join us. United in common purpose, our movement can and will win this fight, striking a blow for our members, our class, our communities,

against those willing to abandon us all in the name of free market ideology. Congress, let's not wake up on November 1, wishing we'd done more. Solidarity, congress.

There was further support for O'Grady's proposal from Dave Prentis, who was then the General Secretary of Unison, Britain's largest union. He declared: 'Already there is talk about going back to normal. Normal, painted as an aspiration. Do not be fooled. Congress, we can never go back to normal. A decade of pain and austerity'.

Kier Starmer himself weighed in. Starmer's comments are especially notable because although he was clearly keen to emphasise the 'back to work' aspect of the TUC's proposals, he also left little doubt that, for many people, continuing the furlough scheme would mean the very opposite:

We all know the furlough scheme can't go on as it is forever. We've never suggested that. But the truth is, the virus is still with us. Infections are rising. Lockdowns are increasing. And for some sectors of the economy – retail, aviation, hospitality, and there are others – for millions of workers and for towns and cities under restrictions, it just isn't possible to get back to work or reopen businesses. That isn't a choice. It's the cold reality of this crisis. So it makes no sense at all for the government to pull support away now in one fell swoop. But with a bit of imagination and if we act in the national interest, a better approach is possible. That's why today I'm calling on the government to work with us, to create new targeted support to replace the job retention scheme, to develop through this a scheme for those sectors that most need it. This needs to be done through urgent talks with the trade unions, with businesses and with the Labour Party... Labour and the British trade union movement need to stand together like never before, to show the British people we've got their back and their future too.

Starmer added, menacingly: 'We will put whatever pressure we can. We've been calling for this over the summer... to put the pressure on the government to say you have got to act.'

In March 2020, the TUC had openly encouraged workers to unilaterally abandon their workplaces. No such open call came in September; the TUC was keen to be giving the impression of 'working with' the government. However, with all the talk of local lockdowns and rising infections and unsafe work-places, the TUC was implicitly warning the govern-ment that furlough would be required in any scenario where staff would be safer if they stayed at home – and the unions had declared themselves the arbiters of that judgement. As the UCU speaker put it: 'Where the government will not act, people and their trade unions must.' Unions intended to force the renewal of the furlough scheme by demanding the right to decide who goes to work and who doesn't and then holding the government responsible for paying all union mem-bers who stayed home. The threat was essentially unchanged from March 2020: we'll cause economic havoc, and we'll blame it on the government if anyone starves.

However, there was one explicit threat of industrial

action from one of the unions at the TUC conference. The threat, which came from PCS, the civil service union, had the potential to put the government in a very awkward position. The General Secretary of PCS is Mark Serwotka. In his conference speech, Serwotka remarked: 'We have been successful... in trying to keep the overwhelming bulk of our members safe. For those who have to be in work, we've tried to keep those workplaces safe, but for the majority we've successfully got them working from home'. (Another PCS member, Paul Williams, the PCS Department for Transport Group President, has written a blog post which gives an insight into how PCS was able to get people working from home: 'Right from the start of the pandemic we have kept our members informed of their rights, in particular their right to remove themselves from a workplace using Section 44 of the Employment Rights Act.') Serwotka continued by warning that the struggle wasn't over: 'In the civil service, the people we represent are being subjected to the most awful political decisions'. He explained as follows: 'The government, to cover up the fact that is [sic] ending the furlough scheme, is now pretending to care for the economy.' Let's be clear about what Serwotka was suggesting here: that the government's primary goal was not to reopen the economy but to end the furlough scheme, to thwart the brave new world the socialists were creating. Only a socialist could say something so twisted and self-centred.

Serwotka went on: '80% of civil servants are expected now to report to a workplace by the end of September. That is irresponsible... the actions of a disgraceful government'. He complained further: 'Contrast this with the Scottish government that today has notified all Scottish civil servants they will continue to work from home until 2021.' Then came the threat:

> Our union and our members are not prepared to stand for that. We will stand against anyone being forced back into a workplace when it is not safe to do so. This week we will start talking to our thousands of reps. We are serving our members and we are prepared to take action if that is what is needed to keep people safe.

The threat was followed up by a clarion call: 'My appeal to this movement is simply this. If we work together we can keep people safe and we can hold this government to account'. And a statement of intent: 'In the here and now we will work with others to keep every trade unionist safe'.

Following the conference, PCS made good on their plans. The first step was sending round a survey on September 17 to all the union's members to get 'their views on coronavirus safety and whether civil servants in England should be forced to return to their workplace'. Presumably the response was congenial – as in, congenial to the PCS leadership – because on September 20 the union took the next step, arranging a 'reps meeting on coronavirus'. An invitation was issued: 'Reps are urged to sign up in advance for an online briefing taking place at 6pm on Wednesday (23) to discuss how to respond to the UK government decision to force civil servants in England to return to workplaces'. On September 22, PCS reiterated the invitation and also reported a stunning escalation: 'At today's meeting with the Cabinet Office, PCS pressed Alex Chisholm to withdraw the threat to force civil servants to return to the workplace'. Chisholm is the Permanent Secretary for the Cabinet Office – basically the highest civil servant in the land, reporting directly to the PM. According to an industry newsletter, Chisholm had told the civil service to 'move quickly' on meeting the 80% target. This had sparked 'pushback from unions, with one saying it could take industrial action'. It's interesting to note the plural *unions*. Dave Penman the General Secretary of the FDA was now weighing in too, calling the government 'Luddites'. Note also the confirmation of PCS's strike threat; the newsletter quoted Mark Serwotka as saying: 'Of course we would be prepared to consider industrial action'. PCS were now making their demands and threats at the highest possible level, just as they had done on March 17.

What happened next was wearily predictable. On the evening of September 22, Johnson announced to the House of Commons that new restrictions were needed. He began with the usual dishonest waffle about the 'science'. He then spoke of the need to 'shelter the economy from the far sterner and more costly measures that would inevitably become necessary later'. The usual preposterous socialist rationalisation. He went on:

I want to stress that this is by no means a return to the full lockdown of March. We are not issuing a general instruction to stay at home. We will ensure that schools, colleges and universities stay open – because nothing is more important than the education, health and well-being of our young people. We will ensure that businesses can stay open in a Covid-compliant way. However, we must take action to suppress the disease.

And the action was: 'We are once again asking office workers who can work from home to do so'. Well, fancy that! The PM was getting in there first, advising working from home before PCS held their meeting the next day and publicly announced their intention to strike over the issue. Johnson emphasised that the only people being advised to work from home were office workers: 'In key public services – and in all prof-essions where homeworking is not possible, such as construction or retail – people should continue to attend their workplaces.' This was the right combin-ation of measures at the right time, you might say.

Further elaborating, Johnson made a shifty comm-ent about Parliament: 'Like Government, this House will be free to take forward its business in a Covid-secure way which you, Mr Speaker, have pioneered'. I am not sure exactly what the PM was getting at here. Perhaps there would be changes to the running of Parliament, orchestrated by the speaker, the Labour MP Lindsay Hoyle. If so, I wonder if Hoyle was instrumental in the closing of Parliament in March 2020. Or perhaps Johnson was citing Parliament's existing Covid-secure methods, so as to exempt MPs from the new wave of restrictions.

Johnson also announced a raft of new measures throughout society, for instance 10pm curfews on pubs and restaurants along with a table service only rule, a decreased limit of 15 people at weddings, limits on participants in team sports, and sterner penalties for breaking all the Covid rules.

In hindsight, we can see clearly what was happ-ening here. The various new measures throughout society were an attempt to craft an overall Covid policy that was consistent with the work from home advice. Where people couldn't work from home, the PM made no intervention; some social contact was unavoidable. But he needed to be seen to be 'doing something' to limit all 'non-essential' social contact, hence the ludicrous arbitrary measures affecting pubs, sport teams, weddings, etc. The new measures were designed to be salient but not completely destructive, because the PM had no desire to shut Britain down again. He summarised his hedging strategy: 'We will not listen to those who say let the virus rip; nor to those who urge a permanent lockdown'.

Johnson most certainly *had* listened to the unions, especially PCS. The Marxist publication the *Morning Star* crowed about the achievement. 'The Tory government was forced into another massive U-turn today as it advised people to work from home if they possibly can', said one article, smugly noting that ministers had previously 'spent weeks advising home workers to return to workplaces'. The article also featured a quote from Mark Serwotka; PCS had been 'vindicated by this government U-turn', he declared, and 'If people can work from home, they should do, until the government has got control of the virus'. The arrogance was astounding! Here was a union leader who had blackmailed our elected government and was now acting as though he was the arbiter of national policy. And more blackmail was to come. As the *Morning Star* noted: 'Trade unions also pointed out that the restrictions come just over a month before the government plans to end the furlough scheme'. Len McCluskey was quoted as saying: 'Without such assistance... this government will be the architect of the community destruction and human despair that will surely follow'. You can witness here direct evidence of a union leader holding the government responsible for the economic destruction that the unions them-selves were unleashing. Francis O'Grady was quoted too: 'The PM says that he will put his arms around the workforce. Let's see him prove it.'

As far as I am aware, PCS is the only union that explicitly threatened industrial unrest in the middle of September 2020 to force through working from home (although I do know that the UCU was threatening to strike in early September, demanding 'regular univ-ersal testing' before face-to-face teaching resumed.) However, given the TUC's Section 44 mutiny back in March, and O'Grady's call to action at the September conference, we can be almost certain that many other work from home mutinies took place throughout the economy in mid-September. In any case, I think the PCS threat alone would have been sufficient for the government to advise all offices to move to working from home. Johnson could hardly advise one thing for the civil service and another thing for other offices, including those in the private sector. Such was the leverage that PCS wielded. And surely they knew it. Maybe that's why, among the TUC's constituent unions, PCS was the only one that went public with a strike threat. That was enough to settle the issue.

Moreover, just as in March, the office closures in September will have dragged in 'nonlaptop' office workers such as porters and cleaners, while also having a knock-on effect on other businesses. Many workers who couldn't work from home would end up being sent home. In turn, the government's U-turn will have triggered many more union mutinies throughout

Britain; the entire economy will once again have become a bubbling cauldron of union unrest. Such was the outcome the TUC had aimed for all along; O'Grady had urged unionists to engage in 'organising, campaigning, lobbying', to 'fight for every job'.

On October 21, the TUC's campaign received a huge boost, as a number of Mayors, trade union general secretaries, Labour MPs and councillors – a total of 131 people – signed a joint statement demanding '80% wage support in an extended furlough scheme' and urging the government to do 'whatever it takes' during the pandemic. The signatories included the Mayor of London Sadiq Kahn, plus Steve Rotheram and Andy Burnham, and the General Secretaries of the unions USDAW, Unite, CWU, GMB, ASLEF, FBU, TSSA, Community, NUJ, CLASS, NEF and the NEU. With another shockwave of economic disruption unleashed, and a powerful lobby holding the government responsible for paying the wages of anyone who was affected by the destruction, the renewal of the furlough scheme became inevitable.

The very next day, October 22, Sunak told the Commons that the furlough scheme would continue. Eight days later, the PM confirmed it publicly. Unions had delivered the body shot. Next came the head shot.


XI


Finally, we have reached the point where the second lockdown can be seen in context and understood.

On October 31, the PM didn't just confirm the renewal of the furlough scheme. He announced that England would go into lockdown for a month, starting from November 5. Let us analyse why this outcome happened, why it happened when it did, and why it happened how it did.

Having begun September complaining about Covid safety in schools, the NEU continued in the same vein, energised by the TUC conference. On September 15, the second day of the conference, Mary Bousted tweeted: 'This is a crisis. It will not go away until school staff are able to access testing easily and get results rapidly'. Bousted's comment was in reference to a *Guardian* report about 'thousands of school leaders' who had written to Gavin Williamson to warn of 'partial rolling closures' due to staff shortages. Many staff were self-isolating after coming into contact with a positive case. The *Guardian* quoted one Head as saying: 'In order to run my school I need to be able to get staff tested quickly and back to work as soon as possible if the test is negative'. Apparently it didn't occur to the teachers just to carry on working if they weren't ill.

A few days later, suddenly there was a flurry of discussion about a 'circuit breaker' lockdown. The concept had originated in Singapore where a short lockdown had been imposed in April. On September 18, the *Guardian* reported that, according to 'government sources', there were 'active discussions' in Downing Street about 'how best to respond to a sharp increase in cases'. A 'fortnight'-long lockdown in England had been mooted, and the idea was 'among those discussed' by SAGE. To 'minimise disruption' the period of new restrictions would encompass the week-long school half term (which ran from October 26-30). The PM was said to be 'keen to avoid' a national lockdown.

On the same day, the *Financial Times* ran a similar story. I think we can assume that ministers were deliberately floating the circuit breaker concept in the media at this point. The *Times Educational Supplement* also ran the story, claiming that SAGE had 'reportedly proposed a two-week national lockdown'. The *TES* quoted a headteacher and a governor who both approved of the proposal. Mary Bousted was quoted too: 'If Sage recommends a two-week half term to suppress Covid and support safer schools and colleges, the NEU would support this.' At first sight, you might assume that SAGE or the government had come up with the idea of a circuit breaker and that Bousted was reacting to the idea. I do not think the situation was that simple. Bousted made a further remark that tells the full story. She said: 'SAGE may not have made this proposal if the government had acted to ensure that the conditions necessary to support school and college full opening, and most importantly an effective test and trace system, had been put in place'. These are *very* revealing words. They strongly suggest that the NEU was the impetus behind all the talk of a new lockdown. As soon as the schools had reopened, the NEU had begun griping about inadequate school safety measures and the test and trace scheme – the usual complaints. SAGE, it seems, was responding to the NEU's griping.

There is more evidence to this effect. On Sept 21, SAGE published a short document suggesting that a circuit breaker lockdown should be 'considered' by the government, along with 'advice to work from home for all those who can'. Given that SAGE's work-from-home recommendation came 24 hours before the government capitulated to the PCS union, we can assume that that recommendation was designed to spin the capitulation. In turn, we can assume that SAGE's circuit breaker recommendation was also designed to spin a (potential) capitulation, and that the NEU – who were keen on a new lockdown – were applying the pressure. In the aftermath of the TUC conference, when PCS started agitating for a work from home policy, ministers will have realised that they were bound to face renewed pressure from the NEU; why shouldn't the teachers 'work from home' too? SAGE was probably asked in September to moot the idea of a minimal lockdown as an insurance policy just in case the NEU threatened to shut down the schools again. A short lockdown would be 'scientific' and could always be extended if the teachers refused to cooperate.

Perhaps you are shocked at the idea of politicians asking scientists to help spin a policy. What is most shocking is that this kind of horse-trading seems to be standard procedure. Graham Medley, a Professor of Infectious Disease, has disclosed how scientific modellers such as himself work with the government: 'We generally model what we are asked to model. There is a dialogue in which policy teams discuss with the modellers what they need to inform their policy'. Indeed, a 'dialogue' of this kind seems to have played a key role in causing Britain's entire coronapanic debacle. In March 2020, a research paper by Professor Neil Ferguson was wheeled out to spin the first lockdown; even the content of Ferguson's paper was probably influenced by the government. I've discussed all this in my essay 'The Road to Lockdown'. If I am right that SAGE mooted the idea of a circuit breaker in September because the government needed to spin a potential capitulation to the NEU, the dynamic was not without precedent.

Would the NEU try to shut the schools again? The prospect seemed increasingly likely. On September 20, Bousted and Courtney wrote a letter to the government 'urging' them 'to take emergency measures if schools and colleges are to keep safe and open'. The letter declared 'you should move towards asymptomatic testing of staff and older pupils' and towards 'a Plan B for education', which would include 'reduction of class sizes' achieved through 'Nightingale Schools'. Yes, you read that right; the NEU wanted new schools to be built, comparable to the seven NHS Nightingale hospitals that had been hastily erected in the spring.

On September 22, the day that the government capitulated to PCS, Courtney popped up to make the most of the occasion. Reiterating the NEU's demand for testing in schools, he wrung his hands about 'some secondary schools that, under public health advice, have had to send home the whole of year 11'. He added: 'This is why the NEU argued for smaller bubble sizes – and smaller class sizes. The Government should have listened'. The ludicrous policy of sending entire year groups home continued throughout the autumn in many schools, as did the policy of isolating individual children who had come into contact with a positive case. Hearing Courtney punitively say 'the government should have listened', you get the impression that the disruption in schools was being *deployed* as a tactic to pressure the politicians. On the same day, Courtney disclosed that 1,000 schools had been 'partially closed' in the previous week... then he reiterated the NEU's latest barmy demands.

A week later, there was a big escalation by the

NEU. The union launched an online 'Covid map', a searchable map/database that would tell parents 'What is the COVID-19 rate around your school?' As reported in the *Daily Mail*, the tool would help 'parents to find out how at risk their children are from coronavirus at school'; the article added that 'one in six state secondary schools could not fully open last week'. Courtney was quoted as saying that the 'website will also encourage parents to support our asks of the Government'. And again Courtney listed the 'asks': 'much quicker testing for staff and students, Nightingale sites for smaller classes, guaranteed home working for vulnerable staff, and more funding for already strained schools and colleges to maintain Covid-security'. What was happening here is obvious: the Covid map was designed to frighten parents so that they would support the NEU's insane demands and – when the government didn't meet those demands – support the ongoing partial schools closures and, if it came to it, full closures.

The *Mail* article also included a shocking revelation: that 'a school leaders union' had 'immediately challenged' the government's edict that masks should be worn in corridors in schools in local lockdown areas only. The union, the article stated, 'will be telling all of its members, regardless of whether they are subject to local lockdown, to ask pupils and staff to wear face coverings in communal spaces'. I have been unable to establish which union this was, but the remark is credible given that the *Mail* article was clearly written with the cooperation of Courtney, who will have been privy to decisions made by his fellow teaching unionists. A few people have corresponded with me to tell me that their children's school was unilaterally requiring masks in corridors in the autumn.

The NEU's agitation continued into October. On October 3, Bousted proclaimed that 'the situation in schools is becoming increasingly untenable'. On the same day, the NEU issued a new press release about a 'Special Conference' that they had held that day. The statement was basically a load of quotes from Bousted. She said that keeping schools safe was 'essential'; 'Only if that is achieved will they remain open'. She cited a statistic: '84% of NEU members in our latest survey have said they do not trust Boris Johnson's Government to keep schools safe.' She added: 'This should be a warning to Government and a clear indication that enough is enough.' Bousted concluded with some cant – 'everything that can be done must be done' to avoid kids 'having to learn at home' – and then she advised 'considering the closure or restriction of other activities to support keeping schools open'. In other words: to keep the schools open, shut other activities down. A new Scargillesque campaign of blackmail was brewing.

A week later, on October 10, Courtney reiterated the NEU's demands, and he highlighted some new data showing that Covid-19 was now spreading fastest among 10-19 olds. (So what? The virus was a cold which was harmless to almost everyone, especially young people.) Four days after that, Bousted shared some NEU guidance about what 'should and shouldn't be happening in your workplace', including inform-ation on how to 'escalate' concerns. A day later, Courtney noted an increase in the number of second-ary schools that were partially closed – the figure was now at 21%.

Meanwhile, as you may remember, events were

escalating in Liverpool and Manchester, and the NEU may have played a part. On September 30, the Liverpool branch of the NEU shared the union's new Covid map and pointed out that 'Virtually all schools in Liverpool are affected', adding: 'The rate of infection in the city is incredibly high. The safety of our members is at risk.' On October 12, the day the city went into a local lockdown, Liverpool's NEU again piped up, complaining that the schools were still open: 'The virus is spreading through schools and our members lives are being put at risk.' You may also remember that Mayor Steve Rotheram had called for a 'circuit breaker' in the city. I don't know if the agitation from the NEU was a decisive factor in the Liverpool lockdown (the UCU were also kicking off there, and probably other unions were doing the same), but there is an intriguing parallel with Manchester where on October 15 a local newspaper reported that 'more than 500 schools' in the region had been 'hit by Covid cases'. That report was two days before Greater Manchester went into a local lockdown. However, I cannot find any evidence that the Manchester branch of the NEU called for the region's lockdown other than one tweet on October 16 supporting a national circuit breaker. Liverpool NEU made the same call on the same day.

The calls were simultaneous because that was the day that the NEU's National Executive officially demanded a circuit breaker lockdown for England. An NEU press release on October 16 declared that the matter was 'urgent': 'schools and colleges should be closed for two weeks at half term for secondary and post-16 students'. Courtney was quoted as saying: 'even if they have few or no symptoms themselves', children 'are still part of spreading the virus to others, including to teachers and other school staff'. Addressing the PM and the Department of Education, Courtney raged that 'scientists have consistently told them that secondary students transmit the virus as much as adults' (in fact, the Chief Medical Officers had explicitly suggested that transmission in schools was largely 'staff to staff... rather than pupil to staff'). Courtney then trumpeted the usual socialist absurdity – 'Taking action now can avoid more disruption later' – and he concluded 'The Government must not just turn a blind eye and pretend all is going to be ok'.

The pressure was mounting on Johnson, and it was coming from all sides. On October 14, Northern Ireland's First Minister Arlene Foster announced that the country's half term holiday, which would begin on October 19, would be extended to two weeks, with pubs and restaurants closing during that period. A similar announcement came in Wales. On October 19, the Welsh First Minister, Mark Drakeford declared a two-week national lockdown, which would run from October 23 to November 9. The *Guardian* reported as follows:

> The Welsh government has repeatedly said it will do everything to keep children in education, but it has not quite been able to keep all schools open. Primary schools and childcare settings will be allowed to open but secondary schools will provide learning online only for the week after half-term.

In other words: *exactly* what the NEU had demanded. Drakeford had 'not quite been able to keep all schools open' – the words are laughable in hindsight.

Notably, the NEU has branches in Northern Ireland, Wales and England, but not Scotland. In Scotland, things panned out differently. On October 7, Sturgeon announced a two-week circuit breaker which would start on October 9; it was then extended for a further week. The schools were to stay open during the lockdown, apart from during the half term, which falls at different times in different parts of Scotland. The main teaching union in Scotland is EIS – the Education Institute of Scotland. The EIS and the NEU are 'sister unions' – they normally work in partnership – but surprisingly their policies diverged in October 2020. The EIS was not in favour of a national lockdown that would encompass the school half term in Scotland. Larry Flanagan, The General Secretary of EIS, wrote to the Scottish government to say: 'It is important for teachers and pupils to have the opportunity of a break without undue confinement'. Granted, Flanaghan also said 'The EIS is not opposed to a "circuit breaker" per se'. However, the union was clearly not trying to force a lockdown at this point; Flanagan noted that 'teachers understand the importance of education and have sought to deliver the best educational experience they can for pupils'. Sturgeon seems to have announced Scotland's circuit breaker for other reasons, unknown to me. Perhaps she simply wanted to add to the pressure on Johnson.

Johnson was certainly receiving pressure from his domestic political rivals. On October 13, Kier Starmer called for a circuit breaker. He told a news conference: 'The government's plan simply isn't working. Another course is needed. That's why I'm calling for a two to three week circuit break in England'. On October 17, Jeremy Hunt, Johnson's main leadership rival within the Conservative party, also backed the policy. Speaking to the BBC, Hunt was asked about a circuit breaker and he replied 'I've always thought that it's better to do things quickly and decisively than to wait until the virus has grown so I have a lot of sympathy with that'. A couple of days earlier, Hunt had called for weekly testing of the entire population.

There was additional support for a circuit breaker from the medical community. As reported by the *Guardian* on October 15, the Chair of the Hospital Consultants and Specialists Association and the Chair of the British Medical Association both backed the proposal, as did the Chief Executive of the Royal Society of Public Health and the President of the Society for Acute Medicine. Further support came from the government's science advisor Sir John Bell, although Bell's comments had a strong whiff of the spin operation about them:

> I can see very little way of getting on top of this without some kind of a circuit breaker because the numbers are actually pretty eye-watering in some bits of the country and I think it's going to be very hard to get on top of this just biting around the edges... I think there will be every effort to keep schools open. If in the end we have to take kids out for two weeks, calm it all down, and then start ideally embedded in a much more rigorous testing regime then that's maybe what we may have to do.

I mean, come on – 'Maybe that's what we may have to do'?! The last sentence simply describes a prospective capitulation to the NEU's demands. And the phrase 'calm it all down' – the government's approach was 'nakedly political', you might say.

Meanwhile, the government was still trying to calm it all down without doing another lockdown. On October 14, the tier system came into effect, a desperate attempt to rationalise England's medley of local restrictions. The country was now separated into three tiers, with indoor mixing banned in tiers 2 and 3. By October 17, when London went into the second tier, more than 28 million people were living in the upper tiers. Speaking in the Commons on October 15, Sunak defended the tiered approach, warning of the 'significant damage' that another national lockdown would do, because 'The entire country would suffer, rather than targeting that support, preventing a lockdown in parts of the country where the virus rates are low'. The next day, Johnson spoke at a press briefing and outlined his own position:

> Some have argued that we should introduce a national lockdown instead of targeted local action and I disagree. Closing businesses in Cornwall, where transmission is low, will not cut transmission in Manchester. So while I cannot rule anything out, if at all possible I want to avoid another national lockdown, with the damaging health, economic and social effects it would have.

Hearing these words back is a reminder that, throughout the pandemic, Johnson kept imposing measures he explicitly didn't agree with. It's also a reminder that he never came clean and declared the whole thing a farce. Instead we had this cynical nonsense about 'avoiding' measures 'if at all possible', and, in the early autumn, we had these cynical local lockdowns designed to patch up local Covid controversies without dragging in the whole country. As ever, we can assume that the virus was an irrelevance in any such controversy. The Covid measures were *all* unscientific and ineffectual; the government's real agenda was always to ensure that unilateral policymaking by unions, local authorities or other groups didn't the undermine the PM's authority.

On October 18, Michael Gove was interviewed by Sky TV. Asked by presenter Sophie Ridge if there would be circuit breaker in England, Gove replied simply 'no'. He then explained that 'It would seem to me to be an error to try to impose on every part of the country the same level of restriction'. But when pressed on the issue, Gove wouldn't rule out a circuit breaker in future: 'We always look at how the disease spreads and we will take whatever steps are necessary to maintain public health'.

Still, we can be near-certain that Johnson didn't want to lock England down again. When discussing with his cabinet colleagues the prospect of a second lockdown, allegedly he shouted 'no more fucking lockdowns' and 'no, no, no, I won't do it' – such is the testimony of Dominic Cummings. Similarly, former SAGE member Jeremy Farrar has quoted Johnson as saying after the first lockdown: 'I don't believe in any of this, it's all bullshit.' In September, Johnson told a commons committee that a second lockdown would be 'completely wrong for this country', and an economic 'disaster'. He even warned that a second lockdown would 'be like Hotel California – with no end in sight'. The analogy is noteworthy, given what we know about the first lockdown. You will remember that the PM 'reviewed' the first lockdown after three weeks, and that he kept on reviewing the restrictions, but each time he was hemmed in by the NEU's refusal to reopen the schools. No wonder Johnson didn't want to capitulate to the NEU again and grant the teachers the two week half term they were demanding in October. He will have been wary of the NEU refusing to return to work again. Once bitten...

On October 21, Johnson berated Starmer in Parliament for supporting a second lockdown; the leader of the opposition was guilty of the 'height of absurdity'. The next day, Johnson made an official statement to the country:

> [Some people] say... we need now to lock the whole place down from John O' Groats to Lands' End. Turn the lights out, shut up shop. Close schools and universities and go back to the same kind of lockdown we had in March and April and May. And I have to say I don't believe that is the right course now. Not when the psychological cost of lockdown is well known to us and the economic cost. Not when it is being suggested that we might have to perform the same brutal lockdown again and again in the months ahead.

No doubt about it – Johnson was twice shy. Indeed, we can assume that the NEU's entire reason for proposing to extend the half term holiday by a week was that if they were given an inch – one week of government-approved 'safety' – they could take a mile; they could justify refusing to return work by reiterating the logic on which their first week off was based.

On October 23, schools in England shut their gates for the half term break, and the debate temporarily simmered down. But one question wasn't going to go away: What would the NEU do next, if they didn't get the two-week holiday they wanted?

On October 28, midway through half term, the answer became clear. Bousted and Courtney were heading into full Scargill mode again. That day, the NEU launched a 'game changing' new app – the 'first of its kind from any trade union'. As announced on the NEU's Twitter page, the app – which was called 'NEU Escalation' – was designed for 'allowing us to understand what's happening in workplaces across the country and helping our reps organise'.

A short accompanying video explained how the app works and 'what we expect you to do with it', in the words of the narrator. After an opening screen ominously displaying the words 'It is coming', the video begins by showing an email with a message from the NEU: 'Reps have asked us to streamline the way members can collectively escalate concerns'. The narrator then goes through the app, step by step. First he opens the homepage, which talks about 'collectivising safety', and 'challenging' any decisions where there are 'safety concerns'. He presses the 'Begin' button and immediately a question pops up: 'Has there been a positive case in your workplace?' 'You can let the NEU know what has been happening in your school', the narrator cheerfully explains. He clicks 'yes' to the question, whereupon there are some questions about whether bubbles or year groups have been sent home.

Then there is a general question: 'What is the biggest concern for you and your members?' The text box automatically has 'Covid-19' written in it, and the narrator studiously adds the words 'in schools', just to emphasise the point. He clicks 'Next' and a bunch of questions arise about what 'stage you and your union group are at'. The options include 'planning an NEU meeting' or 'meet with the Head' or 'your concerns haven't been dealt with by the leadership and you want to escalate further' or 'your union group wants further support'. When the narrator clicks on 'planning an NEU meeting', the next question is 'Would you like support with this step?' An info box gives some further 'guidance': it is 'really important for members to meet (online or socially distanced) to agree their concerns'.

Finally, the narrator presses 'Submit' and a confirmation screen tells him that his answers have been emailed to his 'branch secretary', adding 'If you have asked for support, your local branch will be in touch', and 'We will text you to ask if the issues you have raised have been resolved'. Then the narrator restarts the app and gives a reminder: 'you can access it anytime'.

Let's be clear what the NEU Escalation app was designed to achieve. Whenever there was a Covid case/issue in a school, the NEU's leaders would be notified straightaway, whereupon they would instruct the school's members to participate in a hardline collective response. Bear in mind: not every teacher or every Head was on board with the Covid lunacy. The NEU was fighting *within* schools as well as fighting the government. The new app would give Bousted and Courtney maximum leverage for inflicting their policy aims on schools, thus creating maximum disruption for schools, and, in turn, for the economy and the government. Scargill himself couldn't have dreamt of such a tool in the 70s and 80s when the NUM wanted to shut down as many mines as possible without a national ballot. Since the start of coronapanic, the NEU had wanted to shut down as many schools as possible without a national ballot. Now the leadership was, in effect, armed with thousands of tendrils, gigantic thrashing tendrils that could potentially unleash havoc in schools, emptying them of pupils and teachers in the process.

As well as being a practical tool, the Escalation App was a statement of intent. The NEU had demanded a lockdown, and now they were intending to make sure they got it, via a new surge of disruption. This time the NEU wasn't brash enough to publicly threaten unilateral schools closures, but the government will have been in no doubt regarding the purpose of the Escalation App: to force schools closures, whether partial or full closures. The 'Union news' website was also in no doubt, running the following headline: 'NEU launches app to help teachers escalate action to close unsafe schools'. Later, the *Huffington Post* ran an 'exclusive' article, headlined 'National Education Union Steps Up School Closure Campaign With New "Escalation" App'. The article was subtitled: 'Smartphone app could pave way for local strike action.'

The PM knew what was going on too. And he knew what he knew in March: that if the NEU shut enough schools, he'd be humiliated; he'd be accused of losing control of the situation. Covering up any disruption with local lockdowns would only be effective up to a point. If the disruption in schools was drastic enough, if there was a flood of working parents heading home to look after their kids, the economic damage would be 'phenomenal', to recall Tobias Elwood's term. The media would start to ask: How can the economy function amid such chaos? The NEU was blackmailing the PM into backing down, locking the whole country down and covering up the real reason, just as he did in March.

Johnson didn't cave in. Not yet. On the same day that the NEU released the Escalation App, there was an intriguing development regarding the Covid vaccine, which was still in production at that point. The *Telegraph* reported that the Head of the UK's Vaccine Taskforce, Kate Bingham, had stated that the forthcoming vaccine was 'likely to be imperfect' and 'might not work for everyone'. Also that day, the Environment Secretary George Eustice told Sky News that Bingham's analysis was 'probably right'. I suspect that the story was aired that day as part of an ongoing campaign to steer England away from a second lockdown. In some people's eyes, another lockdown was justifiable as a temporary measure until the vaccine arrived. But if the vaccine was going to be 'imperfect', the idea of 'living with the virus' would seem more logical – why put life on hold if salvation wasn't around the corner? Of course, once the vaccine had arrived, the government's messaging changed drastically; the vaccine became the country's only salvation, never to be questioned.

On the morning of October 30, a Friday, Johnson sent Dominic Raab out to speak to Sky News. Raab doggedly adhered to the government's anti-circuit breaker line: 'It's better to take a targeted approach than have the blunt tool of nationwide restrictions at the very highest possible level'. Raab even alluded to Johnson's 'Hotel California' metaphor: 'A short sharp circuit breaker is something of an enigma. No one can say if you go into a national lockdown how – er – at what point you get out of it'. The schools were due to open on the Monday morning, November 1. This was brinksmanship from the government. You can almost hear Johnson blustering 'No, no, no, I won't do it'. And you can almost hear his inner voice: 'I should have been the Mayor of Jaws and kept the beaches open'. I believe he had decided he wasn't going to back down this time.

But he did back down. The very next day. What changed?

In the late evening of October 30, details of a government meeting were leaked to the press. The meeting, which had been held earlier that evening, was allegedly attended by Rishi Sunak, Matt Hancock, Michael Gove and Boris Johnson. The ministers were presented with some new data by SAGE's scientific modellers, suggesting that 'more than 4,000 people could be dying from coronavirus every day unless a new lockdown is imposed', as the *Independent* put it. The BBC, which also cited the 4,000 figure, noted that Johnson was now 'considering' a new national lockdown. 'The restrictions could be introduced on Wednesday and remain in place until December 1', said the *Mail*, adding that the government's 'scientific advisors' believed that it was now 'too late' for a two week lockdown, hence a longer lockdown would be required. The *Times* quoted a 'senior government source' as saying 'The data is really bad. We're seeing COVID-19 rising all over the country and hospitals are struggling to cope. There has been a shift in our position'. Presumably the 'senior government source' was the person who leaked the story.

The leak required a swift response from Johnson. If the source was credible – and surely it was, otherwise the media wouldn't have gone so big on the story – the

PM had some serious explaining to do. A senior figure in the government was trying to crowbar him into a U-turn. The leak had already prompted renewed calls for a lockdown. The Shadow Health Secretary, Labour's Jonathan Ashworth, barked: 'We are in a deeply serious situation with coronavirus spreading with ferocity. Boris Johnson should have used the school half-term for a time limited circuit break to push infections down, fix test and trace, and save lives. It's urgent Boris Johnson outlines the action he will now take to bring the virus under control.'

Ashworth also made reference to some documents that had been *officially* released by the government on the evening of October 30. The documents, produced by SAGE, claimed that England was on course to breach the 'reasonable worst-case scenario' for Covid infections and hospitalisations. Jeremy Farrar, a SAGE member, popped up on Twitter afterwards and said 'we have to act now'. Hearing this, you may wonder if the PM released the official SAGE documents to spin a second lockdown, and that the 4,000 figure was part of the same PR strategy. I do not think so. There is a difference between an official release and a leak. If the PM intended to spin a new lockdown using the official SAGE documents, those documents would have included the (much more shocking) 4,000 daily deaths claim; the PM wouldn't have omitted that claim while also allowing it to be disclosed in a way that undermined his authority. Nor would he have allowed the lockdown announcement itself to be disclosed in such a way. Moreover, neither the Chief Science Officer Patrick Vallance nor the Chief Medical Officer Chris Whitty echoed Farrar's call for action on October 30. And Dominic Raab would hardly have been sent out to defend the tier system *on the same day* that the PM supposedly intended to start spinning England into a national lockdown. I think the official SAGE documents were designed solely to defend the government against a potential onslaught from the NEU. With a surge of teaching mutinies and schools closures likely the following week, the government would need a 'scientific' basis for suddenly doing a lot of local lockdowns, and the SAGE documents had provided it; 'the reasonable worst-case scenario' was *on course* to be breached, not *already* breached; therein lay a get-out clause if the teachers miraculously backed down. SAGE was not a monolith; the fact that a Covid zealot like Jeremy Farrar was using the official new documents to push for a national lockdown didn't change the fact that the PM was still trying to avoid a national lockdown.

The leak on October 30 was a gamechanger. The government hastily arranged a press conference for the afternoon of October 31. There must have been frantic discussions behind the scenes, because the start time was repeatedly delayed. Initially it was 4pm; then it was changed to 5pm; then, as 5pm approached, the assembled journalists were told it would be 5.30pm; finally, Johnson, Whitty and Vallance appeared at 6pm. The conference began with the two science advisers giving presentations, complete with various terrifying graphs and stats. Vallance's presentation included the 4,000 daily deaths figure. Next, Johnson spoke:

I am afraid that no responsible PM can ignore the message of those figures. When I told you two weeks ago that we were pursuing a local and a regional approach to tackling this virus, I believed then and I still believe passionately that it was the right thing to do. Because we know the cost of these restrictions, the damage they do, the impact on jobs, and on livelihoods, and on people's mental health. No one wants to be imposing these kinds of measures anywhere. We didn't want to be shutting businesses, pubs and restaurants in one part of the country, where incidence was very low, when the vast bulk of infections were taking place else-where… But as we've also seen from those charts, we've got to be humble in the face of nature. In this country alas, as across much of Europe, the virus is spreading even faster than the reasonable worst-case scenario of our scientific advisers, whose models as you've just seen now suggest that unless we act we could see deaths in this country running at several thousand a day.

It's interesting to note that Johnson was now *combining* the (official) 'reasonable worst-case scenario' claim and the (leaked) '4,000 deaths' claim into one lump of spin: he was glossing over the fact that the two claims had been released to the media in very different ways. He continued:

If we let the lines on those graphs grow in the way they could and in the way they're projected to grow, then the risk is that for the first time in our lives, the NHS will not be there for us and for our families.

And with that, Johnson announced: 'From Thursday until the start of December, you must stay home.' He also announced, confirming Sunak's speech to Parliament the previous week, that the furlough scheme would be extended for the duration of the lockdown. Presumably the government hadn't publicly mentioned extending the furlough scheme up until now because they didn't want everyone clamouring after the money; until the lockdown was announced, the main purpose of renewing the furlough scheme was to keep the unions happy behind the scenes.

The lockdown was scheduled to begin on November 5. Just like in March, there was a short delay so the government could prepare the legislation, which sailed through Parliament on November 4 with only 38 votes against. Democracy had again been obliterated.

In the ensuing weeks, the media correctly concluded that Johnson was 'bounced' into the lockdown by the leak; the *Mail* even quoted one 'cabinet ally' who said as much, and who insisted that 'All of this goes against [the PM's] political inclinations'. When the 4,000 daily deaths claim was leaked, you can appreciate that Johnson was placed in an almost impossible position. Having spent the previous eight months 'following the science', he could hardly continue with the tiered approach when the media had been told by a credible source that government scientists were warning of 4,000 daily deaths if there wasn't a lockdown.

So who leaked the story? Who was the so-called 'Chatty Rat', as they were soon nicknamed by the media? You could make a case that it was any of the ministers who attended the meeting on October 30. Back in 2016, Gove had 'stabbed Johnson in the back' by standing against him in the leadership contest. Sunak allegedly orchestrated the flurry of ministerial resignations that ousted Johnson in 2022. Hancock was pushed out of office in 2021 in what looked like a sting operation – perhaps it was vengeance by the PM. And there is another contender who was probably at the meeting: Dominic Cummings. Two weeks after the lockdown began, Cummings was sacked, following unspecified accusations that he had 'briefed against Johnson'. Six months later, 'Number 10 sources' allegedly told three newspapers that Cummings had been 'engaged in systematic leaking'. There is also the fact that Cummings himself has claimed that he and Johnson's aides were plotting to oust the PM within weeks of the 2019 General Election.

The latter allegation takes on a special significance in light of another intriguing disclosure that preceded the second lockdown. In an article about Hunt's support for the lockdown, i newspaper made the following remark:

> The Prime Minister told a Downing Street briefing on Friday he wanted to avoid a second national shutdown 'if at all possible' but 'cannot rule anything out'. Privately, MPs and officials fear he will be 'bounced' into it, i understands.

The article was published on October 17 and was headlined 'Former health secretary Jeremy Hunt backs circuit breaker lockdown as pressure mounts on Boris Johnson'. How could i newspaper have known about Johnson being bounced into the lockdown *two weeks before it happened*, unless someone had planned the manoeuvre in advance? Indeed, given Hunt's prominence within the article, perhaps he was involved in the plan. Hunt could have been colluding with Cummings or any of the ministers mentioned above. Or all of them. Whoever was involved, if there was a plan to bounce Johnson into the lockdown, there was probably also a plan to force him out if he didn't comply.

Johnson was reportedly 'furious' about the leaked lockdown. The *Telegraph* claimed to have 'learnt that the Prime Minister is so angry about being "bounced" into making the announcement earlier that the police may be brought in to investigate a potential offence'. Months later, the *Sunday Times* even alleged that MI5 had been roped in to help the police find the culprit. The *Independent* stated that Johnson 'had not finally decided to go for a lockdown at the meeting with Rishi Sunak, Matt Hancock and Michael Gove on Friday'. My analysis suggests that this is highly likely, and we can deduce Johnson's reasoning. He knew that the NEU would cause trouble when the schools reopened on the Monday. The question was: *how much trouble?* How many schools would the NEU succeed in closing or partially closing using the Escalation App? If the disruption was minimal, Johnson could cover it up with local lockdowns, and justify the new local lockdowns using SAGE'S 'reasonable worst-case scenario' claim. If the disruption was maximal, Johnson would have to issue another national lock-down, and hope that he wouldn't receive too much flak for delaying the measure, and that no one would notice that he was being crowbarred into it by the NEU. The 4,000 daily deaths warning by the scientists was clearly Johnson's insurance policy; he would wheel out that bogus claim if and when he needed to justify a national lockdown. He would tell the country that the situation had changed. For the time being, he was willing to call the NEU's bluff; let them make the first move.

We can also deduce the Chatty Rat's reasoning, whoever they were. *They lost their nerve.* They feared that the NEU was about to cause maximal damage and humiliate the government. If the NEU was about to run amok, and the government was going to have to cover it up with a national lockdown, the most prudent action from a political point of view was to lockdown immediately; the government would receive less flak now, and would ensure that they wouldn't be humiliated. Perhaps the Chatty Rat also feared that if the PM delayed the lockdown any further, the public would realise that the NEU was dictating policy; in turn, the public could latch onto the fact that *every* government policy from the start of the coronapanic had been a spin operation. That disclosure could put a few ministers in very hot water. Better to leak the fake justification for the lockdown now, and ensure that the latest spin operation succeeded.

After Vallance peddled the 4,000 deaths figure on October 31, he was immediately challenged by eminent scientists. The figure was a projection made on October 9, before the tier system came into place. Numerous Covid interventions had been made since then, which the projection hadn't taken into account. Moreover, the projection was based on an R rate of 1.3 to 1.5, but the rate had subsequently fallen to between 1.1 and 1.3. If the model had been correct, the number of daily deaths should have reached 1,000 by the time Vallance cited the 4,000 figure; in fact, the rolling average for that week was 265, falling to 136 on the Monday morning of the next week. 'The assumptions for this model had not been shared transparently', the Office for Statistics Regulation commented a few days later, in an understated rebuke. A more forthright rebuke would be: the 4,000 figure was complete bunk, a total fabrication based on misleading nonsense. Even Whitty and Vallance immediately started to backtrack on the figure. During a grilling by members of the House of Commons Science and Technology Committee on November 3, Vallance said that if he frightened people with the figure, 'I regret that'. Whitty admitted that 'All of us would say that rates will probably be lower than that top peak'.

The truth was, the increase in the rate of infection had slowed by the week preceding the lockdown. The tide was already turning. (And, anyway, Covid-19 was a cold, and there could never be any justification for a lockdown that would achieve nothing but making the situation worse.) Alas, the forces that were arrayed against Johnson were impervious to the hidden truth. Given that the PM wouldn't come clean about the dishonesty of the entire coronapanic debacle, he remained at the mercy of the NEU and his parliamentary colleagues who were selling the country out. He also remained at the mercy of the TUC and the other unions that had forced the continuation of the furlough scheme by agitating for working from home. And he remained at the mercy of public opinion, albeit public opinion that was inflamed by his own lies and the promise of free money. On November 1, a YouGov poll found that 72% of the public backed the second lockdown. Three out of ten people thought the new measures didn't go far enough. Johnson was in charge of a lunatic asylum.

There was, however, a ray of hope. Like a man who lands one last flailing punch as he falls, Johnson had managed to start a fightback even as he was floored. In the midst of the lockdown announcement, Johnson did something extremely surprising: *he announced that he intended to keep the schools open.* Granted, he had insisted for weeks that the schools should stay open. But, then again, he had also insisted that another national lockdown would be 'completely wrong' – and this hadn't stopped him from doing a lockdown. How could the NEU have forced the government into a lockdown without forcing the government into shutting the schools? On the face of it, this outcome seems impossible.

Actually it was based on sensible logic – from the perspective of the PM, or rather, from the perspective of the corner that he had painted himself into by refusing to tell the full truth. Bousted and Courtney were waging a campaign of Scargillesque economic destruction. They wanted to unilaterally shut as many schools as possible, so as to inflict as much economic harm on Britain as possible. They knew that if they forced widespread schools closures, the government would cover up the disruption with a national lockdown. Unless the PM covered up the closures with a lockdown, his authority would be fatally undermined. As far as Johnson was concerned, widespread schools closures *necessitated* a national lockdown. But here's the crucial point: *the reverse was not true.* If the country was *already* in a national lockdown, the schools closures would *automatically be covered up.* There would be no parents forced home to look after the kids, because the parents would already be at home. There would be no bad press about the NEU causing economic disruption, because the economy would already be wrecked, on spurious health grounds. Once Johnson had announced the lockdown, unilateral schools closures were no longer a threat to his authority. The lockdown was like an anti-NEU stab vest: it enabled Johnson to absorb any number of schools closures without being harmed. The NEU could close all the schools, for all it mattered to Johnson now, politically speaking; he could simply blame the closures on the virus and widen the lockdown to include schools. For the time being, he might as well leave the schools open and let the NEU do their worst. If any schools could be salvaged, that was now a political bonus.

Perhaps there was more to it than cynicism. Perhaps Johnson on some level wanted to do the right thing by the kids. And perhaps there was vengeance in his heart: keeping the schools open was a riposte to Bousted and Courtney, after all the trouble the NEU had caused him. On the day that he announced the lockdown, Johnson said: 'I urge parents to continue taking their children to school and I am extremely grateful to teachers across the country for their dedication in enabling schools to remain open.' You can hear that he was making an appeal to the teachers who were being reasonable. There were some.

Relatedly, when announcing the lockdown, Johnson pointed to another surprising policy, one that was designed to support keeping the schools open. He said 'we will not ask people to shield again in the same way'. He explained, 'we are asking those who are clinically extremely vulnerable to minimise their contact with others and not to go to work if they are able to work from home'. I am not sure exactly what the distinction between vulnerable and 'extremely' vulnerable consisted in, but clearly Johnson was not proposing to reissue the same shielding advice that he had paused on August 1 – now the group of people who needed to shield was smaller. He was giving more teachers one less excuse for abandoning the kids.

I think Johnson was quietly confident that the NEU wouldn't succeed in closing all the schools; if he wasn't confident, he wouldn't have been willing to call the NEU's bluff in the first place, that is, before he was bounced into the lockdown. Sky News even suggested that the government was planning to use the tier system to allow different regions to emerge from the national lockdown early. Such a strategy would have been attractive to the PM: if the NEU definitely wasn't causing much trouble in a particular area, there was no reason for the lockdown not to be lifted in that area. However, no such strategy seems to have been pursued. Perhaps Johnson was wary that nervous colleagues would gainsay his decisions again if he got too bullish. Moreover, Johnson was aware that he might even have to *extend* the lockdown if the teachers succeeded in causing massive ongoing disruption. He sent Gove out to deliver the warning to the public. In an interview with Sky News, the Cabinet Office Minister said there was a 'possibility' that the restrictions might continue for more than a month.

Something else Gove said during that interview is notable: 'I do believe that we want to keep schools open and I believe that the measures that we are putting in place will enable us to do so.' Only politicians speak like this! On one hand, Gove was noting that the government merely 'wanted' to keep the schools open – a hint that the situation was in the hands of the teachers. On the other hand, Gove was suggesting that the restrictions would 'enable' the government to keep the schools open – a hint that the teachers might be pacified by a lockdown, insofar as the measures outside of schools would reduce overall transmission and therefore supposedly make schools safer. You will recall that Bousted at one stage had called for 'the closure or restriction of other activities to support keeping schools open'. Well, now the government was giving her what she had called for. Gove even explained that the reason the lockdown might need to be extended was that this action might be necessary to enable the schools to stay open. Of course, he didn't talk explicitly about pacifying the teachers. He made it sound as though reducing overall transmission was *in itself* the crucial variable. But, regardless, Gove was publicly putting pressure on the teachers to fulfil their side of the bargain by not causing any more trouble in schools.

The government took another step to pacify the teachers. On November 4, the Department of Education issued new guidance which stated that children (and staff) should wear masks in corridors in all schools. Teaching unions had demanded mandatory masks for the kids in late July. On August 4, the government's Education Hub website had published an unequivocal response:

Our guidance has been clear and consistent since the beginning of lockdown that we do not expect children to wear face coverings at school. This position is based on scientific advice by Public Health England, which does not currently recommend the use of face coverings in schools, as pupils and staff are mixing in consistent groups. There may also be negative effects on communication and thus education.

Given this statement, there is no way the government would have advised masks in school corridors two months later unless the measure was to pacify the teachers. The measure was announced two days after the schools reopened. Many of the teachers were anxious at that time; perhaps the government issued the mask guidance to help calm them down. Let us also remember that the *Daily Mail* reported in late September that an (unnamed) 'school leaders union' was advising its members to tell all pupils to wear masks in corridors in the autumn. When the schools reopened after half term on November 2, more Heads were bound to be following the union's advice. The government may even have issued the masks in corridors guidance to stay in step with a measure that was happening anyway. As for the NEU, they reacted zealously to the new guidance, declaring: 'Requiring face coverings when moving around secondary schools is welcome, but their use more widely must be considered'. There's no pleasing some maniacs. Even crueller mask mandates were introduced in schools in the coming months, as we will see.

With the second lockdown underway, all that remained to be seen at the start of November was how the NEU would react to the government's decision to keep the schools open. How much damage would the Escalation App do?

Johnson was vindicated. The Chatty Rat was not. There was no collapse of the schools system. Certainly there was widespread disruptive nonsense in schools – bubbles and year groups being sent home, children being asked to self-isolate for no good reason, teachers self-isolating for no good reason, and of course the cruel masks. The NEU ran a story about a rep who had arranged for a 'collective letter' of protest to be sent to a Head who had heroically banned masks in a school; the Head caved in. Courtney wrung his hands about a reported 9,000 schoolchildren self-isolating in Lancashire. But amid all the farce, there were no reports of the education system being decimated, and the government was not compelled to step in and announce that all the schools were closing. By December 1, the final day of the lockdown, 99.2% of state schools were still open. There are around 20,000 state schools in England, suggesting that only around 160 were fully closed – a negligible number, although obviously not for the children or parents involved.

As for partial closures, we can get a rough picture by looking at the decrease in pupil attendance, which the government has quantified. The attendance figure for all state schools was at 87% in early September, was hovering around 90% throughout October, and was still at 89% on November 5 (the Thursday of the first week after half term). Then there was a drop for two weeks – to 83%. No doubt, this was partly due to union disruption; the teachers must have done a lot of 'organising' during that first week back. But also, there was an increase in home schooling during the second lockdown, because some of the parents were paranoid about Covid and some didn't want to subject their kids to the dystopia in schools. All in all, the NEU reduced school attendance by roughly 7% during the second lockdown, whether by forcing full or partial closures or creating a frightening environment. Bousted and Courtney huffed and puffed, but they didn't blow the house down.

And how they huffed! From the moment that the lockdown was leaked, the NEU went into PR overdrive, calling for all schools to be included in the new restrictions; Bousted's suggestion of 'considering the closure or restriction of other activities to support keeping schools open' had turned out to be bogus; the NEU still wanted to close the schools. On October 31, there was an official NEU statement to that effect, along with the launch of a 'close the schools' campaign. By the end of the day – by which time the PM had announced the lockdown – some 70,000 teachers or support staff had signed up to the campaign. During the next week, the NEU incessantly, obsessively, called for schools closures. They wheeled out stats about a rise in infections in schoolchildren; trumpeted a drop in infections over half term; declared a 'health and safety month' beginning on the day the lockdown started; called for people to write to their MPs; issued a new statement claiming that 150,000 teachers now supported the campaign; promoted the Escalation App in conjunction with the call for schools closures; held a reps meeting with some 1,000 attendees; provided quotes for a series of sympathetic media articles; launched a 'major new advertising campaign' asking constituents to lobby their MPs on the issue; enlisted the support of Andy Burnham and Steve Rotheram – the usual suspects; pushed the 'Covid map' to keep up the psychological pressure on parents; and berated Ofsted for saying that kids were being sent home 'too readily'.

After a week, the tsunami of calls for schools closures dried up, and by the middle of the month the NEU had done a *volte face*; now they were lamenting the reduced attendance figures, absurdly blaming the 'disruption' on the government. A week later, they described the reduced attendance as the 'direct result of government negligence', and – even more absurdly – patted themselves on the back for 'working incredibly hard to keep the system running'. The dishonesty was nausea-inducing.

What a repellent organisation the NEU is! From March to December 2020, they mercilessly harangued the government, blackmailing the PM into economy-destroying measures twice, and, all the while, treating the welfare of children as an afterthought, if that. England was clambering back to its feet in September; the economy was tentatively reawakening. The government was planning to scrap the furlough scheme, and the PM was publicly opposed to any new lockdown. But after the TUC and PCS union had laid the groundwork, steamrolling the government into U-turns on furlough and working from home, the NEU seized the moment, rearing up for a new campaign of Scargillesque disruption. They unveiled their new 'Escalation' App, a means – and a threat – to close as many schools as possible. Someone in Johnson's inner circle found the threat too much to bear. This unidentified traitor leaked news of the '4,000 daily deaths' spin operation that the PM was planning to deploy if he needed to justify a national lockdown in the event of a surge in schools closures. The PM himself was willing to face down the NEU's threat, it seems. But he was checkmated by the leak. He admitted defeat and sent England into a new lockdown, albeit with the schools remaining open because now the PM was politically insulated against any disruption that the NEU might cause.

The NEU's 'close the schools' campaign turned out to be a damp squib – all sound and fury with little to show for it. Johnson had blown his second chance to be the Mayor of Jaws and keep the beaches open. According to reports, he raged at his ministers after announcing the second lockdown, shouting that he would rather 'let the bodies pile high in their thousands' than oversee a third lockdown.

Next time, he would be the Mayor of Jaws. Next time, he wouldn't back down. And he very nearly didn't. Alas, next time the NEU went nuclear.

XII

My goal in this essay was to make sense of the second lockdown by situating it in its proper context, namely, Johnson's war against the NEU. That war consisted of three battles, three battles that culminated in three lockdowns. I will now complete the picture by outlining the third lockdown and highlighting its relationship to the second lockdown. The task will be fairly brief – not least because, compared to the first and second lockdowns, the third lockdown was straightforward. It was caused by a sudden, overwhelming act of collective disobedience by NEU members.

When the second lockdown ended on December 2, England reverted to the tier system. Compared to before the lockdown, more areas were now in tier 3. In tiers 2 and 3, indoor mixing was banned. Naturally, the question on everyone's minds was – what about Christmas? One of the goals of the second lockdown was to 'allow ministers to ease restrictions into Christmas', as Sky News put it. Would ministers keep their promise? Well, on November 25, the leaders of the four UK nations announced an 'agreement' that a maximum of three households would be permitted to meet for a maximum of five days over Christmas, in all three tiers. The agreement only lasted a few weeks. During that time there were growing calls for Christmas to be more heavily restricted. The British Medical Association led the calls. On December 15, the BMA issued a press release saying that the government 'must review [the] Christmas Covid plans'. The union's Chair, Chaand Nagpaul, spoke to the *Times* and said 'we need to hear from the government very soon'. The language was clearly menacing. No overt threats were made by the BMA, as far as I know, but the PM will have been in no doubt that he faced another fight with a union.

Johnson responded defiantly on December 16, saying at a Downing Street press conference: 'I want to be clear, we don't want to ban Christmas, to cancel it. I think that would be frankly inhuman and against the instincts of many people in this country. Nor do we want to criminalise plans people may have made for some time'. In Parliament, he mocked Starmer for supporting heavier Christmas restrictions: 'All he wants to do is to lock the whole country down. He's a one-club golfer'. Alas, the BMA refused to back down. That day, Nagpaul told the TV show Good Morning Britain that giving Covid-19 to a relative would be 'the worst Christmas present'. On December 19, he went on LBC radio to warn that the NHS was understaffed by 80,000 people, which was 'the reason why we need to do whatever we can do reduce the pressure on the NHS'. *Whatever we can.* In the evening, the PM caved in, telling the public that 'the situation has deteriorated since I last spoke to you three days ago'; supposedly a 'new variant' of the virus had emerged. As a result, he explained, many areas currently in tier 3 would move into a new 'tier 4'; these areas were all in the south or east of England. In tier 4, no indoor mixing between households was allowed at Christmas. For everyone else, the 'three households' rule would be restricted to Christmas day only. Johnson also emphasised that there would be no relaxation of the rules on December 31, so New Year's Eve was in effect banned. Season's Greetings from the BMA!

Meanwhile, the schools remained battlegrounds after the second lockdown. The attendance level picked up slightly, to around 85% in the first fortnight of December, but that was lower than pre-lockdown levels. By mid-December, the government was threatening court action against any Heads who tried to close schools unilaterally. One Head in Hertfordshire was sent a legal letter by the Schools Minister, instructing him to abandon plans to close the school early. Schools were also at the centre of a sudden surge of aggravation from local authorities. In London, the councils of Greenwich and Islington advised all the schools in the area to close. The Leader of Greenwich Council sent a letter to all Head teachers, asking them to move to online learning because the situation with Covid-19 was 'escalating extremely quickly'. The government responded by launching a legal action against Greenwich Council. Gavin Williamson, the Education Secretary, issued a 'temporary continuity direction', demanding – successfully – the immediate withdrawal of the council's letter to the headteachers. The *Guardian* summarised: 'Although the government has previously threatened legal action, this latest move signals its determination to keep schools open in the run-up to the Christmas holidays and beyond.'

The issue of keeping schools open became more pertinent after the government had caved in to the BMA. The NEU was now re-armed with the same old justification for causing trouble: if mixing between households was banned or heavily restricted across the country, wouldn't this imply that children shouldn't be mixing in schools? On December 21, two days after Johnson announced the new Christmas restrictions, the NEU reared up, predictably. Courtney posted a video in which he outlined the NEU's proposals for how the government can 'improve continuity of education'. (I'll give you a moment to digest that manipulative phrase.) The NEU was now calling for two weeks of online learning at the start of the new term, which was scheduled for January 4, plus weekly testing for the children when the schools reopened, and a programme of vaccination for the school staff to begin during the delay. These calls were communicated to the PM in an open letter. On December 28, the NEU wrote another open letter in which the leadership 'reiterated their call on the Prime Minister to keep schools and colleges closed for at least the first 2 weeks in January'.

The playbook was the same as in October, and so was the battleground. In December, the governments of Scotland, Wales and Northern Ireland all announced that the start of the new school term would be delayed; this time Scotland's EIS was on the same page as the NEU. Now the focus was again on England's schools. And again the government's initial response was to hold the line, with some equivocation. The plan was to reopen only the primary schools on January 4, with the secondary pupils returning over the next few weeks, during which a mass testing programme would be rolled out in secondary schools. On December 28,

Michael Gove told the BBC he was 'confident' that the schools would reopen in the New Year. On December 30, Gavin Williamson confirmed to the commons that 'we will be opening the majority of primary schools, as planned, on Monday 4th January', albeit he pre-empted a possible capitulation by lamenting the 'rapidly shifting situation'. Williamson then issued a public battle cry, writing in the *Mail* on January 2 that 'We must all move heaven and earth to get children back into the classroom'.

Meanwhile, the NEU was also going into PR overdrive, and cranking up the pressure on the government. On December 29, Courtney said he was 'very pleased' with some comments made by the Conservative MP Roger Gale, who had called for 'a clear and definitive statement that schools will not be required to reopen in January until effective vaccination is made available to teaching staff'. On January 1, Bousted spoke to the *Guardian* and said, carpingly: 'Does the government really believe that somehow Covid in England is different than the other countries of the UK?' On the same day, the NEU tweeted that 'The pandemic is worsening hour by hour' and that they had 'called an emergency executive meeting tomorrow. We will then issue new, urgent advice regarding the proposed opening of primary schools on 4 Jan. These developments will affect those returning to work on Monday'. The words were ominous.

The next day, January 2, Courtney boasted that 100,000 people had signed a joint NEU-Unison petition demanding that 'all schools and colleges move immediately to online learning'. He noted approvingly that the National Association of Head Teachers and the Association of School and College leaders were calling on the government to keep the schools closed and had launched a joint legal action to 'challenge the government's position', as the *TES* reported. On January 3, Courtney exclaimed 'Good to hear' in response to the news that the Liberal Democrats were now backing calls for the schools to remain closed until January 18. On the same day, he shared a graph showing that the rate of infection was rising among schoolchildren. By the morning of January 4, the NEU was boasting that 260,000 parents and education staff had signed the petition.

During this period, numerous local authorities were agitating against the government's policy. For instance, on January 2, Brighton and Hove City Council advised all the primary schools in the region to stay shut for two weeks at the start of term. On the same day in Liverpool, the *Echo* newspaper reported 'growing calls' for the region's schools to stay closed, with two local Labour MPs supporting the NEU's proposal. On January 3, Essex's Tory-run council advised primary schools to stay shut until the Wednesday and demanded 'urgent clarity' from the government 'amid rising Covid-19 infection levels in the area'. Reading's Labour-run council declared that they would support any primary schools that decided to stay shut at the start of term. In Birmingham, the council said the same. In Kent, likewise.

The NEU's demand was supported by many local authorities in England, but London was a particular hub of support. On December 30, the government declared that in 22 out of 32 London boroughs the primary schools would remain closed at the start of term. I do not know the reason for the policy divergence between the boroughs, although we can assume that the arbitrariness was rooted in varying levels of local unrest. Williamson explained vaguely that the government's decisions had been based on 'pressure on hospitals'. He added: 'If there's a chance for a borough to have its schools open, I want to see that borough, county district to have its schools open.' In any case, the divergence was soon ironed out when the remaining 10 London boroughs – eight of which were Labour-led – initiated court action against the government, noting that they had higher levels of Covid infection than some of the boroughs where the schools were staying closed. London's Mayor Sadiq Khan weighed in too, explaining that all primary schools in the capital should be 'treated the same'; he reported having 'constructive discussions' on the matter with the Schools Minister. There was also lobbying from 'London Councils', a public sector organisation representing all 32 London boroughs. On January 1, the government caved in, agreeing to keep all the primary schools in London closed. Kevin Courtney bragged: '18 hours for the first government U-turn of 2021.'

Amid the wranglings in London, on December 31 the government suddenly published the minutes of a SAGE meeting that had been held on December 22. The minutes stated that it would be 'highly unlikely' that a policy 'in line with the measures in England in November (i.e. with schools open) would be sufficient to maintain R below 1 in the presence of the new variant'. The minutes also stated that 'R would be lower with schools closed'. The NEU immediately seized upon these statements, publishing a press release with the headline: 'On December 22 SAGE told Government to close schools'. The headline was dishonest. SAGE had said no such thing. The R rate wasn't the be all and end all – Covid was a cold that was harmless to almost everybody – and the government's chief scientific advisors had not deviated from their longstanding stance that schools were safe.

However, the timing of the government's release of these SAGE minutes was suspicious. As usual, the goal seems to have been to spin a capitulation, namely, the decision to close all the primary schools in London. SAGE's equivocal prognostications about the R rate would make the U-turn sound scientific. In turn, if the government ended up U-turning on January 4, the SAGE minutes could spin that capitulation too. It's noteworthy that SAGE also explained that the 'closure of secondary schools [is] likely to have a greater effect than closure of primary schools'. The distinction provided a justification for the government's ongoing efforts to keep as many primary schools open as possible.

Despite the defeat in London, the government pressed on with the plan to reopen primary schools throughout the rest of the country. On January 2, Amanda Spielman the Chief Inspector of Ofsted wrote an article in the *Sunday Telegraph* in support of the government's position. 'There is a real consensus that schools should be the last places to close and the first to re-open', she insisted; 'We cannot furlough young people's learning or their wider development'.

The next day, Johnson was interviewed on TV by Andrew Marr. The PM made his strongest case yet for keeping the schools open, albeit he also let loose the usual flurry of equivocation. I will quote liberally from the 29-minute interview because it corroborates my analysis of all three lockdowns, leaving no doubt as to the kind of rearguard action the government was fighting. Johnson told Marr: 'Schools are safe. Very, very important to stress that.' He repeated the point: 'The risk to kids, to young people, is really very, very, very small. The risk to staff is very small.' Again and again, he emphasized: 'Schools are safe, there is absolutely no doubt about it'; 'There is no doubt in my mind that schools are safe'. He declared that 'The priority has got to be children's education'. He even portrayed keeping the schools open as a health issue: 'For public health reasons, we think in the large majority of the country it is sensible to continue to keep schools open'. This remark was especially significant, because by emphasising the health aspect, Johnson was taking the fight onto the enemy's own territory. *Of course* children's health would suffer if they were confined to their houses and deprived of contact with their peers. And of course the rest of the public would suffer too during a lockdown. Only a maniac would suggest otherwise.

The PM was well aware that failing to reopen the schools would politically push him into issuing new national restrictions. He indicated that he understood the harms of the lockdown policy, speaking about the 'damage to the long-term prospects of young people' and the 'damage to people's mental health'. He attacked the lockdowns as inherently absurd: 'If you look at all these examples of firebreaks or circuit breakers, all they do is buy you some temporary respite.' He was defiant when the pot-stirring Andrew Marr raised the possibility of a 'tier 5', perhaps with a 'curfew system'. 'You've spoken about tier 5, I haven't', Johnson batted back at him. And when Marr asked him 'Are you going to take legal action against councils like Brighton for instance which is just unilaterally closing its primary schools?' Johnson responded: 'We'll work very hard with authorities across the country to get our message across.'

But there was the rub; Johnson knew that with the NEU and its allies working against the government's agenda, the matter of the schools reopening was ultimately out of his hands. Hence, in the interview he undermined all his honest pronouncements by digging himself the usual array of political bolt-holes, just in case the NEU caused problems the following morning. Johnson waffled about being 'humble in the face of this virus' and 'grappling with a new variant of the virus which is surging particularly in London and the South East'; this was a shifty reference to the fact that his attempt to reopen the schools in London had been thwarted, and that Brighton Council was likely to thwart him too. On the subject of the renegade local authorities, he said 'My message to such councils is that they should be guided by the public health advice which is at the moment that schools are safe'. Note those three words: 'at the moment'. When Marr asked Johnson if he could guarantee that all schools would be open by January 18, he could not. He said 'we will keep this under constant review' and 'we're entirely reconciled to doing what it takes to get the virus down, and that may involve tougher measures in the weeks ahead'. He warned of further local measures: 'It may be that we need to do things in the next few weeks that will be tougher in many parts of the country... I'm fully, fully reconciled to that'. He explained that the tier system is a 'tough system and, alas, probably about to get tougher'; clearly he was aware that if the NEU forced any schools closures, he would have to cover it all up with local lockdowns. And finally, with two small words, he summarised his own powerlessness: 'In principle it's a good thing to keep schools open'.

Just like in the run up to June 1, Johnson was nervous. And once again, he had every reason to be. Bousted and Courtney were preparing a similar campaign to the one they had waged then. As I mentioned earlier, the NEU convened 'an emergency executive meeting' on January 2. At the meeting, the executive finalised a 'strategy paper' on how to close the schools. Later that day, the NEU issued a press release, with a headline that summed up the strategy: 'The NEU advises primary members it is unsafe to return to work'. The text of the press release noted that the advice also applied to staff in 'special needs schools, and early years settings'. The executive explained their decision as follows: 'We will not sit by and see the worsening of a health catastrophe'. There was also a little bit of needle from the NEU: 'In December, we called for schools to be closed for two weeks at the start of the spring term, in order to provide a circuit breaker and lower infections. Our view was ignored.' The union was now 'calling on all primary schools to move to remote learning for the first two weeks of January'.

This time, the NEU would not be ignored. They backed up their demands with a new action plan: 'We are writing to employers, urging them to look at the advice of SAGE... and we are urging our members, on the basis of that science, to use our model letter to inform their headteacher that it is unsafe for them to be in school'. The model letter was supplied online, but has subsequently been removed. It was a Section 44 letter – an expression of the signatory's right to avoid the workplace on health and safety grounds. Meanwhile, another teaching union, GMB, came out in support of the schools closures, and supplied its members with two letters. GMB explained: 'The best way we can protect you is by asking you to issue: Letter 1 (Request for a Revised Risk Assessment) then Letter 2 (Working from Home letter if you feel unsafe)'. The second letter included the statement: 'Until we are convinced that the risk assessment undertaken covers all pertinent areas then we will have no choice other than to advise our members that they should not be returning to work'. Curiously, however, GMB didn't publicly advise its members not to return to work; the union couldn't say with 'legal certainty' that its members who worked in schools should stay home, because most of those members were support staff, not teachers. Two other unions – NASUWT and Unison – also supported the schools closures, but NASUWT followed GMB in not issuing the stay home advice, whereas Unison followed the NEU and advised its members to avoid the workplace and submit Section 44 letters. Additionally, there were public declarations of support for the schools closures from three other unions: NAHT, ASCL and CWU.

As for the other part of the NEU's action plan – the leadership contacting 'employers' to exert pressure – they were likely to receive a sympathetic response. The *Guardian* reported that the NAHT (the National Association of Head Teachers) planned to 'issue guidance to headteachers, which will recommend they take no action against staff who refuse to return to work because they feel it is unsafe'. In the same article, there were also quotes from Courtney and various other senior figures in education, all supporting the schools closures.

There was further PR by the NEU on January 2. Courtney was interviewed on BBC radio. 'Why are you advising teachers not to go back to school?' was the interviewer's somewhat soft opening question. Courtney replied: 'We're following the science'. Then there was an even softer question: 'Isn't it a bit late to call for this now?' No word of criticism for the advice itself. No mention of the fact that the NEU was riding roughshod over the government's official policy. Courtney's response was: 'We're really sincerely sorry... but you have to put this at the door of government'. Breathtaking dishonesty. Courtney concluded the interview by reiterating the NEU's strategy, namely, 'our advice to our members that it's not safe' to return to work and that 'they can use Section 44 of the Health and Safety Act to insist on their right to work in safe situations'. He added, euphemistically, that 'if members do that, then headteachers can make a rational decision to start that online working'.

The NEU's press release and other media activities were an attempt to galvanise teachers and parents – to encourage an uprising against the schools reopening. In all of this, the NEU's leaders were emulating the strategy that they had deployed in May, but going further: their decision to go public this time with their Section 44 advice was a massive escalation. The NEU also emulated their earlier strategy by organising another online members' meeting. A Zoom call was scheduled for the morning of January 3, which was a Sunday; the teachers were due to return to work the next morning. The purpose of the call was for the leadership to directly explain the NEU's advice to reps, members and the public. The event turned out to be another massive escalation, because of the sheer number of participants.

The NEU has claimed that the Zoom call on January 3 again broke the world record for a trade union meeting, with an incredible 100,000 people viewing the entire hour-long call and 400,000 people viewing at least part of it. With the leadership repeating their latest advice to staff – 'it would be, in our view, unsafe for you to attend the workplace in schools and colleges which were open to all students' – the meeting launched a huge teaching mutiny. By the evening, the NEU was already reporting that 'thousands of our members across the country have sent S44 letters to their heads'. We can assume that many of the Section 44 letters had multiple signatories. As a blogger later relayed on the Independent Left website, 'The NEU strategy was explicitly one of collective action... In literature and mass online meetings the advice was that if possible, school branches should send a single, collective letter, signed by as many staff as possible'. The *TES* put it even more starkly: 'National teacher walk-out over Covid safety expected'.

On the morning of January 4, the government was still holding the line. In the words of politics reporter, John Johnson: 'There was an all staff meeting of civil servants at the Department of Education today where they were told there was no plans to close schools and no plans to cancel exams'. He added, portentously: 'Hearing there will now be another tomorrow morning, presumably to row back entirely on all of it.' As the day unfolded, the scale of the teaching mutiny became clear. At 8.25am, the NEU claimed that Section 44 letters had been handed in in 6,000 schools.

There are 16,769 primary schools in England, but 2,196 of them are in London, and those were already closed. So the NEU, it seems, disrupted the reopening of at least 40% of primary schools throughout the rest of the country. As the *TES* summarised, at midday on January 4: 'Teachers in 6,000 primaries "don't go in"'. Bear in mind that the figure may have increased throughout the day. Also bear in mind that each letter was probably signed my multiple teachers. One commentor, a man called Tony Dowling, who describes himself as a 'teacher, socialist, trade unionist' has given an indication of the overall numbers involved: 'Hundreds of thousands of teachers and school workers were encouraged and inspired by meeting together to take up the advice of their union and to use the model letter saying they would not work in unsafe schools'. There are 264,804 primary school teachers *in total* in the UK. If the mutiny was on anything like the scale that Dowling suggests, the schools would have been rendered inoperable. A few months later, Bousted said 'at least 25% of primary members signed Section 44 letters' on that day, which would suggest a lower figure than 'hundreds of thousands', but then again, the NEU wasn't the only union involved in the mutiny. The *Guardian* has recently reported that 'a quarter of all primary school teachers... signed "Section 44" letters, refusing to enter their classroom', which would put the figure at around 66,000 mutineers.

Adding fuel to the fire were the numerous local authorities backing the NEU over the government. In the aforementioned article, the *TES* asserted: 'Council leaders in Wolverhampton, Norfolk, Slough, Manchester, County Durham, Lancashire, Birmingham and

Gateshead have all now said they will support the decision of headteachers who do not think it is safe for their school to open'. Furthermore, some familiar faces popped up on January 4 to pile on the pressure. At 11.58am, Jeremy Hunt proclaimed on Twitter that 'we need to close schools, borders, and ban all household mixing RIGHT AWAY'. Incredibly, ten minutes later the NEU tweeted a 'thank you' to Hunt. At 2.22pm, Mark Serwotka from PCS declared 'Our union whole-heartedly supports the NEU and Unison in their campaign to make schools safe'.

There was also a joint statement that day from six teaching unions: NEU, GMB, NAHT, NASUWT, UNISON and Unite, declaring that 'Unions have called for a pause in the reopening of schools', and that 'The government's chaotic handling of the open-ing of schools has caused confusion for teachers, school staff and parents alike'. The statement included a quote from Francis O'Grady: 'Instead of creating chaos for parents and exposing workers to risks, the Prime Minister should be talking to trade unions about what steps are needed to make sure all schools are Covid-secure.' As ever, the dishonesty was breath-taking. The unions were blaming the government for chaos that *they themselves were causing*. On the morn-ing of January 4, Courtney gave an interview to Sky News, in which he declared that 'It is not safe for primary schools to be open at the moment, and at least for the first two weeks of term'. The idea that this charlatan was in any position to pronounce that schools weren't safe, or that they would be safe in two weeks' time, was preposterous beyond belief. Courtn-ey then confirmed the NEU's position: 'We think that teachers and support staff are within their rights to say that they won't work in full classes in schools. We think that's helping headteachers make the right decision.'

Later in the day, the screw was turned even tighter on Johnson. Kier Starmer gave a round of interviews in which he urged the PM to announce a new national lockdown. 'The virus is out of control – everybody can see that', Starmer blustered; 'You only need to go out on the streets now to see lots of people out and about... We need to go back to where we were in March with very, very strong messaging about staying at home'. He added: 'I'm afraid that the closure of schools is now inevitable, and therefore that needs to be part of the national plan for further restrictions.' Starmer was 'afraid' to say this, because only 24 hours earlier his stance had been quite different: he had backed a new national lockdown but he had *declined* to back the mutinying teachers. On the morning of January 4 the Shadow Education Secretary Kate Green reiterated the party line: 'We don't think schools should close; we want schools to remain open; the right place for children to be, if they can, is safely in school'. Yet here was Starmer, in the late afternoon, saying 'We must introduce a national lockdown now. Tragically, that must mean school closures', as though he was backing the school closures *because* he was backing the lockdown. He made no mention of *why* the schools were closing, why he had U-turned. Many teachers were angry that Starmer hadn't supported the January 4 mutiny; there was no way he was about to start a public argument with them when the government was on the back foot. Without even a hint as to the appalling callousness that the teaching unions had displayed towards the nation's children, Starmer called for schools closures, so as to appear to be leading the argument, to be pre-empting the PM's inevitable U-turn.

Of course, Starmer wasn't the only leader displaying extreme dishonesty. Johnson was about to do the same, presumably telling himself that it was justified because he was clinging on to power, so as to stop even less honest people from taking power. At 8pm on January 4, Johnson addressed the nation. He started with the usual 'science' spiel: 'There is no doubt that in fighting the old variant of the virus, our collective efforts were working and would have continued to work. But we now have a new variant of the virus.' He warned of rising numbers of Covid patients, hospitals under pressure, deaths increasing. And he delivered the direst news: 'In England, we must therefore go into a national lockdown which is tough enough to contain this variant'.

He then addressed the issue of the schools, saying: 'Because we now have to do everything we possibly can to stop the spread of the disease, primary schools, secondary schools and colleges across England must move to remote provision from tomorrow'. Obviously, this was astonishing news, given that the previous morning Johnson had told the public 'The risk to kids, to young people, is really very, very, very small', and that 'The risk to staff is very small' and that 'Schools are safe, there is absolutely no doubt about it'. He had some explaining to do, and he acknowledged this: 'Parents whose children were in school today may reasonably ask why we did not take this decision sooner.' By way of an answer, Johnson said 'I want to stress that the problem is not that schools are unsafe for children'; rather, 'schools may nonetheless act as vectors for transmission, causing the virus to spread between households'. Of course, the logic was absurd. If schools were safe for children and adults, then the idea of the virus spreading among households in which children and adults live was, on the whole, nothing to worry about either. Johnson's answer was pure bunk. The real reason for the decision to close the schools was that the NEU's colossal teaching mutiny made opening the schools unviable.

The NEU's teaching mutiny had also triggered the lockdown. There is simply no way that Johnson would have tried to reopen all the schools on January 4 if his plan was to shut them all on the same day and lock the entire country up in the evening. The schools closures would cause colossal economic damage. The purpose of the lockdown was to cover up both the NEU mutiny and the economic damage and to buy the PM an indefinite period of time in which he could try to get the schools open again while spinning the delay as scientific; if the NEU refused to cooperate, Johnson could pretend the schools were staying closed for epidemiological reasons. His strategy was essentially the same as in March 2020, only this time Johnson had covered up an actual mutiny not just a potential mutiny; he had shifted the narrative even more drastically, and got away with it – again.

Perhaps you will argue that Johnson was planning to lock the country down but keep the schools open, and that he wanted to get the schools open first. Perhaps he brought the date of the lockdown forward when the NEU mutinied, but he was planning to lock-down anyway. It's logically possible but not remotely plausible. If Johnson was planning a lockdown, he would have locked down *first* and then tried to reopen the schools. A lockdown would have cushioned him against failure; if he had locked down first, he could have let the mutinying teachers do their worst, kept as many schools open as possible, and blamed the closures on the virus, just as he did in June and November. By trying to open the schools *before* locking down, Johnson opened himself up to a massive humiliation, which he only narrowly avoided by hastily announcing the lockdown. And, remember: planning any sort of lockdown went against every instinct Johnson had displayed since day 1 of the coronapanic debacle. He would only lockdown if he was forced into it. Also remember that, after the first lockdown, he promised himself he would be the Mayor of Jaws next time. The only reason he had caved in the second time was because of the leak, and, even then, he had successfully managed to keep the schools open. This time, he was determined that he would try to keep the schools open without doing a lockdown first. He would call the NEU's bluff.

A few months later, Bousted accused Johnson of engaging in 'brinksmanship' on January 4. She was right about that. She and Courtney knew very well that they were waging a Scargillesque campaign, and that the PM was trying to thwart them. Johnson called the NEU's bluff because he was overconfident after his success in keeping the schools open during the second lockdown. He didn't reckon with the massive escalation that the NEU unleashed on January 4. Thanks to the Zoom call on January 3, and the Section 44 advice that the leadership conveyed to the meeting's 400,000 participants, the NEU was able to disrupt the reopening of a large swathe of the nation's schools the next day. Just like Starmer, Johnson was forced onto the backfoot, drastically changing his previous position. He offered only the merest hint of the NEU mutiny, saying forlornly 'we have been doing everything in our power to keep schools open'. Once again, the public believed they were being locked up for health reasons. Indeed, the public were so heavily duped (or deranged), a YouGov poll found that 62% of people believed that Johnson had made the 'wrong decision' to open the schools for a day; apparently he had put the nation's health at risk in doing so.

The NEU, for their part, issued a press release at 8.45pm on January 4. The opening words were: 'No one wanted schools and colleges to be shut again'. (Sometimes I don't know whether to laugh or cry when I'm researching this stuff.) The text continued, 'but the evidence clearly pointed to the necessity for this to happen weeks ago'. Then the NEU made an incredible attempt to shift the blame: 'Government must take responsibility for this closure because it has allowed COVID-19 to become, again, out of control.' On the same day, the union also posted a tweet saying 'If the government wants schools to stay open, then they have a funny way of showing it'.

In fact, Bousted and Courtney didn't really think the government was responsible for the schools closures. In the ensuing days, the NEU boasted about what happened on January 4. An email was sent round on January 5 to the union's members, saying 'You did it!... You agreed with our advice that it was not safe for primary schools to be open'. The NEU posted many gloating tweets that day too. 'Thank you to all the people thanking the NEU for what we've done', said one. Another one included a video of the PM saying that schools were safe on January 3; the tweet said, sarcastically: 'Well this went well didn't it. The Government didn't step up, so we did'. Another said 'The Prime Minister wouldn't #MakeSchoolsSafe so we did'.

On January 6, an 'NEU spokesperson' was quoted in the *Mail*, explaining in fairly unequivocal terms what had gone on:

Last week we had to do our job as a union by informing our members that they have a legal right to refuse to work in unsafe conditions which are a danger to their health and to the health of their school communities and more generally. The NEU makes no apologies for advising members of their rights. 400,000 people joined our Zoom call on 2 January [sic] to hear further details about our advice. The NEU and its members are relieved that the Prime Minister eventually listened to the arguments being put to him.

On the same day, Kevin Courtney posted a video on Facebook of him speaking at a 'People Before Profit' meeting. I will quote his somewhat garbled words at length because they are self-incriminating:

It is, I believe, only because the NEU and Unison were taking some sort of campaigning steps around it, and, in the NEU, that we had a meeting on Sunday morning... where 400,000 people watched that meeting for part of the time, and where thousands of our members and thousands of Unison members had sent letters to their headteacher saying that they thought it was unsafe for community and unsafe for them, for those primary schools to be open, at that point, on that Monday morning, and many Head Teachers agreeing with them. And I think that was the material decision that changed Boris Johnson's mind. The data did not change between Sunday and Monday... But I think they could not cope with the idea that it could grow out of control, that people would take the question of safety into their own hands.

Courtney followed up these comments with further demands: 'I just want to say there are some things the government should now do to put this right'. One of the demands was: 'They have to furlough the parents who have to stay at home.' These words indicate that Courtney was well aware that the school closures would cause economic damage and that the government would be pushed into colluding in the damage. He was well aware that the UK economy would be decimated by the exodus of working parents, and that the government would now have to pick up the tab. Economic damage had been at the heart of the NEU's strategy since March 2020. Indeed, a few months after January 4, Courtney intimated that he also knew that the schools closures would push the government into doing a lockdown. While discussing a recent decrease in Covid cases, he remarked 'This is the combined effect of the lockdown (which the PM had to be forced into) and the spread of the vaccinations'. These words weren't quite an explicit admission from Courtney, but be in no doubt: he knew that the government would cover up both the teaching mutiny and the economic damage by issuing a lockdown on January 4.

The blatant causal relationship between the schools closures on January 4 and the lockdown announcement later that evening confirms the core claim of this essay: that the NEU caused all three lockdowns. If there was any doubt that the NEU's threats in March 2020 and October 2020 prompted the government to capitulate, leading to the total shutdown of the economy, there can be no doubt about what happened on January 4, 2021; the NEU's threats became real, and the lockdown capitulation was instant. In turn, given that we know with certainty that the NEU's campaign of Scargillesque disruption could trigger a lockdown once, on January 4, we are entitled to conclude that the other two lockdowns were triggered in the same way. The threat of schools closures may not have become real in March and October, but the government's rearguard action was the same either way: don't let the public know that the NEU is calling the shots; cover it all up with a lockdown spin operation. Of course, in the case of the second lockdown, the government needed a bit of an extra push, from the Chatty Rat, but the NEU was still the ultimate driver of the events.

In this light, an interesting question arises regarding the second lockdown: Why didn't the NEU deploy their January 4 strategy in November? The NEU's threats had already triggered the lockdown itself, but why didn't the leadership then go further and force the schools closures too? The likely reason is that the strategic value of a mass walkout was lower in November than in January. After all, a mutiny on that scale didn't come with zero risk for the NEU. If the public wised up to what was going on, the NEU could be discredited. Moreover, the legality of the mutiny on January 4 was highly questionable. A union cannot legally organise a national strike without a national ballot. The 'advice' that the NEU leadership issued to the membership – it would be 'unsafe for you to attend the workplace' – was dangerously similar to organising a national strike. At least one teaching union, GMB, got cold feet on January 3 and refused to issue the advice publicly, for legal reasons. In November when the country was already in lockdown, the NEU probably concluded that the payoff of a national teaching walkout wasn't worth the risk. There was no point pursuing a strategy that was potentially both unpopular and illegal if the main objective – maximal economic damage – had already been achieved. Instead, the NEU tried to close as many schools as possible using the Escalation App, which did not imply such a drastic departure from the rules agreed by the government at the time.

In contrast, the potential payoff of a mass walkout was much greater in January. The NEU knew that the action could force Johnson into a lockdown, a lockdown that wasn't going to happen otherwise. And perhaps there was another factor in play. When Johnson kept the schools open during the second lockdown, Bousted and Courtney will have felt somewhat humiliated. They may have wanted to take revenge in January with a huge counter offensive. Or perhaps a certain amount of desperation had crept in. When Johnson called the NEU's bluff again and refused to back down on reopening the schools, perhaps the leadership panicked, remembering that their efforts had failed in November. They gambled, went nuclear, blurring the line between Scargillism and outright illegality; they all-but called for a national walkout without a national ballot.

A week later, there was a curious exchange between the government and the NEU and Unison. With the schools remaining open for the children of key workers, the two unions had removed the Section 44 advice from their websites – some of the teachers would need to go to work to teach the minority of children who were still in school. Gavin Williamson responded by saying in Parliament 'I'd like to thank both the National Education Union and UNISON for recognising the fact that the action that they took and the advice that they gave their members on Sunday was incorrect and that they have withdrawn that advice'. NEU and Unison immediately responded by publishing an open letter saying that they had only removed the advice because of the 'radical change of Government direction'. The letter emphasised that removing the advice 'emphatically does not mean we believe face-to-face work with full or near full classes in schools is safe in the current circumstances – far from it. Neither does the removal of this advice from our websites indicate that we do not believe it was the right advice to give at the time'.

Two things are notable about this exchange. First, consider Gavin Williamson's claim that the action that the NEU took on January 4 was 'incorrect'. What a strange adjective to use! Did Williamson mean 'illegal', but he didn't want to say it, because this would open an enormous can of worms for the government? Or did he mean 'not illegal but morally wrong'? Or perhaps the government was trying to decide one way or another at that point.

Second, consider the way that the NEU and Unison slapped Williamson down. They continued to insist that they supported the closure of the schools for most pupils, on safety grounds. Yet, as a matter of fact, the two unions had removed the advice from their websites, rather than qualifying it. You cannot help but wonder if they too were starting to wonder if their action had been illegal.

Regardless, the die was cast. The government had been manoeuvred into another lockdown. Now, other socialist unions would do their bit to keep the lunacy going. On the evening of January 4, the BMA announced their support for the lockdown, saying 'without these tougher measures, the further this virus will spread, potentially taking more lives and damaging the NHS beyond repair'. On January 5, Unison wrote an open letter 'urging employers to review their workplace risk assessments and safety measures' and demanding 'updated guidelines' from the government. On the same day, Unite bellowed: 'The government must today set out a full programme of income support for working people.' Also that day, the RMT called for 'an industry-wide approach to manage the serious risks to both staff and passengers raised by the new COVID variant'.

The NEU continued being disruptive too. On January 5, they held another Zoom meeting, this time with 58,000 attendees. The meeting was on how to 'make schools safe'. A few weeks later, the union published a long report called 'NEU Education Recovery Plan', which detailed 'how to reopen schools and colleges in a safe and sustainable way' and promised that the NEU would 'work hard to get the Government to accept the proposals in this plan so that our members can return to school'. The report griped that 'Ministers have consistently set their sights on returning all students to full-time education rather than planning to return them safely'. The NEU's latest proposals for 'safe' schools included: 'social distancing', 'constraints on mixing', 'lower numbers of pupils in classrooms', 'rotas', 'more staff', 'erecting marquees on school sites and identifying and bringing back into use unused public buildings', 'Education staff... vaccinated as a priority', and 'increased use of face coverings – masks should be worn by secondary-aged students in classrooms as well as all other areas of the school'. The NEU had first demanded masks in classrooms back in December. The reiteration of the demand did not bode well for the beleaguered schoolchildren.

The NEU timed the released of their Recovery Plan to precede a speech that the PM gave to Parliament on January 27. Johnson told MPs that the government had 'launched the biggest vaccination programme in British history'. Over the next year, he continued to place a heavy emphasis on vaccination, attempting to spin the country back to freedom using vaccine-acquired immunity as the premise. It's ironic that Covid zealots proceeded to ignore the vaccine harms (including an estimated 20,000 deaths in the UK), having previously rejected natural herd immunity on the basis of the harms the policy would allegedly cause. Johnson also told Parliament that, in February, the government will publish 'our plan for taking the country out of lockdown'. The plan would 'set out our approach towards reopening schools'. The reopening date was scheduled for March 8. Reopening the schools, Johnson explained, was contingent on vaccin-ating 'everyone in the four most vulnerable groups'. He made no mention of vaccinating teachers, or of the NEU's other demands.

On February 19, the NEU, accompanied by eight other teaching unions, issued a statement:

We are increasingly concerned that the government is minded to order a full return of all pupils on Monday 8 March in England. This would seem a reckless course of action. It could trigger another spike in Covid infections, prolong the disruption of education, and risk throwing away the hard-won progress made in suppressing the virus over the course of the latest lockdown.

The NEU insisted, however, that their latest statement didn't signify an 'intent to stand in the way of the full reopening of schools and colleges'. What the statement was calling for, rather, was 'a cautious approach with wider school and college opening phased over a period of time'. I think this distinction can be taken with a large pinch of salt. A phased reopening of schools wouldn't have enabled the full reopening of the country; the lockdown would have dragged on, and the NEU knew it. Moreover, they would likely have continued to be obstructive if the government had agreed to a phased reopening. The NEU was trying to appear to be reasonable while still causing trouble.

Johnson was undeterred. He intended to press ahead with a full reopening. On February 22, he gave a speech to Parliament, in which he outlined what he was now calling the government's 'roadmap' for reopening Britain. With the priority groups vaccinated as planned, he confirmed the March 8 date for reopening schools. He then intoned: 'Mr Speaker, all the evidence shows that classrooms are the best places for our young people to be. That's why I've always said that schools would be the last to close and the first to reopen.' Please take a moment to consider what was happening here. The schools would be the 'first to reopen' because, as far as the PM was concerned, he couldn't reopen the economy with a quarter of the workforce missing and with the uncooperativeness of the teaching unions still hanging over him. He would try to reopen the schools first, and, if successful, the rest of the country would follow. On that note, he also dug the requisite bolt-holes, should anything go horribly wrong on March 8: 'We can't, I'm afraid, rule out re-imposing restrictions at local or regional level if evidence suggests they are necessary to contain or suppress a new variant which escapes the vaccines'. Finally, he offered some words of hope: 'A wretched year will give way to a spring and a summer that will be very different and incomparably better than the picture we see around us today'.

Why was Johnson so optimistic? Well, partly it was because he was again in the position of having nothing to lose; he might as well try to get as many schools open as possible, and cover up any failures with 'scientific' local lockdowns. But I think there was more to his optimism than that. I think something changed between February 19 and March 1: the NEU backed down. On March 1, the NEU held another large Zoom meeting, in which the leadership were now adopting a more conciliatory tone. A socialist writer named Tania Kent, who attended the meeting, recounted the occasion in an article. The NEU, she howled, was now 'backing the reopening of schools and the economy at the expense of health and lives of educators, students and parents'. The leadership had conceded on the issue of a phased reopening: now the union would grudgingly support a 'big bang' reopening. Instead of continuing to disrupt the government's plans, the NEU executive promised merely that they would 'monitor' the situation after the Easter break and possibly request more measures after that.

Kent also recounted that the Zoom call on March 1 was accompanied by a 'chat line', whereby members could type their responses to the proceedings in real time. She noted that when Bousted and Courtney conceded on the issue of the schools reopening, for several pages 'the only word visible was "ballot"': basically, the members were demanding that the NEU arrange a ballot for a national strike. The demand was ignored, the meeting continuing in the foreground, until someone on the chat line commented: 'Don't pretend you can't follow the chat, it's one word'. I will quote Kent at length, regarding what happened next:

> Bousted finally responded, saying, 'I have looked at the chat line and people are saying "ballot" and getting frustrated... The national executive discussed this and came to the conclusion that a national ballot is not the right way to go ahead. What is the right way to go ahead is to ensure school by school, that the return is as safe as possible. Given that infection rates are falling, hospitalisation rates are falling and given that the vaccine rollout is taking place, the executive agreed this is not the way forward'... She chastised the audience, 'You can't simply say "ballot" and expect it to take place... So it is an easy thing to say "ballot", but that is not going to stop the school return on March 8 and nor is it something we think will be achievable, and nor do we think it is the appropriate action under these new circumstances'.

Kent's recollections provide a fascinating insight, but

actually the meeting is available online, and I too have watched it. On the recorded version you cannot see the chat line. However, I can confirm that there were other clear indications of a climbdown from the NEU executive at the meeting. Robin Bevan, the NEU President, opened the proceedings by insisting: 'Our advice and guidance tonight has to be context specific. We can't give one message for every workplace.' As well as rejecting the idea of an official strike, the leadership were now rejecting the idea of advising another national walkout. Courtney explained: 'We used Section 44 in January and it led to a quicker change of policy'. However, he continued: 'We can't say Section 44 is always the right decision in all circumstances. It is not sensible to use Section 44 without advice from your union's regional office... That is because [of] the requirements that Section 44 has about having an imminent serious danger. You need talk to the union before you use that provision.' Courtney also indicated that that NEU had conceded on the issue of priority vaccination for teachers; he explained that the union didn't have strong grounds for complaint given that the most vulnerable groups in society had had the opportunity to be vaccinated. He noted further that the union had done a survey of 44,000 members and found there was 'more or less an even split' for and against reopening primary schools (the issue of reopening secondary schools was less polarised, with 71% against). He even questioned the sacred science of Covid safety in schools, saying 'Quite unlike January, scientists now have much more mixed views'. Bousted agreed: 'Scientists are not now united. There are different opinions, based on different readings of the science.' Incredibly, she tried to shift the focus away from the virus; she recited the harms that were accruing to children while the schools were shut – kids without laptops, or without space to work at home, or without parents who were capable of teaching them. 'For some children and young people', she observed, 'lockdown has made them less safe and… some will have suffered real trauma'. Suddenly the kids seemed to matter again: 'Whilst people are concerned about safety, they are also really concerned about their pupils.'

There is no doubt that the NEU executive had – at least temporarily – abandoned their Scargillesque campaign by March 1, 2021. To be sure, they were still maintaining the despicable lie that any of the Covid madness was ever justified; they were still expressing concern about the planned reopening of schools; and they were still intending to ensure that insane Covid protocols would be in place when the pupils returned to school. But Bousted summed up the union's new position: 'We hope that return will go well.' She and her colleagues were clearly on the defensive. You could sense a bit of an atmosphere at the meeting, the executive trying to justify their new stance to the members, many of whom apparently weren't impressed. Kent, for her part, urged teachers to join a breakaway group called the 'Educators Rank-and-File Safety Committee', which had been founded in the USA in August 2020 and was now operating in Britain too. The new committee had scheduled an online event, for March 6. Kent invited her readers to join in, 'to find out more about the policies we adv-ance for the closure of schools and, where they are forced to be open, the measures that must be adopted to protect lives'.

Bousted's phrase 'under these new circumstances' is intriguing. In the context, she was referring to the vaccine rollout and the falling infection rates, but I wonder if there was more to the phrase. The virus, after all, was always a pretext. Recall Gavin Williamson's suggestion that the NEU's 'action' on January 4 was 'incorrect'. Let's speculate that the government had decided that the action was in fact *illegal*. How then could they deter the NEU from doing something similar again? Well, all that would be required was a credible threat by the government to prosecute the NEU if they didn't start cooperating. A legal action against the NEU would send Bousted and Courtney to jail and put an instant end to the war. Granted, the government was also deeply compromised by the events of January 4, and Johnson himself could end up in jail if the truth emerged. But that wouldn't make the threat of legal action any less of a deterrent to the NEU. The threat was one of mutually assured destruction. We can even speculate that if such a threat was made, it wasn't necessarily delivered by Johnson himself. If MI5 were bought in to investigate the second lockdown, perhaps they were still involved in the unfolding events, acting on the government's behalf or even unilaterally. If a third party issued the threat of legal action, the threat would be more credible. In any case, if there was a credible threat of legal action against the NEU, the government and the NEU were now in a boxers' clinch. Both would keep jabbing at each other, but neither would launch their heaviest punches, because the prospect of mutually assured destruction would weigh too heavily on them both. The government would try not to provoke the NEU into further Scargillism, and the NEU would try not to provoke the government or anybody else into prosecuting them.

When March 8 came around, the schools reopened under these 'new circumstances'. The NEU and the government may have come to an uneasy truce, but, alas, the children were bearing a heavier burden than ever. The government had agreed to a few of the NEU's demands, the PM no doubt being conscious of the fact that there was still a lot of unrest among the teachers. During the March 1 Zoom call, Courtney noted that the NEU's survey had found that 'A clear majority of respondents in both primary and secondary schools supported mask wearing for pupils'. When the children returned to school, the secondary pupils were forced to wear masks in classrooms; this measure, which the NEU had been pushing for for months, was recommended as a 'temporary extra measure' by the government's roadmap. My blood boils when I think of those poor kids, sitting there for 6 hours in pointless stifling dehumanising masks, being treated worse than terrorists, purely because the adults were being cowards. Cowards, hiding behind the suffering of children. Cowards, avoiding an honest discussion, avoiding reality. In addition, the secondary pupils were forced to take thrice-weekly Covid tests in school. Swabs were shoved up the noses of healthy kids, with many of the kids being sent home when they tested positive for a harmless illness that they didn't even have any symptoms of. A great evil engulfed schools in March 2021, even greater than in June and November 2020.

It feels wrong to draw any positives from such an abominable situation. Yet there was one ray of hope: the schools were open. And with that, England gradually reopened, as per the three remaining steps of

Johnson's roadmap. The plan was that non-essential shops and outdoor venues would open in mid-April, followed by indoor venues in mid-May, followed by the lifting of all restrictions in June. The staggered nature of the plan was a ruse to enable the government to backtrack more easily if the teachers caused any more problems. They didn't: the truce with the NEU held firm. By May 17, the PM had grown confident enough to withdraw the masks in schools guidance. The kids had suffered enough, their degradation enabling the government to coax the teachers back to work. That said, teaching unions did object to the withdrawal of the guidance. The NEU and four unions wrote a letter of protest on May 17. And on June 8, the NEU joined with three unions to demand the reintroduction of the masks. In the meantime, many headteachers simply continued mandating the masks. But the government didn't reinstate the guidance. For once, Johnson had successfully called the unions' bluff.

Actually, there may have been slightly more to it than that. The government's original plan was that every Covid restriction throughout the country would be lifted on June 21, but on June 14 Johnson announced that there would be a month-long extension of the lockdown. The BMA had called for the extension, and the government had caved in. In addition, the teaching unions' agitation over the masks may have been playing on Johnson's mind: perhaps he decided that politically the safest course of action was to delay the full reopening until the end of term, just like he did for the first lockdown. The school holidays were a 'natural firebreak', he told the country on July 12. He could unlock everything during the holidays because schools closures couldn't stop him. And that is what he did.

On July 19, in the week that the school term ended, Johnson declared England free of government Covid mandates.

Of course, that wasn't quite the end of the corona-panic debacle. As July 19 approached, there was a burst of protest from almost every corner of the public sector. In my essay 'The Unions and the U-turns', I listed 25 unions that were opposed to 'Freedom Day'. In the months after July 19, most public sector organisations ignored the government and continued to uphold mask mandates and other psychotic Covid restrictions. And, as the summer drew to a close, the government was once again colluding in the psychosis. On September 21, a programme of mass vaccination was rolled out in secondary schools. The programme had been demanded in the summer by the NEU, GMB, UNISON and Unite. The government U-turned, capitulating to the unions once again, despite the Joint Committee on Vaccination and Immunisation saying that a Covid vaccine rollout for healthy schoolchildren was unnecessary, because the benefits would not outweigh the 'potential risks'.

A few months later, there were further government capitulations. As I predicted would happen, on November 27 the government issued mask mandates for shops and trains, following demands from USDAW and the RMT. A new 'variant' of Covid, called 'Omicron', was doing the rounds, we were told. On December 8, the government went further, announcing the full implementation of a 'Plan B' – making masks compulsory in most indoor venues and 'asking' people to work from home, the latter request following 'pressure from PCS', as the union put it. However, the furlough scheme had ended on September 31, and was not renewed, which dampened down the overall workplace exodus. Moreover, the fact that there was explicitly no mask guidance for hospitality venues meant that people were still mixing freely in at least one situation, which leant further impetus to employers and employees who wanted to keep their workplaces open. The country had had a taste of freedom over the summer, and many people were now ignoring the masks guidance where it applied as well as the new guidance on home working.

The government's announcement on November 27 also included 'recommending' masks in corridors in secondary schools. This didn't go far enough for the NEU and NASUWT, the two unions immediately demanding the reintroduction of masks in classrooms. A month later, on January 2, 2022, the government caved in to that demand too. As the NEU gloated in a press release: 'Finally, the government have been forced to recognise, and react to, the scale of the Omicron variant and its potential impact on education. The recommendation on wearing face masks in secondary school classrooms is overdue'.

The government must have been nervous in the New Year, given what had happened the same time last year. The NEU was still under pressure from its own members. It looks like the masks in classrooms guidance was issued to reassure the teachers, to reduce the likelihood that – with or without the NEU's support – there would be another mass walkout. A few weeks later, with the start of term undisturbed, the government again scrapped the masks in schools guidance, much to the chagrin of the NEU; Bousted called the move 'premature'. But the NEU was floundering by now. The demented policy of forcing schoolchildren into masks had – at last – received significant pushback from the public, including a growing awareness that the policy was being driven by teaching unions.

Meanwhile, the government colluded in one final disgrace. On December 15, Covid vaccine passes were mandated 'for entry into nightclubs and settings where large crowds gather', as the official statement put it. On Freedom Day, Johnson had warned that this measure might be introduced in the autumn, but on September 12 the Health Secretary Sajid Javid had said that in fact the government would not go ahead with the plan. Alas, following pressure from NHS Confederation and the BMA, the government caved in. Suddenly the British public was faced with the outrageous and farcical requirement of providing evidence of being vaccinated against a cold before they could access numerous public venues. The BMA then proceeded to call for further restrictions over Christmas, but this time the government didn't cave in. Perhaps Johnson gambled – correctly – that the doctors would settle for the mandatory Covid Passes.

There may have been another factor in the BMA's impotence over Christmas 2021. On November 9, the government announced a plan to introduce mandatory Covid vaccination for all NHS staff. The mandate was due to come in in April, meaning that the latest date on which staff could get their first jab to be fully vaccinated in time was February 3. On January 31, the government suddenly abandoned the plan, amid pushback from medical unions, including the Royal College of Nursing, the Royal College of Midwives and the Royal College of GPs. There were warnings that 123,000 NHS staff could be forced out if the mandate was implemented. Even the BMA said abandoning the plan was the 'right decision'. You cannot help but wonder. Was the NHS jab mandate another threat of mutually assured destruction by the government? The mandate was in no one's interests: neither the government nor the NHS/medical unions would benefit from an exodus of medical staff. But that doesn't mean the NHS and its unions wouldn't have been alarmed by the prospect. Perhaps that's partly why the BMA backed down over Christmas. Perhaps Johnson had started making a few demands of his own.

After Christmas, Johnson felt sufficiently confident to announce another Freedom Day. On January 19, the government withdrew not only the masks in schools guidance from that day onwards, but declared that *all* Covid regulations in England, including mandatory Covid Passes, would be withdrawn in a week's time. Perhaps the latter decision resulted from another of Johnson's 'demands'. If my speculations are right, the government successfully subdued the NEU, the BMA and NHS Confederation by way of threats of mutually assured destruction.

And let me offer one final piece of speculation, taking us right back to where this essay started: the Partygate scandal, all those wine and cheese parties that were held in Downing Street during the lockdowns. The public were never told who exactly had attended the parties. Photographs were published in the media but many of the faces were pixelated out. I wonder if a few union leaders were in attendance. Of course, it doesn't make sense that Johnson himself would have leaked the pictures. But anti-lockdowners within the Conservative party could have done so, thus issuing a warning to the PM a*nd* the unions. A media outcry about union leaders demanding restrictions then fraternising at Downing Street during the lockdowns would have brought the entire scandal of the corona-panic debacle crashing down, and crashing into public consciousness. The union leaders would have been deterred by the prospect, and the PM would have been incentivised to push back even harder against their demands. Anti-lockdowner rivals of Johnson would have relished both outcomes, along with the bonus that the PM would be politically damaged by the leaked pictures even without the full story emerging.

All these speculations may or may not be true. What is certainly true is that the government's second attempt at Freedom Day was about to be consolidated by a dramatic new development, 1500 miles away. On February 24, Russia invaded Ukraine. Russia's President Vladmir Putin was no doubt emboldened by two years of Western self-immolation. The invasion jolted the West back to sanity. Like tantrumming toddlers distracted by a surprising new stimulus, Covid zealots snapped out of their hypochondria and began waving Ukraine flags. Pity the Ukrainians. And pity the Russian soldiers enlisted into this new lunacy. But, for Britain, calm descended: the coronapanic debacle was over. It fizzled out just fast as it had burst into being.


# XIII

At the start of March 2020, the British government told the public that a new coronavirus was doing the rounds. The PM and his chief scientists insisted that the illness would be mild for the overwhelming majority, including the overwhelming majority of elderly people. The public were advised to carry on as normal, to wash their hands more often, and to self-isolate if unwell.

By the end of March, Britain had been plunged into a surreal nightmare. With mass hysteria and a spontaneous union-led shutdown convulsing the nation, the PM put the economy into an induced coma. He led a process that was happening whether he liked it or not. The lockdown was a spin operation, but the lie spiralled out of control, ushering in two more years of union unrest, accompanied by a relentless parade of government U-turns, leading to further insane Covid restrictions, as Johnson attempted to navigate a political path through the lunacy.

In the middle of this maelstrom of dishonesty came the second lockdown, an enigma that can only be explained by zooming out and seeing the coronapanic debacle in its entirety. When unions started unliterally shutting Britain down in mid-March 2020, the PM hastily advised social distancing. He also conceded to the unions' demands for a furlough scheme. In turn, on March 17 when the NEU threatened a Scargillesque campaign of unilateral schools closures, the PM caved in further, shutting the schools and sending the whole country into lockdown, to cover up the phenomenal economic damage that the schools closures would inflict. As the lockdown dragged on, amid months of failed attempts to reopen the schools, Johnson hit upon the idea of local lockdowns, enabling him cover up any pockets of unrest without issuing national restrictions. His attempt to reopen the schools in June was largely a failure, but at the end of the school term he reopened the economy. A summer of local lockdowns followed, including Muslim lockdowns. Meanwhile, further deranged Covid rules – including mask mandates – were imposed on workplaces, shops and public transport, at the behest of unions.

By the autumn, the country was staggering back to its feet. Alas, a campaign by the TUC and an overt strike threat by PCS union forced the government to renew the furlough scheme. Then, in October, with the NEU going into full Scargill mode again, the country faced the looming threat of another lockdown. At first, the PM insisted that new national restrictions would be wrong. But someone in his cabinet leaked the fake science which the PM was preparing to wheel out should he be forced to capitulate to the NEU. The leak bounced Johnson into the second lockdown, which he announced at the end of October. At the same time, he achieved a small win by keeping the schools open, albeit he conceded to the NEU's cruel demand for the children to wear masks in corridors. The implacable NEU leadership proceeded to use their new 'Escalation App' to try to close as many schools as possible. The campaign turned out to be a damp squib: most schools stayed open during November, with only a small dip in pupil attendance.

After Christmas, which was heavily restricted as a result of pressure from the BMA, the NEU avenged Johnson's previous win. At a huge Zoom meeting on January 3, Bousted and Courtney advised the union's membership that schools were unsafe. The advice triggered a national walkout by teachers on January 4, when Johnson tried to reopen primary schools. The PM immediately covered up the mutiny by issuing the third lockdown later that evening. Three months later, the schools reopened. The children were now being forced to wear masks in classrooms, another cruel NEU demand to which the PM had conceded. Once again, the children were bearing the brunt of the adults' cowardice and lies. But January 4 was the beginning of the end. Bousted and Courtney retreated from their Scargillesque campaign a few months later. The coronapanic debacle gradually unravelled over the following year.

No words of condemnation are adequate for the NEU, this barbarous so-called teaching union that perpetrated mass child abuse and dragged the rest of Britain into a hell from which the country may never recover. And no words of condemnation are adequate for Bousted and Courtney, the sociopaths who led the NEU's attack on the nation and its children. However, having read this whole essay, you are probably as shellshocked as I am after writing it, so I will not dwell any longer on the crimes. I will merely draw a handful of general conclusions.

First, let me reiterate that the coronapanic debacle was a socialist atrocity. If Johnson had had his way, the government would have pursued herd immunity and kept the country open. But the socialists had other ideas. The Chinese Communist Party blitzed Britain with pro-lockdown propaganda. Socialist unions enga- ged in a concerted mutiny to damage the economy and damage the government. And Remainers – generally on the left – likewise saw the Covid-19 pandemic as an opportunity to cause trouble and discredit Brexit in the process. For a year, working people such as delivery drivers and shop workers were imprisoned and enslaved while socialists luxuriated at home and pretended to care about other people. Socialist teachers were especially exploitative, relentlessly disrupting the education system and treating the welfare of children as an afterthought.

Second, the coronapanic debacle was an atrocity in which many conservatives were complicit. Most conservatives either directly supported the first lockdown or offered no overt resistance. The vast majority of those who spoke out spoke out too late. And of course – as the socialists never tire of pointing out to me – the coronapanic debacle was overseen by a Conservative government. People will debate forever whether Johnson's capitulation in March 2020 was the right decision – he saved Brexit, some will say – but no sane person can fail to be extremely dismayed by the two years of dishonesty that followed. Neither the PM, nor anyone in his cabinet, nor any of his colleagues in Parliament, nor any prominent party members, nor any well-known conservatives in the media, ever showed enough backbone to confront the socialists directly. Instead, we had the hideous spectacle of powerful Conservatives wriggling and writhing under an immensely manipulative assault, trying to keep their authority intact, pretending that any of the Covid lunacy was ever worthwhile, as they span their way out of an atrocity that they had spun their way into.

This dynamic should alarm us not just intrinsically, but because of its implications. What sort of 'democracy' is this when the entire Conservative establishment will allow itself to be bullied and humiliated for two years by public sector socialists, without offering so much as a whimper of defiance? Throughout the coronapanic debacle, the government pretended to be in charge, lying and lying and lying, to make the policies of unelected socialist maniacs seem palatable to a British electorate that had in fact voted for

Conservative governance. If no one in the Conservative establishment would tell the public what was actually happening during an assault of such consequence, why should we expect them to tell the truth in future when they are being bullied by socialists over any other matter? Given what we now know, we can expect all elected Conservative politicians to be spin doctors for a permanent socialist bureaucracy. Under such circumstances, democracy is a sham. Conservatives must start talking honestly about the compromises that they are making with public sector socialists. Let the electorate decide if such compromises are tolerable. Let the electorate decide with their eyes open, fully informed by faithful political representatives, instead of being lied to by snake oil salesmen who sell socialist malevolence as conservative policy.

Third, the coronapanic debacle was an atrocity in which the media were complicit – from the start and throughout. I am not just talking about all the fearmongering and sensationalism in the media. I am not just talking about the journalists who explicitly supported the lockdowns and other deranged Covid measures, or the journalists who hid and therefore implicitly supported the measures. I am not just talking about the journalists who failed to ask questions. And I am not just talking about the many conservative journalists who abandoned their principles. All this was utterly disgraceful.

I am also talking about the journalists who started out as lockdown supporters and then reinvented themselves as lockdown sceptics. These latecomer journalists have systematically covered up the full truth about the coronapanic debacle. For a start, they have buried the facts about March 2020: that the PM abandoned the scientific policy of herd immunity because of a massive socialist mutiny, a mass panic, and a media that offered almost zero support for freedom. Instead of talking honestly about what happened, the latecomer journalists have insisted that the first lockdown was a sensible scientific policy that 'went on too long', or – even more absurdly – they have claimed that the lockdown was 'planned' by way of an international conspiracy. They don't talk about what really caused the first lockdown, and, accordingly, they don't condemn what really happened, because they don't want to admit that they themselves made a mistake in supporting it.

The latecomer journalists have also avoided talking about the fact that almost all the Covid restrictions for two years came about in a similar way to the first lockdown. The fundamental dynamic behind the coronapanic debacle – socialist unions bullying the government into restrictions – has been 100% ignored by the latecomer journalists, because the topic is like a trail that leads back to their own cowardice at the start. My message to these journalists is this: it's OK to make a mistake, but only if you take responsibility and try to make amends; it's not OK to cover up mistakes. Or perhaps I'm being extremely naïve here. No latecomer journalists have ever discussed the fact that Britain was bombarded with Chinese Communist Party-derived pro-lockdown propaganda in March 2020. No journalists at the *Telegraph*, for instance, have ever discussed what went on at the newspaper, which allegedly published more than 50 articles paid for by the CCP in early 2020. Many media outlets and journalists no doubt have a lot to hide. Perhaps some are (still) receiving CCP money. Or money from the

British government. Or money from unions. Fake lockdown sceptics who carefully obscure the real causes of the lockdown would no doubt be an asset to any organisation that has committed crimes during the last two years.

As for the tiny minority of journalists who did oppose the lockdown from the start, they too have avoided talking about the unions, perhaps to spare the blushes of their colleagues.

After January 4, the entire coronapanic debacle should have swiftly unravelled. No one should have been left in any doubt as to what had happened that day: in broad daylight, a union had openly defied the government, and the PM had covered it up, spinning the capitulation into a phony health measure. In turn, the full truth should have emerged: that the same dynamic had occurred repeatedly since March 2020. But, incredibly, no one in the media even mentioned the truth about January 4. Or ever has. Literally no journalist has ever discussed the fact that the third lockdown was blatantly caused by an NEU mutiny. The entire episode has been memory-holed like Tiananmen Square. I spent the whole of 2021 desperately trying to draw attention to the events of January 4, but as far as I know I am still the only person in Britain who has ever publicly discussed what happened (aside from the gloating socialists who've been slightly less than explicit in their discussions). I'm also the only commentator who has discussed the fact that unions boast of "forcing" the government into the furlough scheme. The silence is bewildering. Where is the media? We cannot fix our democracy until the public knows the truth about January 4, March 2020 and the second lockdown. We cannot get justice for any of the harms done, including those of mass vaccination, until we dispatch the idea that the harms were justified by sound policy. The public needs to understand that the coronapanic debacle was union-driven, pointless and dishonest from the start and all the way through.

Fourth, and finally, and most importantly, let me remind you of who suffered the most during the coronapanic debacle: children. There must be justice for the kids, and they must receive an apology. They must be told that none of the Covid lunacy will ever be repeated. They must be told that there was nothing scientific or morally acceptable about what was done to them or to the whole country. They must be told that the entire episode was nothing but a confection of socialist malice and conservative cowardice.

In the process, the kids must be told that the fundamental premise of the lockdown was deranged from the start. If you want the government to ban everyone from leaving the house and to dole out free money until everyone is 'safe' from a virus, you're not going to get normality back any day soon, not while vested interests are still demanding more safety and more money. No such twisted undertaking should ever have been contemplated. Human rights are sacrosanct, never to be sacrificed at the altar of any virus. Even if there's an unmild virus, you don't get to hijack the government and confiscate people's rights and enslave a subset of the population and divide families and deprive children of an education and trash the economy and use other people's future taxes so you can hide indefinitely in your house.

The coronapanic debacle was a disgrace that Britain can put firmly in the past only when the future of the children is put front and centre of the discussion. An honest discussion and a proper reckoning is urgently needed for the sake of the children. Do not let them down. Never again.

September 4, 2022

Printed in Great Britain
by Amazon

42809048R00159